Beyond Human Design

Beyond Human Design

Turbocharge Your Practice with Integrated Channels in All Four Worlds

Eleanor Haspel-Portner, Ph.D.

Beyond Human Design: Turbocharge Your Practice with Integrated Channels in All Four Worlds

Copyright © 2024 Noble Sciences, LLC.

All rights reserved.
This book or any portion thereof may not be reproduced or used in any manner whatsoever without the express written permission of the publisher except for the use of brief quotations in a book review.

Library of Congress Control Number: 2024913152

ISBN:
978-1-931053-16-7, 978-1-931053-17-4 (Paperback)
978-1-931053-15-0 (Ebook)

BODY, MIND & SPIRIT / Human Design
PSYCHOLOGY / Personality
HEALTH & FITNESS / Alternative Therapies
BODY, MIND & SPIRIT / New Thought
SELF-HELP / Personal Growth / Success

Book Design by Michelle M. White

Other titles by Eleanor Haspel-Portner
Cosmic Guidance
Cosmic Secrets
Astrology Essentials
First Degree Reiki Manual
Second Degree Reiki Manual & Workbook
Marriage in Trouble: A Time of Decision

Author's websites
www.nobleenergywellness.com
www.DrEleanor.com
www.moptu.com/DrEleanor

*To students of Human Design
who have the wisdom and integrity to seek the truth
of science and to follow it Beyond Human Design™ into the depths
of consciousness as they embrace their full potential.*

Table of Contents

Introduction to Integrated Channels   1

Channel 1-8   7

Integrated Mental and Spiritual/Archetypal Worlds
(Scorpio-Taurus/Gemini)   8

Mental World
(Scorpio-Taurus/Gemini)   9

Spiritual/Archetypal World
(Scorpio-Taurus/Gemini)   10

Channel 2-14   11

Integrated Mental and Emotional/Angelic Worlds
(Taurus-Scorpio/Sagittarius)   12

Mental World
(Taurus-Scorpio/Sagittarius)   13

Emotional/Angelic World
(Taurus-Scorpio/Sagittarius)   14

Channel 3-60   15

Integrated Mental and Emotional/Angelic Worlds
(Aries/Taurus-Capricorn/Aquarius)   16

Mental World
(Aries/Taurus-Capricorn/Aquarius)   17

Emotional/Angelic World
(Aries/Taurus-Capricorn/Aquarius)   18

Channel 4-63   19

Integrated Mental and Emotional/Angelic World
(Leo-Pisces)   20

Mental World
(Leo-Pisces)   21

Emotional/Angelic World
(Leo-Pisces)   22

Channel 5-15   23

Integrated Mental and Spiritual/Archetypal,
Emotional/Angelic, and Physical/Biological Worlds
(Sagittarius-Gemini/Cancer)   25

Integrated Mental, Spiritual/Archetypal,
and Emotional/Angelic Worlds
(Sagittarius-Gemini/Cancer)   27

Integrated Mental, Spiritual/Archetypal,
and Physical/Biological Worlds
(Sagittarius-Gemini/Cancer)   29

Integrated Mental, Emotional/Angelic,
and Physical/Biological Worlds
(Sagittarius-Gemini/Cancer)   31

Integrated Spiritual/Archetypal, Emotional/
Angelic, and Physical/Biological Worlds
(Sagittarius-Gemini/Cancer)   33

Integrated Mental and Spiritual/Archetypal Worlds
(Sagittarius-Gemini/Cancer)   35

Integrated Mental and Emotional/Angelic Worlds
(Sagittarius-Gemini/Cancer)   36

Integrated Mental and Physical/Biological Worlds
(Sagittarius-Gemini/Cancer)   37

Integrated Spiritual/Archetypal and
Emotional/Angelic Worlds
(Sagittarius-Gemini/Cancer)   38

Integrated Spiritual/Archetypal and
Physical/Biological Worlds
(Sagittarius-Gemini/Cancer)   39

Integrated Emotional/Angelic and
Physical/Biological Worlds
(Sagittarius-Gemini/Cancer)   40

Mental World
(Sagittarius-Gemini/Cancer)   41

Spiritual/Archetypal World
(Sagittarius-Gemini/Cancer)   42

Emotional/Angelic World
(Sagittarius-Gemini/Cancer) 43

Physical/Biological World
(Sagittarius-Gemini/Cancer) 44

Channel 6-59 — 45

Integrated Mental World and Emotional/
Angelic and Physical/Biological World Portals
(Virgo-Virgo) 47

Integrated Mental World and Physical/
Biological World Portals
(Virgo-Virgo) 48

Integrated Emotional/Angelic and
Physical/Biological World Portals
(Virgo-Virgo) 49

Mental World
(Virgo-Virgo) 50

Channel 7-31 — 51

Integrated Mental and Emotional/Angelic Worlds
(Leo-Leo) 52

Mental World
(Leo-Leo) 53

Emotional/Angelic World
(Leo-Leo) 54

Channel 9-52 — 55

Integrated Mental and Emotional/Angelic Worlds
(Sagittarius-Cancer) 56

Mental World
(Sagittarius-Cancer) 57

Emotional/Angelic World
(Sagittarius-Cancer) 58

Channel 10-20 — 59

Integrated Mental World, Spiritual/Archetypal,
and Emotional/Angelic Portals
(Sagittarius/Capricorn-Gemini) 61

Integrated Mental World and
Spiritual/Archetypal Portal
(Sagittarius/Capricorn-Gemini) 62

Integrated Spiritual/Archetypal and
Emotional/Angelic Portals
(Sagittarius/Capricorn-Gemini) 63

Mental World
(Sagittarius/Capricorn-Gemini) 64

Channel 10-57 — 65

Integrated Mental World and Spiritual/
Archetypal and Emotional/Angelic Portals
(Capricorn/Libra-Sagittarius) 67

Integrated Mental World and
Spiritual/Archetypal Portal
(Capricorn/Libra-Sagittarius) 68

Integrated Mental World and
Emotional/Angelic Portal
(Capricorn/Libra-Sagittarius) 69

Mental World
(Capricorn/Libra-Sagittarius) 70

Emotional/Angelic World Portal to the
Spiritual/Archetypal World Portal
(Capricorn/Libra-Sagittarius) 71

Channel 10-34 — 73

Integrated Mental and Emotional/Angelic Worlds
(Sagittarius/Capricorn-Sagittarius) 74

Mental World
(Sagittarius/Capricorn-Sagittarius) 75

Emotional/Angelic World
(Sagittarius/Capricorn-Sagittarius) 76

Channel 10-34-57 — 77

Integrated Mental, Spiritual/Archetypal
Portal and Emotional/Angelic Portal
(Sagittarius/Capricorn-Sagittarius-Libra) 79

Integrated Mental, Spiritual/Archetypal and Emotional/Angelic Portals
(Sagittarius/Capricorn-Sagittarius-Libra) 81

Channel 10-20-34 83

Integrated Mental World, Spiritual/Archetypal, and Emotional/Angelic Portals
(Sagittarius/Capricorn-Gemini/Sagittarius) 85

Channel 10-20-57 87

Integrated Mental World and Spiritual/Archetypal and Emotional/Angelic Portals
(Sagittarius/Capricorn-Gemini/Sagittarius-Libra) 89

Channel 10-20-34-57 91

Integrated Mental World, Spiritual/Archetypal, and Emotional/Angelic Portals
(Sagittarius/Capricorn-Gemini/Sagittarius-Libra) 93

Channel 11-56 95

Integrated Mental and Emotional/Angelic Worlds
(Sagittarius-Cancer/Leo) 96

Mental World
(Sagittarius-Cancer/Leo) 97

Emotional/Angelic World
(Sagittarius-Cancer/Leo) 98

Channel 12-22 99

Integrated Mental World, the Physical/Biological World, and The Spiritual/Archetypal World Portal
(Gemini-Pisces) 101

Integrated Mental World and Portal of the Spiritual/Archetypal World
(Gemini-Pisces) 102

Integrated Mental and Physical/Biological Worlds
(Gemini-Pisces) 103

Integrated Spiritual/Archetypal Portal and Physical/Biological Worlds
(Gemini-Pisces) 104

Mental World
(Gemini-Pisces) 105

Physical/Biological World
(Gemini-Pisces) 106

Channel 13-33 107

Integrated Mental and Emotional/Angelic Worlds
(Aquarius-Leo) 108

Mental World
(Aquarius-Leo) 109

Emotional/Angelic World
(Aquarius-Leo) 110

Channel 16-48 111

Integrated Mental and Emotional/Angelic Worlds
(Gemini-Libra) 112

Mental World
(Gemini-Libra) 113

Emotional/Angelic World
(Gemini-Libra) 114

Channel 17-62 115

Integrated Mental, Emotional/Angelic, and Portal to the Spiritual/Archetypal World
(Aries-Cancer) 117

Integrated Mental, Emotional/Angelic Worlds
(Aries-Cancer) 118

Integrated Mental and Portal to the Spiritual/Archetypal Worlds
(Aries-Cancer) 119

Mental World
(Aries-Cancer) 120

Emotional/Angelic World
(Aries-Cancer) 121

Channel 18-58 123

Integrated Mental and Emotional/Angelic Worlds
(Libra-Capricorn) 124

Mental World
(Libra-Capricorn) 125

Emotional/Angelic World
(Libra-Capricorn) 126

Channel 19-49 — 127

Integrated Mental, Emotional/Angelic, Physical/Biological World and Portal to the Spiritual/Archetypal Worlds
(Aquarius-Aquarius) 129

Integrated Mental, Physical/Biological World and Portal to the Spiritual/Archetypal Worlds
(Aquarius-Aquarius) 130

Integrated Physical/Biological World and Portal to the Spiritual/Archetypal Worlds
(Aquarius-Aquarius) 131

Integrated Mental World and Portal to the Spiritual/Archetypal World
(Aquarius-Aquarius) 132

Integrated Mental and Physical/Biological Worlds
(Aquarius-Aquarius) 133

Mental World
(Aquarius-Aquarius) 134

Physical/Biological Worlds
(Aquarius-Aquarius) 135

Channel 20-57 — 137

Integrated Mental and Spiritual/Archetypal Worlds
(Gemini-Libra) 138

Mental World
(Gemini-Libra) 139

Spiritual/Archetypal World
(Gemini-Libra) 140

Channel 20-34-57 — 141

Integrated Mental and Spiritual/Archetypal Worlds and Emotional/Angelic Portal
(Gemini-Sagittarius-Libra) 143

Channel 20-34 — 145

Integrated Mental World, Spiritual/Archetypal and Emotional/Angelic World Portals
(Gemini-Sagittarius) 147

Integrated Mental World and Spiritual/Archetypal Portal
(Gemini-Sagittarius) 148

Integrated Mental World and Emotional/Angelic World Portal
(Gemini-Sagittarius) 149

Integrated Spiritual/Archetypal and Emotional/Angelic World Portals
(Gemini-Sagittarius) 150

Mental World
(Gemini-Sagittarius) 151

Channel 21-45 — 153

Integrated Mental and Physical/Biological Worlds
(Aries-Gemini) 154

Mental World
(Aries-Gemini) 155

Physical/Biological World
(Aries-Gemini) 156

Channel 23-43 — 157

Integrated Mental and Emotional/Angelic Worlds
(Taurus-Scorpio) 158

Mental World
(Taurus-Scorpio) 159

Emotional/Angelic World
(Taurus-Scorpio) 160

Channel 24-61 — 161

Integrated Mental and Emotional/Angelic Worlds
(Taurus-Capricorn) 162

Mental World
(Taurus-Capricorn) 163

Emotional/Angelic World
(Taurus-Capricorn) 164

Channel 25-51 — 165

Integrated Mental and Physical/Biological Worlds
(Pisces/Aries-Aries) 166

Mental World
(Pisces/Aries-Aries) 167

Physical/Biological World
(Pisces/Aries-Aries) 168

Channel 26-44 — 169

Integrated Mental and Physical/Biological Worlds
(Sagittarius-Scorpio) 170

Mental World
(Sagittarius-Scorpio) 171

Physical/Biological World
(Sagittarius-Scorpio) 172

Channel 27-50 — 173

Integrated Mental and Spiritual/Archetypal Worlds
(Taurus-Libra/Scorpio) 174

Mental World
(Taurus-Libra/Scorpio) 175

Spiritual/Archetypal World
(Taurus-Libra/Scorpio) 176

Channel 28-38 — 177

Integrated Mental and Spiritual/Archetypal World
(Scorpio-Capricorn) 178

Mental World
(Scorpio-Capricorn) 179

Spiritual/Archetypal World
(Scorpio-Capricorn) 180

Channel 29-46 — 181

Integrated Mental and Emotional/Angelic Worlds
(Leo/Virgo-Virgo/Libra) 182

Mental World
(Leo/Virgo-Virgo/Libra) 183

Emotional/Angelic World
(Leo/Virgo-Virgo/Libra) 184

Channel 30-41 — 185

Integrated Mental and Physical/Biological Worlds
(Aquarius/Pisces-Aquarius) 186

Mental World
(Aquarius/Pisces-Aquarius) 187

Physical/Biological Worlds
(Aquarius/Pisces-Aquarius) 188

Channel 32-54 — 189

Integrated Mental and Physical/Biological Worlds
and Gate 54 Portal to The Emotional/Angelic World
(Libra-Capricorn) 191

Integrated Mental World and Portal Through
Gate 54 to Emotional/Angelic World
(Libra-Capricorn) 192

Integrated Mental and Physical/Biological Worlds
(Libra-Capricorn) 193

Integrated Physical/Biological World and Gate
54 Portal to The Emotional/Angelic World
(Libra-Capricorn) 194

Mental World
(Libra-Capricorn) 195

Physical/Biological World
(Libra-Capricorn) 196

Channel 34-57 — 197

Integrated Mental, Spiritual/Archetypal
Portal and Emotional/Angelic Portal
(Sagittarius-Libra) 199

Integrated Mental and Spiritual/Archetypal Worlds
(Sagittarius-Libra) 201

Integrated Mental World and Portal
to the Emotional/Angelic
(Sagittarius-Libra) 202

Integrated Spiritual/Archetypal Portal
and Emotional/Angelic Portal
(Sagittarius-Libra) 203

Mental World
(Sagittarius-Libra) 204

Channel 35-36 — 205

Integrated Mental and Physical/Biological Worlds
(Gemini-Pisces) 206

Mental World
(Gemini-Pisces) 207

Physical/Biological World
(Gemini-Pisces) 208

Channel 37-40 — 209

Integrated Mental and Physical/Biological Worlds
(Pisces-Virgo) 210

Mental World
(Pisces-Virgo) 211

Physical/Biological World
(Pisces-Virgo) 212

Channel 39-55 — 213

Integrated Mental and Physical/Biological Worlds
(Cancer-Pisces) 214

Mental World
(Cancer-Pisces) 215

Physical/Biological World
(Cancer-Pisces) 216

Channel 42-53 — 217

Integrated Mental, Spiritual/Archetypal,
and Physical/Biological Worlds
(Aries-Cancer) 219

Integrated Mental, Spiritual/Archetypal Worlds
(Aries-Cancer) 221

Integrated Mental and Physical/Biological Worlds
(Aries-Cancer) 223

Mental World
(Aries-Cancer) 224

Spiritual/Archetypal World
(Aries-Cancer) 225

Physical/Biological World
(Aries-Cancer) 226

Channel 47-64 — 227

Integrated Mental and Emotional/Angelic Worlds
(Virgo-Virgo) 228

Mental World
(Virgo-Virgo) 229

Emotional/Angelic World
(Virgo-Virgo) 230

Acknowledgments — 231

About the Author — 233

Introduction to Integrated Channels

When I first saw the Mandala for the Human Design System, I recognized it as a synthesis of the Kabbalistic Tree of Life, Chakras, Astrology, and the Hexagrams of the I-Ching. In my training, I had studied all of these systems but had never seen them integrated. I pursued studying the Human Design System, and because of my background, Ra Uru Hu asked me to validate it Scientifically.

From 1999 to 2003, Ra Uru Hu (Allan Krakower) and I had a legal business partnership. Ra asked my husband, a medical doctor, and me to document the Human Design System clinically and statistically. Ra, Marvin, and I agreed that Marvin and I would market and present the Human Design material and its research to a professional audience; he believed they would be interested in the system's science and documentation. Ra intended to address the Human Design System more superficially for the general public.

My background in social science research gave me the tools I needed to do the first statistical studies on the Human Design System. The research initially involved 30,000 cases divided into five matched groups on all variables necessary to fulfill the criteria of a reliable scientific, astrological, and statistical study.

At the time, I documented that the Human Design Body Graph is a viable construct and that some of Ra's hypotheses about how it worked held. The Type, Definition, Centers, and Profile were structurally sound. I found that:

- There are Five distinct Types: the Manifestor, Generator, Projector, Reflector, and Manifesting Generator.
- The definition of Types is valid: Single, Split, Triple Split, and Quadruple Split.
- The profile shows a specific mathematical regularity in accord with the structure of the Hexagrams; it occurs with the same regularity in the population as would be mathematically predicted. No interpretation can be inferred about the meaning of the lines or profiles from these statistics. This statistic proves that the body graph calculations and structure are sound.

- The Dream and Sleep Matrices are sound and delineate Types as defined in the 64 Gate Matrix.

- The definition of a Center does not predict medical conditions. For example, an open heart Center does not predispose a person to a heart attack compared to someone with a defined heart Center. The data showed that medical conditions occur independently of Center definitions or the activation or non-activation of Gates and lines.

- The Dream and Sleep Matrices integrate essential functional information for interpreting the Body Graphs and how someone expresses their design. Ra recognized that integrating the Matrices shows the complex interactions of the Worlds.

In 2003, Ra and I dissolved our legal contract. I separated from the Human Design Community to continue my work that, based on science, expanded the Human Design calculations to include all Four Worlds: the Mental, Spiritual, Emotional, and Physical Worlds. I pursued additional components of the Human Design System because I found that the calculation for the design of a sleeping mammal was missing from Ra's model. In addition, he had not been given the Matrix for the Emotional/Angelic World. Ra confirmed that the "Voice" told him, "There was the existence of the Matrix I was hypothesizing. Within a short time, I was given a copy of the Emotional/Angelic World Matrix by the "Voice," which speaks to and guides me.

Several factors led me to identify the calculation for the sleep design of a mammal, which was missing from the information Ra gave me. Because I had twin kittens whose birth data I had to the second, I could differentiate them on a physiological level and explain their health differences. When I used astrologically sound and logical calculations for the charts, I was astonished to find that when using solar degrees, solar minutes, lunar degrees, and lunar minutes, both prenatally and postnatally, the charts delineated actual critical developmental periods in early human development.

Verifying developmental sequences in a baby when using astrological calculations confirmed the integrity of the Human Design calculations as significant in many ways previously not even considered. The developmental aspects of the charts bring in a new level of psychological and physiological verification of the data. It confirms through different disciplines that the information coded into the Human Design Matrix is also valid in other Worlds.

Because the Human Design System synthesizes the Tree of Life, chakras, astrology, and Hexagrams, it logically must include those systems and the details and data of those systems must support and align with the Human Design information. In other words, they must be synergistically related and correlate. In Noble Energy Maps® that go Beyond Human Design©, I use all Four Worlds and look at how they integrate consciousness. The Tree of Life has 10 Centers and 32 Paths of Intelligence active in the 10 Centers in Four Worlds. The Worlds in the Tree of Life correlate with the Worlds I have delineated in my calculations.

When you multiply 32 paths of intelligence by 12, it equals 384. When you multiply the 64 hexagrams of the I-Ching by their six lines you again get 384. This correspondence again validates the structural integrity of the systems synthesized in the Body Maps. However, it requires further exploration and documentation than I have done to date.

As I continued working with my clients and their charts, I noticed that the Four Worlds were essential in helping clients navigate relationships with others and themselves. I began to recognize which World a client was functioning in or talking from, and I then used a congruent language and communication style. As I delved into Noble Energy Maps® and the eight maps that combine into the Integrated Energy Map, I realized that as the Worlds combine energetically, the nuance of their expression shifts accordingly.

Over the past 20 years, I have done more than 15,000 Noble Energy Maps® for clients, friends, and family. In reading the Integrated Maps, I combined the nuances of the Channels for each World and when activated in more than one World.

There are a hundred forty-eight Channels when using the Integrated Noble Energy Maps®. In the simplest case where only two Matrices are involved in a channel, three possible Channel combinations have their own energetic slant. In the most complex Channels, there are many ways the Channels can connect, and sometimes they connect through what I call a Portal.

A Portal is a Gate that connects to a different World. For example, Gate 34 joined Gate 57, making Channel 34-57. Gate 34 is in the Mental World and acts as a Portal to the Emotional/Angelic World. Gate 57 is a Gate in the Mental World and acts as a Portal to the Spiritual World. Thus, Channel 34-57 functions in three Worlds and has different nuances depending on which Worlds are activated. For example, the Mental World only in Gate 57 gives the Channel a different energy than if it is in the Spiritual World in Gate 57. Look at the various combinations of how this Channel can be formed by combinations of Gates and Worlds. As you read over the Channels, think about how their meaning might change experientially by their different combinations of energy.

Channel 34-57 Integrated Channels & Possible Combinations

- Integrated Mental, Spiritual/Archetypal Portal and Emotional/Angelic Portal Channel 34-57 (Sagittarius-Libra)
- Integrated Mental and Spiritual/Archetypal Worlds Channel 34-57 (Sagittarius-Libra)
- Integrated Mental World and Portal to the Emotional/Angelic 34-57 (Sagittarius-Libra)
- Integrated Spiritual/Archetypal Portal and Emotional/Angelic Portal Channel 34-57 (Sagittarius-Libra)
- Mental World Channel 34-57 (Sagittarius-Libra)

Thus, this book gives you all the iterations for all the Channels possible in Integrated Noble Energy Maps®. There are 148 Channels. Use this book as a manual, and do not attempt to memorize all the nuances. You will learn how to read Noble Energy Maps® and the nuances as you practice doing readings. In addition, your perceptive, creative intelligence will guide you when you are familiar with the energy of each Channel and how each Gate energetically varies depending on the World it is in.

I have worked with the Four Worlds and their Integration for over 20 years using Noble Energy Maps®. As a clinical psychologist, using Noble Energy Maps® gives clear insights into how my clients use their energy and how empathic and vulnerable they are to the energy around them. Recognizing the Worlds and the Portals to the Worlds makes nuances of how someone functions clear. Many of my clients experience inner validation for who they have known themselves to be. This validation empowers them, and they excel beyond their expectations when they feel recognized on a soul level and are guided to follow the complexities of how they know what they know, i.e., their inner knowing.

Each Channel has Action Points and Empowerment Statements that give practical guidance for optimizing the energy of the Channels in daily life. By following these guidelines, the energy of each Channel is anchored and grounded. A resource page at the end of this book links you to all the resources and their source.

It is my honor and privilege to present this material. As you open to the Four Worlds and to living as an Integrated Being in multiple dimensions, your resilience, joy of living, and capacity to manifest your highest potential become a reality.

Eleanor Haspel-Portner, Ph.D.
Mount Pleasant, SC
May 2024

Channel 1-8

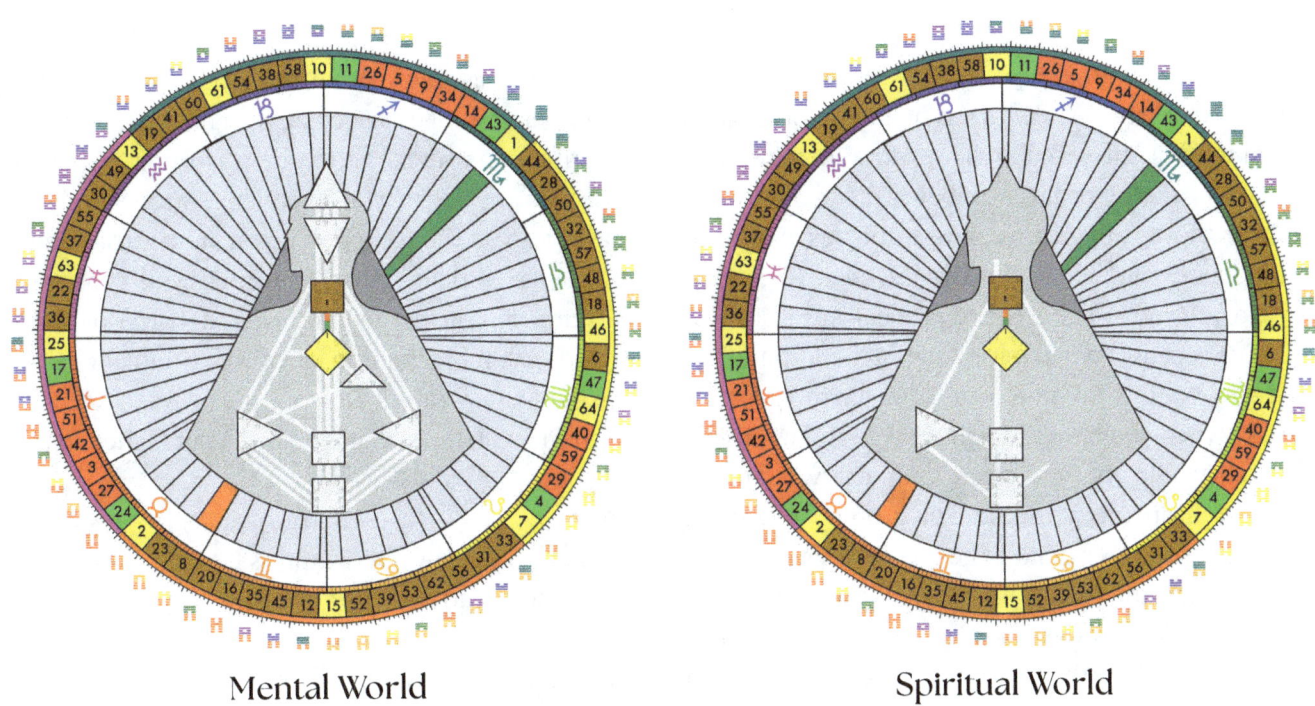

Mental World · Spiritual World

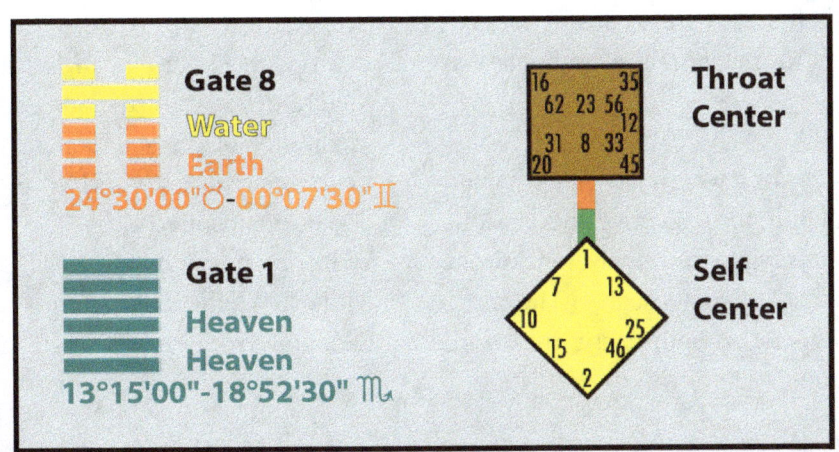

Channel 1-8

Integrated Mental and Spiritual/Archetypal Worlds
Channel 1-8 *(Scorpio-Taurus/Gemini)*

Keywords: Creative Expression, Inspiration, Unity, Self-Direction, Strength

You are creative and inspirational.

You are a creative person who wants to express your creativity in a way that is helpful to others and can make a difference in the world. When inspired, you feel a sense of aliveness because of your excitement about your creative power. You thrive on your uniqueness and focus more on the creative process than your goal. The creative process is transformational because something is born out of nothing. You have great creative potential. Thus, anything is possible when you have the right energy and intention. You have the power to create your reality and manifest your dreams. With the right attitude and focus, it is possible to manifest the life you desire. When meditating, tune in to your creative spark that ignites your soul. Write down any ideas or thoughts and pay attention to how they may inspire you toward action or deepen your inner process. Pay attention to how you function in the Four Worlds and the timing of what turns on and off in you energetically to maximize your capacity to manifest in alignment with your highest Self.

Creative energy activates when you sleep. When you dream, content from the collective unconscious becomes partially accessible to your awareness spiritually and consciously to some degree. The more you meditate and practice spirituality, the more accessible this information becomes to your conscious mind. Your active creativity and your drive to contribute to your life and work in a meaningful way give you joy. When you experience a connection that gives you the feeling that you are contributing to your life work in a way that deepens your sense of life purpose, you feel an inner sense of harmony and joy. To maximize the impact of this spiritual channel, meditate, write down your dreams, and keep a journal in which you dialogue with your higher Self.

Your Keys to Empowerment
- When you feel inspired, express yourself Creatively.
- Be Self-directed.
- Find common ground with those you love.
- Pay attention to how you function in the Four Worlds and behave accordingly.

Action Points for Manifesting Your Dreams
- Meditate daily using the Sun/Moon Meditation or Transcendental Meditation.
- Keep a journal handy and write down your inspired ideas.
- Write down your dreams. Dialogue with your Higher Self.
- Recognize your inner strength and act accordingly.

Mental World
Channel 1-8 *(Scorpio-Taurus/Gemini)*

Keywords: Creative Expression, Inspiration, Unity, Self-Direction, Strength

You are creative and inspirational.

You are a creative person who wants to express your creativity in a way that is helpful to others and can make a difference in the world. When inspired, you feel a sense of aliveness because of your excitement about your creative power. You thrive on your uniqueness and focus more on the creative process than your goal. The creative process is transformational because something is born out of nothing. You have great creative potential. Thus, anything is possible when you have the right energy and intention. You have the power to create your reality and manifest your dreams. With the right attitude and focus, it is possible to manifest the life you desire. When meditating, tune in to your creative spark that ignites your soul. Write down any ideas or thoughts and pay attention to how they may inspire you toward action or deepen your inner process. Pay attention to how you function in the Four Worlds and the timing of what turns on and off in you energetically to maximize your capacity to manifest in alignment with your highest Self.

Your Keys to Empowerment
- When you feel inspired, express yourself Creatively.
- Remain open to new possibilities and always envision what you want to manifest.
- Find common ground with those you love.
- Pay attention to how you function in the Four Worlds and behave accordingly.

Action Points for Manifesting Your Dreams
- Meditate daily using the Sun/Moon Meditation or Transcendental Meditation
- Keep a journal handy and write down your inspired ideas.
- Use the Four Worlds Clarity Worksheet to track your ideas.
- Keep a journal to dialogue with your Higher Self.

Spiritual/Archetypal World
Channel 1-8 *(Scorpio-Taurus/Gemini)*

Keywords: Creative Expression, Inspiration, Unity, Self-Direction, Strength

You are creative and inspirational.

Creative energy activates when you sleep. When you dream, content from the collective unconscious becomes partially accessible to your awareness spiritually and consciously to some degree. The more you meditate and spend spiritual time, the more accessible this information becomes to your conscious mind. With your active creativity, you feel driven to contribute to your life and work in a way you think is meaningful. Imagination heightens your experience of a connection, and you feel that you are contributing to your life work in a way that deepens your sense of life's purpose. You feel an inner sense of harmony and joy. To maximize the impact of your spirituality, meditate, write down your dreams, and keep a journal in which you dialogue with your higher Self.

Your Keys to Empowerment
- When you feel inspired, express yourself Creatively.
- Love what you do and do what you love.
- Recognize your strength and use it to stand for what you know is right for you.
- Pay attention to how you function in the Four Worlds and behave accordingly.

Action Points for Manifesting Your Dreams
- Meditate daily using the Sun/Moon Meditation or Transcendental Meditation.
- Keep a journal handy and write down your creative ideas.
- Spend time in nature for inspiration.
- Dialogue with your Higher Self.

Channel 2-14

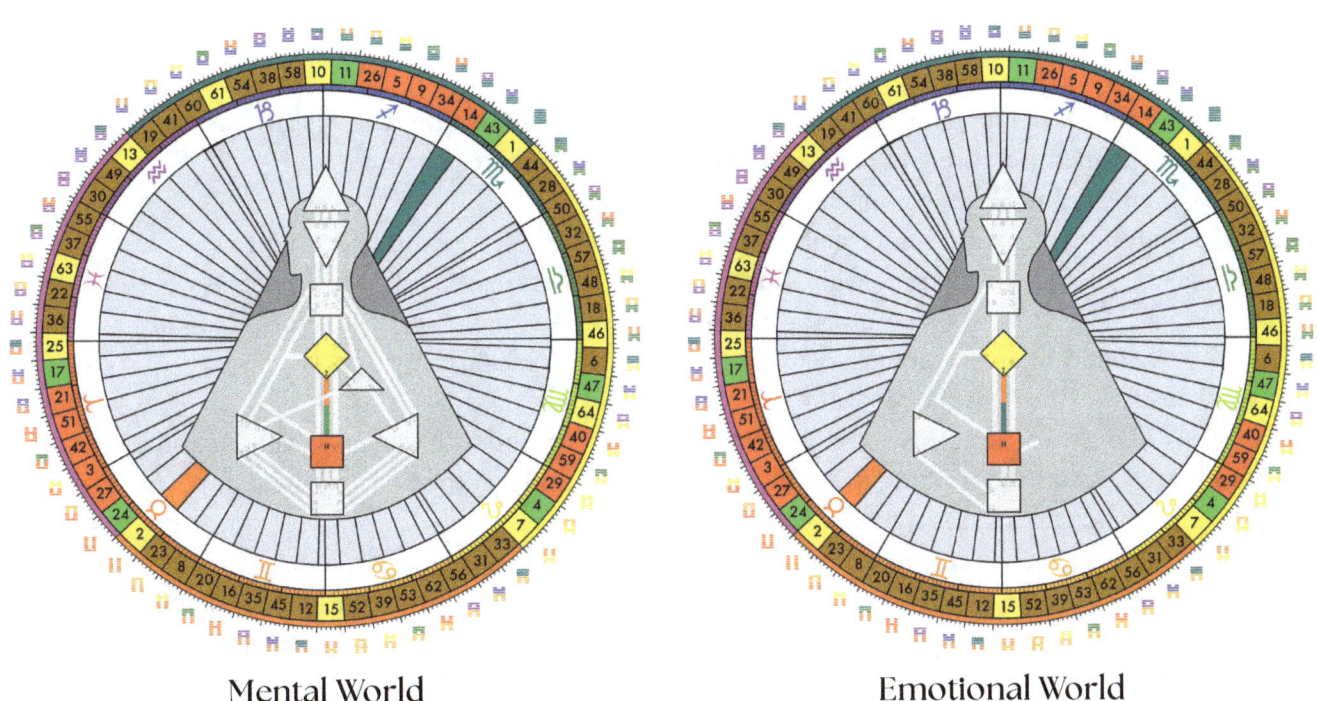

Mental World   Emotional World

Channel 2-14

Integrated Mental and Emotional/Angelic Worlds
Channel 2-14 *(Taurus-Scorpio/Sagittarius)*

Keywords: Directional Intelligence, The Beat, Self-Direction, Keeper of the Keys, Sovereignty

You are at your best when you honor what is right for you.

You do well with clear intentions and direction that honors your highest purpose and connects you to the cosmic energy flow. When you tap into the direction that truly resonates with you and is aligned with your highest goals, you are in sync with your deep Self and will likely attract others to you with your energy and confident aura. You must be clear that you are heading in the right direction and have clear intentions. You have a clear sense of how to orient yourself in the world and toward others, and when you combine strength and clarity with your determination used gracefully, you are a powerhouse.

Because of your powerful presence, maintain a humble and modest attitude and keep your strength internal while radiating kindness and love.

It is wise for you to ask some Clean Questions like: Am I facing the right direction? Am I in the right space? Am I in the right mindset? Be clear that you align in all Four Worlds to gain optimal clarity about your self-direction. Use Clean Questions and the Four Worlds Clarity exercise.

Your Keys to Empowerment
- Be clear that you align in all Four Worlds to gain optimal clarity about your self-direction.
- Always stand up for what you know is your "right direction."
- Stay focused on your goals without distraction.
- You attract others when you exude confidence.

Action Points for Manifesting Your Dreams
- Meditate Daily using the Microcosmic Orbit and Transcendental Meditation
- Use the Four Worlds Clarity Exercise
- Use the Sun/Moon Meditation regularly.
- Ask yourself Clean Questions like:
  – Am I facing in the right direction?
  – Am I in the right space?
  – Am I in the right mindset?

Mental World
Channel 2-14 *(Taurus-Scorpio/Sagittarius)*

Keywords: Directional Intelligence, The Beat, Self-Direction, Keeper of the Keys, Sovereignty

You are at your best when you honor what is right for you.

You do well when you have clear intentions and a clear direction that honors your highest purpose and connects you to the cosmic energy flow. When you tap into the path that truly resonates with you and is aligned with your highest goals, you are in sync with your deep Self and will likely attract others to you with your energy and confident aura. Because of your strength and powerful presence, you must remain modest and humble so those in your presence remain trusting and open to your input. Be mindful of your strength and use it strategically and wisely.

You must be clear that you are heading in the right direction and have clear intentions. It is wise to ask some Clean Questions like: Am I facing the right direction? Am I in the right space? Am I in the right mindset? Be clear that you align in all Four Worlds to gain optimal clarity about your self-direction. Use Clean Questions and the Four Worlds Clarity exercise.

Your Keys to Empowerment
- Be clear that you align in all Four Worlds to gain optimal clarity about your self-direction.
- Always stand up for what you know is your "right direction."
- Stay focused on your goals without distraction.
- Remain humble and modest to stay in touch with the divine.

Action Points for Manifesting Your Dreams
- Meditate Daily using the Microcosmic Orbit
- Work with the Four Worlds Clarity Exercise
- Be mindful of your strength and use it strategically and wisely.
- Ask yourself Clean Questions like:
  – Am I facing in the right direction?
  – Am I in the right space?
  – Am I in the right mindset?
  – Am I in the right mindset?

Emotional/Angelic World
Channel 2-14 *(Taurus-Scorpio/Sagittarius)*

Keywords: Directional Intelligence, The Beat, Self-Direction, Keeper of the Keys, Sovereignty

You are at your best when you honor what is right for you.

You are firmly in touch with the core of yourself if you take the time to tune in and reflect on what is right for you and what you experience as most aligned with you along your life path. When you are deeply committed to knowing yourself and your life path, you may find that other people gravitate to you and want to be in your presence because they feel a sense of ease with your self-assurance and self-directedness. Because you have a solid internal self-identity, your presence energetically communicates who you are and whether you are following your true path. Take the time to know yourself and what is right for you regarding your life path. Nothing is more important than your overall health and well-being. Meditate daily, do the Microcosmic Orbit before you fall asleep at night, write in your journal using the Four Worlds Clarity Exercise, and when you know what is right for you, stand up for it and yourself.

Your Keys to Empowerment
- Be clear that you align in all Four Worlds to gain optimal clarity about your self-direction.
- Always stand up for what you know is your "right direction."
- Stay focused on your goals without distraction.
- Always make sure you align with your deepest Self.

Action Points for Manifesting Your Dreams
- Meditate Daily using the Microcosmic Orbit
- Use the Four Worlds Clarity Exercise Daily
- Stand firm when you know you are heading in the right self-direction.
    - Ask yourself Clean Questions like:
    - Am I facing in the right direction?
    - Am I in the right space?
    - Am I in the right mindset?

Channel 3-60

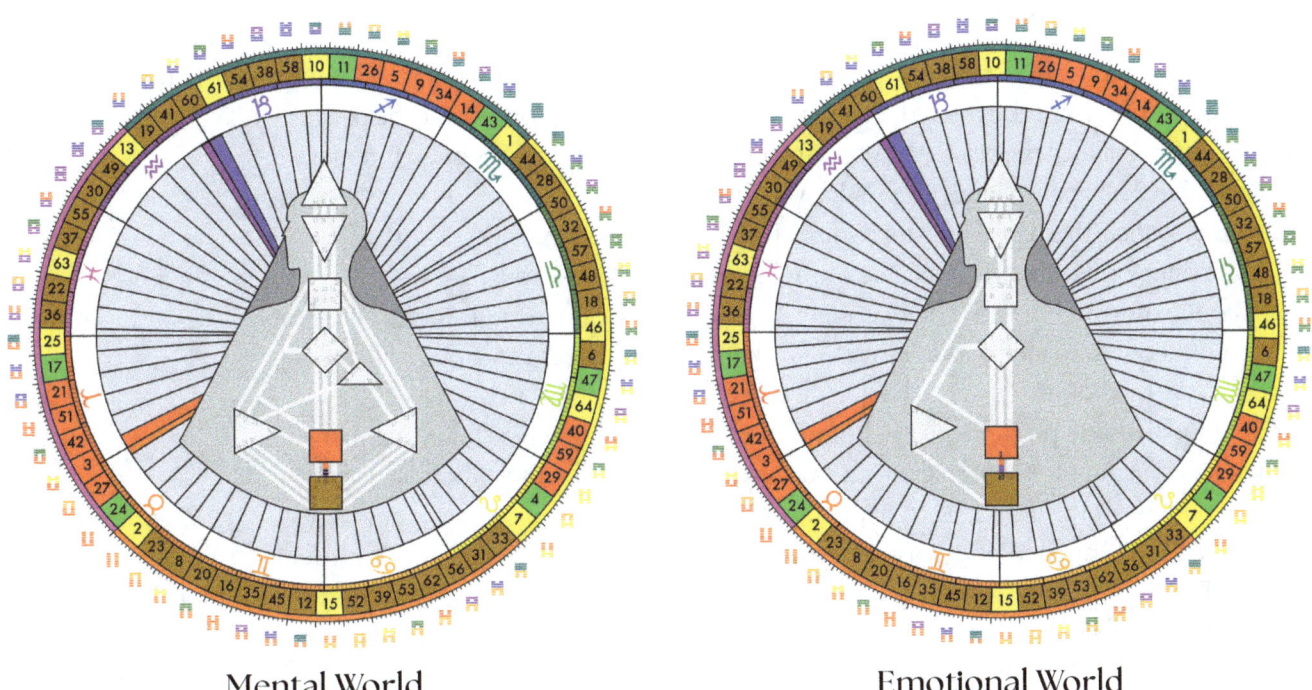

Mental World   Emotional World

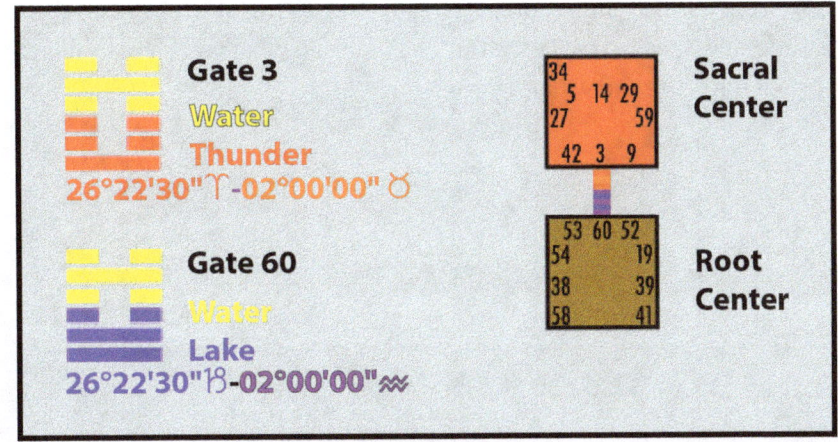

Channel 3-60

Integrated Mental and Emotional/Angelic Worlds
Channel 3-60 *(Aries/Taurus-Capricorn/Aquarius)*

Keywords: Process, Mutation, Acceptance, Energy Fluctuations

When you feel your energy shifting, tune in to what you trust and wait for clarity.

You have an acute awareness that change is a natural part of life. You recognize the value in change that serves a higher purpose. Each breath you take has an inhale, a pause, and an exhale. When you breathe, notice the pause and recognize that your breath transforms you as you exhale. You are not the same person who inhaled. Thus, you feel an inherent connection to how your awareness changes and how mutations create questions related to existence that you probe regularly. Sometimes, you may feel frustrated when challenged because you don't understand what needs to happen to release stuck energy. Patience and trust are your friends here. Because you are acutely aware that change is a natural part of life, staying rooted in trust and faith are critical calming forces. When you are considering a question that puzzles you, or when you are considering a course of action, take all the time you need to meditate using a breathing meditation that allows you the time and space to access your deep knowing; pose your question and wait for your consciousness to reveal the answer you need. Your process takes time; be patient with yourself and others with whom you interact.

Your Keys to Empowerment
- Trust your Process.
- Understand you are changeable.
- Accept and love yourself by monitoring your self-talk.
- Recognize that your energy fluctuates. Wait for clarity.

Action Points for Manifesting Your Dreams
- Meditate using a breathing meditation such as the Sun/Moon Meditation.
- Write down your questions and wait for answers.
- Write down the steps you plan to take to reach your goals.
- Take all the time you need to make decisions. Be certain what you choose aligns with your values.

Mental World
Channel 3-60 *(Aries/Taurus-Capricorn/Aquarius)*

Keywords: Process, Mutation, Acceptance, Energy Fluctuations

When you feel your energy shifting, tune in to what you trust and wait for clarity.

You are acutely aware that change is a natural part of life. Each breath you take has an inhale, a pause, and an exhale. When you breathe, notice the pause and recognize that your breath transforms you as you exhale. You are not the same person who inhaled. Thus, you feel an inherent connection to how your awareness changes and how mutations create questions related to existence that you probe regularly. Your curious mind wants answers, and with patience and probing, you will find them. When you are considering a question that puzzles you, or when you are considering a course of action, take all the time you need to meditate using a breathing meditation that allows you the time and space to access your deep knowing; pose your question and wait for your consciousness to reveal the answer you need. Trust your process.

Your Keys to Empowerment
- Trust your Process.
- Understand you are changeable.
- Accept and love yourself by monitoring your self-talk.
- Take time alone to consider what is right for you and wait for clarity.

Action Points for Manifesting Your Dreams
- Meditate using a breathing meditation such as the Sun/Moon Meditation.
- Write down your questions and wait for answers.
- Waiting for clarity before committing to something is healthy for you.
- Take all the time you need to align internally.

Emotional/Angelic World
Channel 3-60 *(Aries/Taurus-Capricorn/Aquarius)*

Keywords: Process, Mutation, Acceptance, Energy Fluctuations

When you feel your energy shifting, tune in to what you trust and wait for clarity.

You recognize the value in change that serves a higher purpose. Sometimes, you may feel frustrated when challenged because you don't understand what needs to happen to release stuck energy. Patience and trust are your friends here. Because you are acutely aware that change is a natural part of life, staying rooted in trust and faith are critical calming forces. When you breathe, notice the pause, and recognize that your breath transforms you as you exhale. You are not the same person who inhaled. Thus, you feel an inherent connection to how your awareness changes and how mutations create questions related to existence that you probe regularly. When you consider a question that puzzles you, or when you consider a course of action, take all the time you need to meditate using a breathing meditation that allows you the time and space to access your deep knowing; pose your question and wait for your consciousness to reveal the answer you need. Trust your process.

Your Keys to Empowerment
- Trust your Process.
- Understand you are changeable.
- Breathing meditations such as Microcosmic Orbit can balance your energy.
- Recognize that your energy fluctuates. Wait for clarity.

Action Points for Manifesting Your Dreams
- Meditate using a breathing meditation such as the Sun/Moon Meditation.
- Write down your questions and wait for answers.
- Dialogue with your Higher Self to gain self-awareness.
- Take all the time you need to make decisions. Be certain what you choose aligns with your values.

Channel 4-63

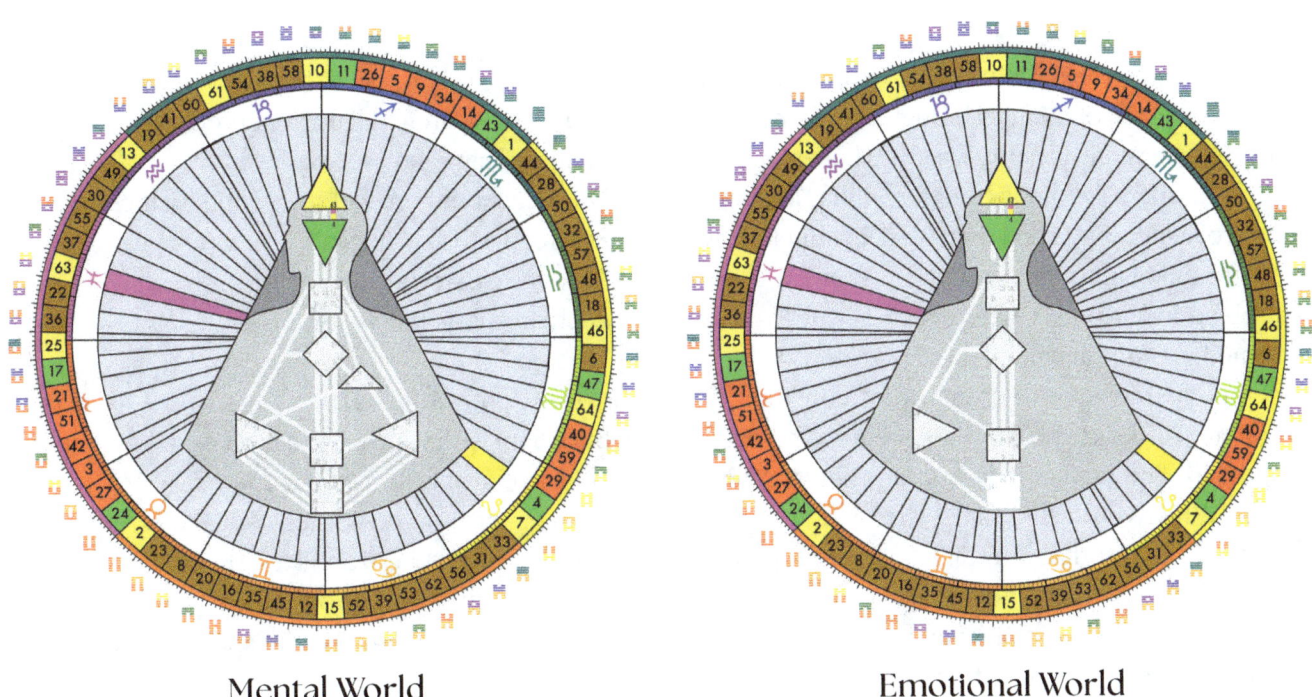

Mental World   Emotional World

Channel 4-63

Integrated Mental and Emotional/Angelic World
Channel 4-63 *(Leo-Pisces)*

Keywords: Hypothesizing, Logic, Patience, Testing

You are a deep thinker with many interests to explore.

You are a natural researcher who likes to hypothesize about all kinds of things. Through your questioning and wonderment, you find what you believe is based on logic and solid theories. Before you commit to a path of action, you need to trust that your effort will be grounded in truth and integrity. While you enjoy probing and are inquisitive, especially when you find something intriguing and a little beyond your easy comprehension, you also want to be confident that you are on solid ground. Be patient with yourself and trust the timing of how you process information. When you feel satisfied that you are on the right track, trust that you will know how to proceed toward your goals. When challenged about your strong beliefs or questions, you may react emotionally. Practice detachment from emotional reactions while you process information and formulate your internally guided perspective. Take time to breathe and reset your attitude.

Your Keys to Empowerment
- You are a researcher. Trust your process of questioning and probing.
- Do not act until you feel at ease and balanced.
- Stay focused on your goals.
- Recognize that your energy fluctuates. Wait for clarity.

Action Points for Manifesting Your Dreams
- Be patient with yourself. Your process takes time.
- Logic is essential for you. If it doesn't seem right to you, do not act.
- You like to hypothesize and test things. Enjoy your process without attachment.
- When stressed, pause, breathe, and rebalance.

Mental World
Channel 4-63 *(Leo-Pisces)*

Keywords: Hypothesizing, Logic, Patience, Testing

You are a deep thinker with many interests to explore.

You are a natural researcher who likes to hypothesize about all kinds of things. Through your questioning and wonderment, you find what you believe is based on logic and solid theories. Before you commit to a path of action, you need to trust that your effort will be grounded in truth and integrity. While you enjoy probing and are inquisitive, especially when you find something intriguing and a little beyond your easy comprehension, you also want to be confident that you are on solid ground. Be patient with yourself and trust the timing of how you process information. When you feel satisfied that you are on the right track, trust that you will know how to proceed toward your goals.

Your Keys to Empowerment
- You are a researcher. Trust your process of questioning and probing.
- Make sure your commitments are grounded.
- When on mental overload, take a break and breathe.
- Recognize that your energy fluctuates. Wait for clarity.

Action Points for Manifesting Your Dreams
- Be patient with yourself. Your process takes time.
- Logic is essential for you. If it doesn't seem right to you, do not act.
- You like to hypothesize and test things. Enjoy your process without attachment.
- Stay emotionally detached while considering alternative actions.

Emotional/Angelic World
Channel 4-63 *(Leo-Pisces)*

Keywords: Hypothesizing, Logic, Patience, Testing

You are a deep thinker with many interests to explore.

When challenged about your strong beliefs or questions, you may react emotionally. As a natural researcher who likes to hypothesize about all kinds of things, you base your questioning and wonderment on logic and solid theories. Before you commit to a path of action, you need to trust that your activity will be grounded in truth and integrity. While you enjoy probing and are inquisitive, especially when you find something intriguing and a little beyond your easy comprehension, you also want to be confident that you are on solid ground. Be patient with yourself and trust the timing of how you process information. When you feel satisfied that you are on the right track, trust that you will know how to proceed toward your goals. Practice detachment from emotional reactions while you process information and formulate your internally guided perspective. Using a pause to breathe and reset your attitude can go a long way for you in keeping your sense of inner calm and balance.

Your Keys to Empowerment
- You are a researcher. Trust your process of questioning and probing.
- Do not act until you feel at ease and balanced.
- Recognize that your energy fluctuates. Wait for clarity.
- When experiencing mental overload, take time to meditate using Transcendental meditation or the Sun/Moon Meditation.

Action Points for Manifesting Your Dreams
- Be patient with yourself. Your process takes time.
- Logic is essential for you. If it doesn't seem right to you, do not act.
- You like to hypothesize and test things. Enjoy your process without attachment.
- Take time to consider whether the answers satisfy your hypotheses.

Channel 5-15

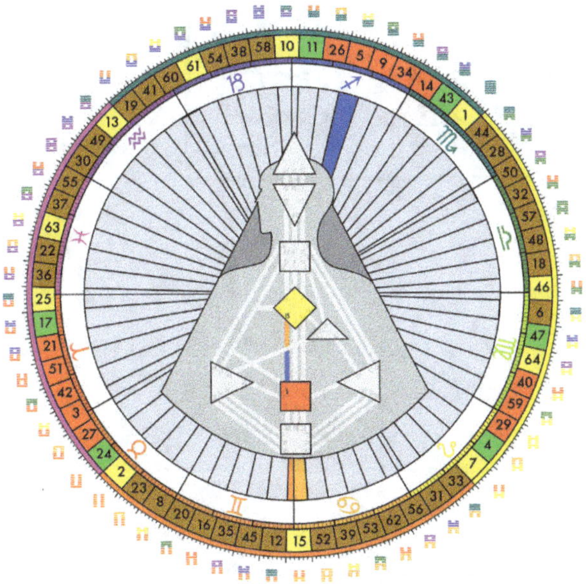

Mental World

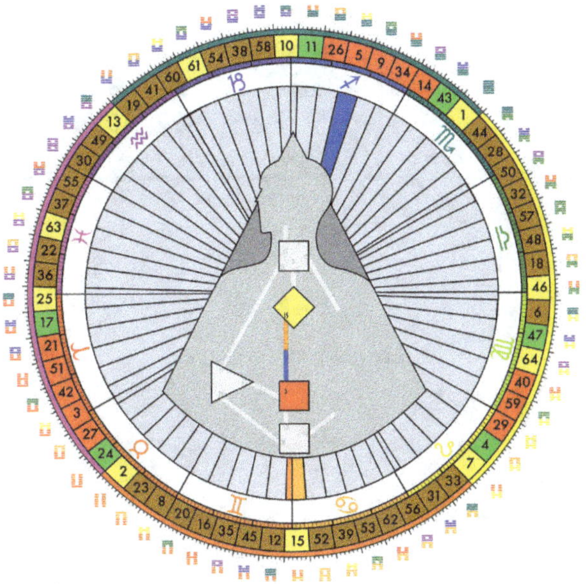

Spiritual World

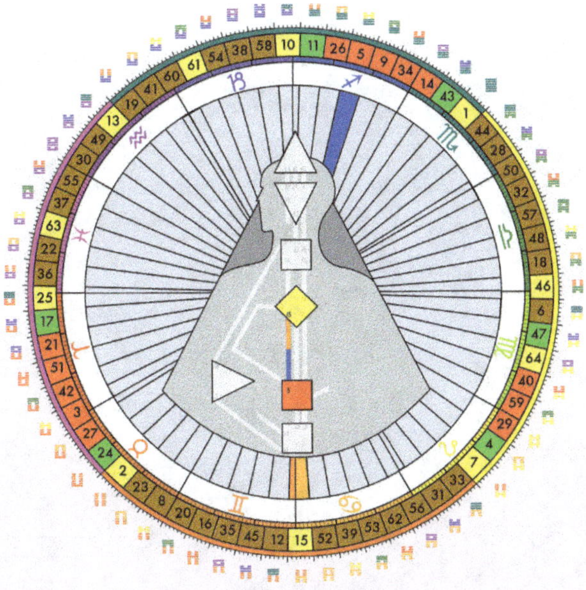

Emotional World

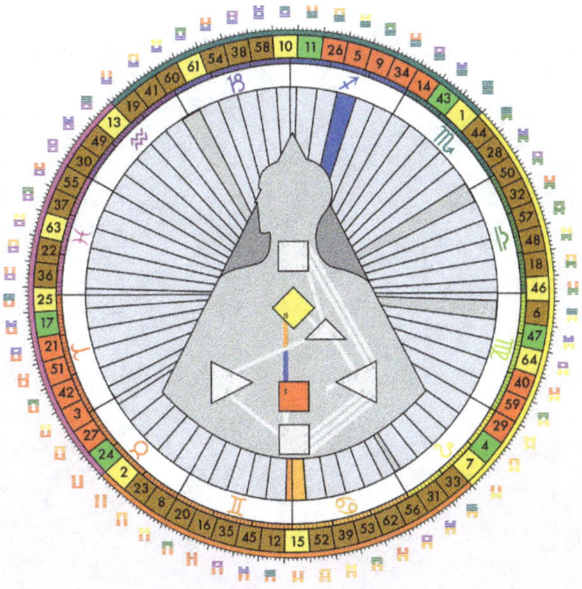

Physical World

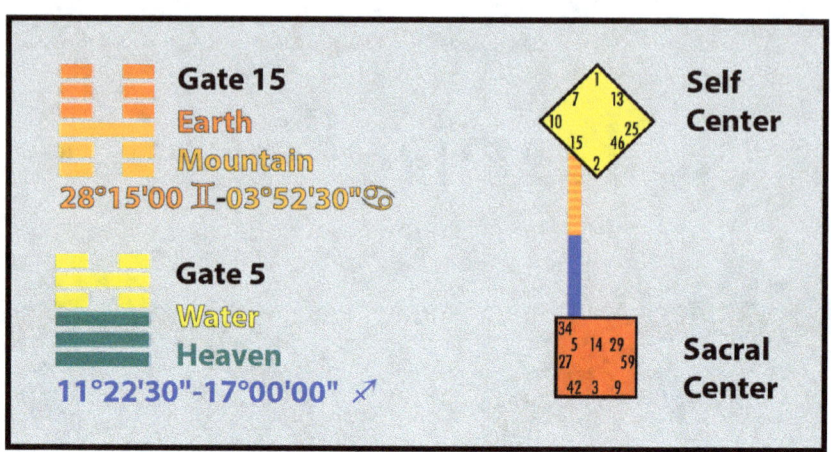

Channel 5-15

Integrated Mental and Spiritual/Archetypal, Emotional/Angelic, and Physical/Biological Worlds
Channel 5-15 *(Sagittarius-Gemini/Cancer)*

Keywords: Being in the Flow, Multidimensionality, Rhythm, Transcendence, Assuredness, Wisdom, Wavelength

You align with energy that feels right for you and have a good sense of timing.

Your multidimensional awareness sets you apart from others who do not recognize energy and how it flows. You know you are part of a greater consciousness and trust your inner integration. You are committed to your integrity regarding knowledge and how to orient yourself for your highest goals. When you face opposition to what you know to be right from deep within, stand up for yourself and do not compromise your integrity. Being in the flow and true to yourself reveals your divinity. Recognizing the energy of inner alignment is within your reach.

You feel intuitively that there is more than just this three-dimensional world. You, in fact, know intuitively that you live in the Mental, Spiritual, Emotional, and Physical Worlds and that they work together as a unified whole. Thus, you attune yourself to other people, especially to animals and nature. You feel an affinity and health benefit when you have a close relationship with your pets because they carry the spiritual/archetypal energy that activates that energy in your unconscious. This energy supports and enhances your instinctive consciousness. Honor your inner sense of what is right for you, and do not waiver.

Because you are so deeply connected to all four worlds, you may sometimes recognize patterns and rhythms that others do not perceive. When your awareness penetrates beyond what others perceive, you may feel impatient. Rather than disengaging from your perceptions, stand up for what you know with kindness and love. This shift in your attitude can transform your emotions as well as the emotions of those around you. Recognize your strength and consciousness.

Your sense of timing is instinctively excellent, and when you know that the time is right to act, if you honor your instinct, you usually find your actions and instincts to be correct. Take time daily to go within and experience your deep Self so you can stand firm against any experiences that are misaligned with you and your values. Do not waiver.

Your Keys to Empowerment

- You recognize your multidimensional nature and honor it.
- Only act when you know that action aligns with your deep Self.
- Your wisdom and knowing guide your life and its timing.
- You are confident and self-assured when you are "in the flow."
- You know more than you think you know. Trust yourself and stay aligned.

Action Points for Manifesting Your Dreams

- Only act when you feel aligned in all Four Worlds: the Mental, Emotional, Spiritual, and Physical.
- Your integrity is crucial to you. Do not compromise when you know you are internally aligned.
- Take time to meditate and consider all variables before making commitments.
- Ask yourself: "Does what I am considering move me closer to my goals, and is it in the right energy?"
- Be clear to release all preconceived ideas about your path forward and go within to learn what path is right for you.

Integrated Mental, Spiritual/Archetypal, and Emotional/Angelic Worlds
Channel 5-15 *(Sagittarius-Gemini/Cancer)*

Keywords: Being in the Flow, Multidimensionality, Rhythm, Transcendence, Assuredness, Wisdom, Wavelength

You align with energy that feels right for you and have a good sense of timing.

Your multidimensional awareness sets you apart from others who do not recognize energy and how it flows. You know you are part of a greater consciousness and trust your inner integration. You are committed to your integrity regarding knowledge and how to orient yourself with your highest goals. When you face opposition to what you know to be right from deep within, stand up for yourself and do not compromise your integrity. Being in the flow and true to yourself reveals your divinity. Recognizing the energy of inner alignment is within your reach.

You feel intuitively that there is more than just this three-dimensional world. You, in fact, know intuitively that you live in multiple dimensions and that they work together as a unified whole. You may have a great sense of timing regarding when to move forward on projects and when to stay still. In addition, you attune yourself to other people, especially animals and nature. You feel an affinity and health benefit when you have a close relationship with your pets because they carry the spiritual/archetypal energy that activates that energy in your unconscious. This energy supports and enhances your instinctive consciousness. Honor your inner sense of what is right for you, and do not waiver.

Because you are so deeply connected to other dimensions, you may sometimes recognize patterns and rhythms that others do not perceive. When your awareness penetrates beyond what others perceive, you may feel impatient. Rather than disengaging from your perceptions, stand up for what you know with kindness and love. This shift in your attitude can transform your emotions as well as the emotions of those around you. Recognize your strength and consciousness.

Your sense of timing is instinctively excellent, and when you know that the time is right to act, if you honor your instinct, you usually find your actions and instincts to be correct. Take time daily to go within and experience your deep Self so you can stand strong against any experiences that are misaligned with you and your values. Do not waiver.

Your Keys to Empowerment
- When you are aligned energetically, you know and feel confident.
- You act only when you know that action aligns with your deep Self.
- Your wisdom and knowing guide your life and its timing.
- Trust yourself and honor your timing.

Action Points for Manifesting Your Dreams
- Only act when you feel balanced and aligned.
- Your integrity is crucial to you. Do not compromise when you know you are internally aligned.
- Take time to meditate and consider all variables before making commitments
- Ask yourself: "Does what I am considering move me closer to my goals, and is it in the right energy.

Integrated Mental, Spiritual/Archetypal, and Physical/Biological Worlds
Channel 5-15 *(Sagittarius-Gemini/Cancer)*

Keywords: Being in the Flow, Multidimensionality, Rhythm, Transcendence, Assuredness, Wisdom, Wavelength

You align with energy that feels right for you and have a good sense of timing.

Your multidimensional awareness sets you apart from others who do not recognize energy and how it flows. You know you are part of a greater consciousness and trust your inner integration. You are committed to your integrity regarding knowledge and how to orient yourself with your highest goals. When you face opposition to what you know to be right from deep within, stand up for yourself and do not compromise your integrity. Being in the flow and true to yourself reveals your divinity. Recognizing the energy of inner alignment is within your reach.

You feel intuitively that there is more than just this three-dimensional world. You, in fact, know intuitively that you live in multiple dimensions and that they work together as a unified whole. You may have a great sense of timing regarding your physical health and body rhythm. In addition, you attune yourself to other people, especially animals and nature. You feel an affinity and health benefit when you have a close relationship with your pets because they carry the spiritual/archetypal energy that activates that energy in your unconscious. This energy supports and enhances your instinctive consciousness. Honor your inner sense of what is right for you, and do not waiver.

Because you are so deeply connected to all Four Worlds, you may sometimes recognize patterns and rhythms that others do not perceive. When your awareness penetrates beyond what others perceive, you may feel impatient. Rather than disengaging from your perceptions, stand up for what you know with kindness and love. If you feel emotionally reactive, you may have picked up energy from someone else. Use your creative intelligence to remain balanced. This shift in your attitude can transform your emotions as well as the emotions of those around you. Recognize your strength and consciousness.

Your sense of timing is instinctively excellent, and when you know that the time is right to act, if you honor your instinct, you usually find your actions and instincts to be correct. Take time daily to go within and experience your deep Self so you can stand strong against any experiences that are misaligned with you and your values. Do not waiver.

Your Keys to Empowerment
- You recognize your multidimensional nature and honor it.
- Pay attention to what aligns with your Physical needs.
- Your wisdom and knowing guides your life and its timing.
- You know more than you think you know. Trust yourself and stay aligned.

Action Points for Manifesting Your Dreams
- Only act when you feel aligned.
- Your integrity is crucial to you. Do not compromise when you know you are internally aligned.
- Take time to meditate and consider all variables before making commitments.
- Take time for Self-Care and meditation.

Integrated Mental, Emotional/Angelic, and Physical/Biological Worlds
Channel 5-15 *(Sagittarius-Gemini/Cancer)*

Keywords: Being in the Flow, Multidimensionality, Rhythm, Transcendence, Assuredness, Wisdom, Wavelength

You align with energy that feels right for you and have a good sense of timing.

Your multidimensional awareness sets you apart from others who do not recognize energy and how it flows. You know you are part of a greater consciousness and trust your inner integration. You are committed to your integrity regarding knowledge and how to orient yourself with your highest goals. When you face opposition to what you know to be right from deep within, stand up for yourself and do not compromise your integrity. Being in the flow and true to yourself reveals your divinity. Recognizing the energy of inner alignment is within your reach.

You feel intuitively that there is more than just this three-dimensional world. You, in fact, know intuitively that you live in multiple dimensions and that they work together as a unified whole. You may have a great sense of timing regarding your physical health and body rhythm. In addition, you attune yourself to other people, especially animals and nature. You feel an affinity and health benefit when you have a close relationship with your pets because they carry the spiritual/archetypal energy that activates that energy in your unconscious. This energy supports and enhances your instinctive consciousness. Honor your inner sense of what is right for you, and do not waiver.

Because you are so deeply connected to all Four Worlds, you may sometimes recognize patterns and rhythms that others do not perceive. When your awareness penetrates beyond what others perceive, you may feel impatient. Rather than disengaging from your perceptions, stand up for what you know with kindness and love. If you feel emotionally reactive, you may have picked up energy from someone else. Use your creative intelligence to remain balanced. This shift in your attitude can transform your emotions as well as the emotions of those around you. Recognize your strength and consciousness.

Your sense of timing is instinctively excellent, and when you know that the time is right to act, if you honor your instinct, you usually find your actions and instincts to be correct. Take time daily to go within and experience your deep Self so you can stand strong against any experiences that are misaligned with you and your values. Do not waiver.

Your Keys to Empowerment
- You recognize your multidimensional nature and honor it
- Pay attention to what aligns with your Physical needs.
- Your wisdom and knowing guides your life and its timing.
- You know more than you think you know. Trust yourself and stay aligned

Action Points for Manifesting Your Dreams
- Only act when you feel aligned.
- Your integrity is crucial to you. Do not compromise when you know you are internally aligned.
- Take time to meditate and consider all variables before making commitments.
- Take time for Self-Care and meditation.

Integrated Spiritual/Archetypal, Emotional/Angelic, and Physical/Biological Worlds
Channel 5-15 *(Sagittarius-Gemini/Cancer)*

Keywords: Being in the Flow, Multidimensionality, Rhythm, Transcendence, Assuredness, Wisdom, Wavelength

You align with energy that feels right for you and have a good sense of timing.

You need time to process information because your multidimensional awareness sets you apart from others who do not recognize energy and how it flows. You know you are part of a greater consciousness and trust your inner integration. You are committed to your integrity regarding knowledge and how to orient yourself with your highest goals. When you face opposition to what you know to be right from deep within, stand up for yourself and do not compromise your integrity. Being in the flow and true to yourself reveals your divinity. Recognizing the energy of inner alignment is within your reach.

You feel intuitively that there is more than just this three-dimensional world. You, in fact, know intuitively that you live in multiple dimensions and that they work together as a unified whole. You may have a great sense of timing regarding your physical health and body rhythm. In addition, you attune yourself to other people, especially animals and nature. You feel an affinity and health benefit when you have a close relationship with your pets because they carry the spiritual/archetypal energy that activates that energy in your unconscious. This energy supports and enhances your instinctive consciousness. Honor your inner sense of what is right for you, and do not waiver.

Because you are so deeply connected to your inner process, you may sometimes recognize patterns and rhythms that others do not perceive. When your awareness penetrates beyond what others perceive, you may feel impatient. Rather than disengaging from your perceptions, stand up for what you know with kindness and love. If you feel emotionally reactive, you may have picked up energy from someone else. Use your creative intelligence to remain balanced. This shift in your attitude can transform your emotions as well as the emotions of those around you. Recognize your strength and consciousness.

Your sense of timing is instinctively excellent, and when you know that the time is right to act, if you honor your instinct, you usually find your actions and instincts to be correct. Take time daily to go within and experience your deep Self so you can stand strong against any experiences that are misaligned with you and your values. Do not waiver.

Your Keys to Empowerment
- You recognize your multidimensional nature and honor it.
- Pay attention to what aligns with your Physical needs.
- You need time to process things. Take all the necessary time until you feel ready to integrate what you know.
- Trust yourself and stay aligned.

Action Points for Manifesting Your Dreams
- Only act when you feel aligned.
- Your integrity is crucial to you. Do not compromise when you know you are internally aligned.
- Take time to meditate and consider all variables before making commitments.
- Self-care is important for your health and inner balance.

Integrated Mental and Spiritual/Archetypal Worlds
Channel 5-15 *(Sagittarius-Gemini/Cancer)*

Keywords: Being in the Flow, Multidimensionality, Rhythm, Transcendence, Assuredness, Wisdom, Wavelength

You align with energy that feels right for you and have a good sense of timing.

Your multidimensional awareness sets you apart from others who do not recognize energy and how it flows. You know you are part of a greater consciousness and trust your inner integration. You are committed to your integrity regarding knowledge and how to orient yourself for your highest goals. When you face opposition to what you know to be right from deep within, stand up for yourself and do not compromise your integrity. Being in the flow and true to yourself reveals your divinity. Recognizing the energy of inner alignment is within your reach.

You feel intuitively that there is more than just this three-dimensional world. You, in fact, know intuitively that you live in the Mental, Spiritual, Emotional, and Physical Worlds and that they work together as a unified whole. Thus, you attune yourself to other people, especially to animals and nature. You feel an affinity and health benefit when you have a close relationship with your pets because they carry the spiritual/archetypal energy that activates that energy in your unconscious. This energy supports and enhances your instinctive consciousness. Honor your inner sense of what is right for you, and do not waiver.

Your sense of timing is instinctively excellent, and when you know that the time is right to act, if you honor your instinct, you usually find your actions and instincts to be correct. Take time daily to go within and experience your deep self so you can stand strong against any experiences that are misaligned with you and your values. Do not waiver.

Your Keys to Empowerment
- You recognize your multidimensional nature and honor it.
- You act only when you know that action aligns with your deep Self.
- Your wisdom and knowing guide your life and its timing.
- You are confident and self-assured because you are "in the flow."

Action Points for Manifesting Your Dreams
- Only act when you feel aligned in all Four Worlds: the Mental, Emotional, Spiritual, and Physical.
- Your integrity is crucial to you. Do not compromise when you know you are internally aligned.
- Take time to meditate and consider all variables before making commitments.
- Ask yourself: "Does what I am considering move me closer to my goals, and is it in the right energy?"
- Be clear to release all preconceived ideas about your path forward and go within to learn what path is right for you.

Integrated Mental and Emotional/Angelic Worlds
Channel 5-15 *(Sagittarius-Gemini/Cancer)*

Keywords: Being in the Flow, Multidimensionality, Rhythm, Transcendence, Assuredness, Wisdom, Wavelength

You align with energy that feels right for you and have a good sense of timing.

Your multidimensional awareness sets you apart from others who do not recognize energy and how it flows. You know you are part of a greater consciousness and trust your inner integration. You recognize that you exist in Four Worlds, i.e., the Mental, Emotional, Spiritual, and Physical Worlds, and you often feel tuned into high-frequency consciousness and think outside of the ordinary ways people around you think. Your timing and energy awareness allow your power of manifesting to be timed to what you want to have happen. At best, you act at the right time and in the right manner.

Stay true to what aligns deeply within you and wait to act until you feel the inner imperative whispering to you that the time to act is now.

You are committed to your integrity regarding what you know and how to orient yourself for your highest goals. When you face opposition to what you know to be right from deep within, stand up for yourself and do not compromise your integrity. Being in the flow and being true to yourself reveals your divinity to you and to others. Recognizing the energy of inner alignment is within your reach. Take time daily to go within and experience your deep Self so you can stand strong against any experiences that are misaligned with you and your values. Do not waiver. Be courageous and trusting in your Higher Self to know what actions are right. Stand up for what you know, and do not compromise when pressured by those less conscious than you.

Your Keys to Empowerment
- You recognize your multidimensional nature and honor it.
- You act only when you feel that action aligns with your deep Self.
- Quiet meditation time is essential for your health and inner balance.
- You are confident and self-assured when you are "in the flow."

Action Points for Manifesting Your Dreams
- Only act when you feel aligned in all Four Worlds: the Mental, Emotional, Spiritual, and Physical.
- Your integrity is crucial to you. Do not compromise when you know you are internally aligned.
- Take time to meditate and consider all variables before making commitments.
- Ask yourself: "Does what I am considering move me closer to my goals, and is it in the right energy?"
- Be courageous and trusting in your Higher Self to know what actions are correct. Stand up for what you know. Do not compromise when pressured by those less conscious than you.

Integrated Mental and Physical/Biological Worlds
Channel 5-15 *(Sagittarius-Gemini/Cancer)*

Keywords: Being in the Flow, Multidimensionality, Rhythm, Transcendence, Assuredness, Wisdom, Wavelength

You align with energy that feels right for you and have a good sense of timing.

Your multidimensional awareness sets you apart from others who do not recognize energy and how it flows. You know you are part of a greater consciousness and trust your inner integration. You are committed to your integrity regarding what you know and how to orient yourself for your highest goals. When you face opposition to what you know to be right from deep within, stand up for yourself and do not compromise your integrity.

You have a strong sense of patterns and rhythms that align and resonate with your body chemistry. When something physically misaligns with your frequency, you instinctively sense it and want to move away from that person or situation. Your health and peace of mind must honor your instinctive sensibilities and timing. Pay attention to patterns in your life, discern what uplifts you, and eliminate what no longer serves you. Take time for Self-Care and especially balance it in all Four Worlds.

Being in the flow and true to yourself reveals your divinity to others. Recognizing the energy of inner alignment is within your reach. Take time daily to go within. Experience your deep Self and stand firm against any experiences that misalign with you and your values. Do not waiver.

Your Keys to Empowerment
- You recognize your multidimensional nature and honor it.
- You act only when you know that action aligns with your deep Self.
- Your wisdom and knowing guides your life and its timing.
- Take time to ensure you are physically aligned and "in the flow."

Action Points for Manifesting Your Dreams
- Only act when you feel aligned in all Four Worlds: the Mental, Emotional, Spiritual, and Physical.
- Your integrity is crucial to you. Do not compromise when you know you are internally aligned.
- Take time for Self-Care and only act when you know you are rested and clear-headed.
  – Ask yourself: "Am I in a rested and honoring my deep Self?"
  – Consider your body rhythm and listen to its guidance.

Integrated Spiritual/Archetypal and Emotional/Angelic Worlds
Channel 5-15 *(Sagittarius-Gemini/Cancer)*

Keywords: Being in the Flow, Multidimensionality, Rhythm, Transcendence, Assuredness, Wisdom, Wavelength

You align with energy that feels right for you and have a good sense of timing.

Your multidimensional awareness sets you apart from others who do not recognize energy and how it flows. You know you are part of a greater consciousness and trust your inner integration. Your sense of timing is instinctively excellent, and when you know that the time is right to act, if you honor your instinct, you usually find your actions and instincts to be correct.

You acknowledge that you exist in Four Worlds, and you often feel tuned into high-frequency consciousness and think outside of the ordinary ways people around you think. Your timing and energy awareness allow your power of manifesting to be timed to what you want to have happen. At best, you act at the right time in the proper manner.

Stay true to what aligns deeply within you and wait to act until you feel the inner imperative whispering to you that the time to act is now. Be courageous and trust in your Higher Self to know what actions are correct. Stand up for what you know, and do not compromise when pressured by those less conscious than you.

You attune yourself to other species, and you do well when you are in the presence of your pets. The reason for this affinity and health benefit for you of having a close relationship with another mammal is that they carry the spiritual/archetypal energy that activates that energy in your unconscious, supporting you and enhancing your intuitive consciousness. Honor your inner sense of what suits you, and do not waiver.

Your Keys to Empowerment
- You recognize your multidimensional nature and honor it.
- You act only when you know that action aligns with your deep Self.
- Take time alone to meditate to be certain that wisdom and knowing guides your life and its timing.
- When you are "in the flow," you have a sense of well-being that empowers you.

Action Points for Manifesting Your Dreams
- Only act when you feel aligned in all Four Worlds: the Mental, Emotional, Spiritual, and Physical.
- Your integrity is crucial to you. Do not compromise when you know you are internally aligned.
- Be alert to your inner process and commit to what resonates deep within you.
- You know what you know. Stay firm on your inner guidance.

Integrated Spiritual/Archetypal and Physical/Biological Worlds
Channel 5-15 *(Sagittarius-Gemini/Cancer)*

Keywords: Being in the Flow, Multidimensionality, Rhythm, Transcendence, Assuredness, Wisdom, Wavelength

You align with energy that feels right for you and have a good sense of timing.

Your multidimensional awareness sets you apart from others who do not recognize energy and how it flows. You know you are part of a greater consciousness and trust your inner integration. Your sense of timing is instinctively excellent, and when you know that the time is right to act, if you honor your instinct, you usually find your actions and instincts to be correct.

You have a sense of patterns and rhythms that align and resonate with your body chemistry.

When something physically misaligns with you, you instinctively sense it and want to move away from that person or situation. Your health and peace of mind must honor your instinctive sensibilities and timing for acting if that is your option. Pay attention to patterns in your life and discern what uplifts you and what you can eliminate.

You are attuned to other species, and you do well when in the presence of your pets. The reason for this affinity and health benefit for you of having a close relationship with another mammalian species is that they carry the spiritual/archetypal energy that activates that energy in your unconscious, supporting you and enhancing your intuitive consciousness. Honor your inner sense of what suits you, and do not waiver.

Your Keys to Empowerment
- Meditation is crucial for your sense of being part of a larger whole that empowers you.
- Act only when you know that action aligns with your deep Self.
- Your wisdom and knowing guide your life and its timing.
- Feeling confident and self-assured makes you "in the flow."

Action Points for Manifesting Your Dreams
- Only act when you feel aligned in all Four Worlds: the Mental, Emotional, Spiritual, and Physical.
- Your integrity is crucial to you. Do not compromise when you know you are internally aligned.
- Be alert to your inner process and commit to what resonates deep within you.
- Pay attention to what feeds your soul and what detracts from your momentum toward your goals. Commit to what moves you forward toward your goals and eliminate unnecessary task

Integrated Emotional/Angelic and Physical/Biological Worlds
Channel 5-15 *(Sagittarius-Gemini/Cancer)*

Keywords: Being in the Flow, Multidimensionality, Rhythm, Transcendence, Assuredness, Wisdom, Wavelength

You align with energy that feels right for you and have a good sense of timing.

Your multidimensional awareness may set you apart from others who do not recognize energy and how it flows. You know you are part of a greater consciousness and trust your inner integration. You acknowledge that you exist in Four Worlds, and you often feel tuned into high-frequency consciousness and think outside of the ordinary ways people around you think.

Your timing and energy awareness allow your power of manifesting to be timed to what you want to have happen as it relates to patterns and rhythms that align and resonate with your body chemistry. When something physically misaligns with your frequency, you instinctively sense it and want to move away from that person or situation. Your health and peace of mind must honor your intuitive sensibilities and timing for acting if that is your option. Pay attention to patterns in your life and discern which uplifts you and which ones may be eliminated.

At best, you act at the right time in the proper manner. Stay true to what you know aligns deeply within you and wait until you feel the inner imperative that is the time to act. Be courageous and trusting in your Higher Self to know what actions are correct. Stand up for what you know, and do not compromise when pressured by those less conscious. Take time for Self-Care and especially balance it in all Four Worlds.

Your Keys to Empowerment
- You recognize your multidimensional nature and honor it.
- You act only when you know that action aligns with your deep Self.
- Your wisdom and knowing guide your life and its timing.
- You are confident and self-assured because you are "in the flow."

Action Points for Manifesting Your Dreams
- Only act when you feel aligned in all Four Worlds: the Mental, Emotional, Spiritual, and Physical.
- Your integrity is crucial to you. Do not compromise when you know you are internally aligned.
- Be alert to what facilitates your awareness and avoid stressful encounters.
- Take time to meditate and use breathing to rebalance and realign.

Mental World
Channel 5-15 *(Sagittarius-Gemini/Cancer)*

Keywords: Being in the Flow, Multidimensionality, Rhythm, Transcendence, Assuredness, Wisdom, Wavelength

You align with energy that feels right for you and have a good sense of timing.

Your multidimensional awareness sets you apart from others who do not recognize energy and how it flows. You know you are part of a greater consciousness and trust your inner integration of knowing. You are committed to your integrity regarding what you know and how to orient yourself for your highest goals. When you face opposition to what you know to be right from deep within, stand up for yourself and do not compromise your integrity. Being in the flow and being true to yourself reveals your divinity to you and others. Recognizing the energy of inner alignment is within your reach. Take time daily to go within and experience your deep Self so you can stand strong against any experiences that are misaligned with you and your values. Do not waiver.

Your Keys to Empowerment
- You recognize your multidimensional nature and honor it.
- You act only when you know that action aligns with your deep Self.
- Your wisdom and knowing guides your life and its timing.
- Following what is aligned personally and cosmically makes you feel empowered and "in the flow."

Action Points for Manifesting Your Dreams
- Only act when you feel aligned in all Four Worlds: the Mental, Emotional, Spiritual, and Physical.
- Your integrity is crucial to you. Do not compromise when you know you are internally aligned.
- Be alert to what facilitates your awareness and avoid stressful encounters.
- Before acting, be certain that you are aligned with your goals.

Spiritual/Archetypal World
Channel 5-15 *(Sagittarius-Gemini/Cancer)*

Keywords: Being in the Flow, Multidimensionality, Rhythm, Transcendence, Assuredness, Wisdom, Wavelength

You align with energy that feels right for you and have a good sense of timing.

Your multidimensional awareness sets you apart from others who do not recognize energy and how it flows. You know you are part of a greater consciousness and trust your inner integration of knowing. Your sense of timing is instinctively excellent, and when you know that the time is right to act, if you honor your instinct, you usually find your actions and instincts to be correct. You have a sense of living in multiple dimensions; thus, you have an affinity for all living beings, and you do well when you are in the presence of your pets. The reason for this affinity and health benefit for you of having a close relationship with another mammalian species is that they carry the spiritual/archetypal energy that activates that energy in your unconscious, supporting you and enhancing your intuitive consciousness. Honor your inner sense of what is right for you, and do not waiver.

Your Keys to Empowerment
- You recognize your multidimensional nature and honor it.
- You act only when you know that action aligns with your deep Self.
- You sense when energy supports you and when you need to wait.
- You are confident and self-assured because you are "in the flow."

Action Points for Manifesting Your Dreams
- Only act when you feel aligned in all Four Worlds: the Mental, Emotional, Spiritual, and Physical.
- Your integrity is crucial to you. Do not compromise when you know you are internally aligned.
- Listen for your inner voice of wisdom before acting.
- Take time for yourself before committing to actions, and remain open and flexible if you need to revise your plans.

Emotional/Angelic World
Channel 5-15 *(Sagittarius-Gemini/Cancer)*

Keywords: Being in the Flow, Multidimensionality, Rhythm, Transcendence, Assuredness, Wisdom, Wavelength

You align with energy that feels right for you and have a good sense of timing.

Your multidimensional awareness may set you apart from others who do not recognize energy and how it flows. You know you are part of a greater consciousness and trust your inner integration of knowing. You recognize that you exist in Four Worlds, and you often feel tuned into high-frequency consciousness and think outside of the ordinary ways people around you think. Your timing and energy awareness allow your power of manifesting to be timed to what you want to have happen. At best, you act at the right time and in the right manner. Stay true to what you know aligns deeply within you and wait to act until you feel the inner imperative that whispers to you that the time to act is now. Be courageous and trusting in your Higher Self to know what actions are right. Stand up for what you know, and do not compromise when pressured by those less conscious than you.

Your Keys to Empowerment
- You recognize your multidimensional nature and honor it.
- You act only when you know that action aligns with your deep Self.
- Your wisdom and knowing guide your life and its timing.
- When you know you are on the right path for yourself, you have integrity and strength.

Action Points for Manifesting Your Dreams
- Only act when you feel aligned in all Four Worlds: the Mental, Emotional, Spiritual, and Physical.
- Your integrity is crucial to you. Do not compromise when you know you are internally aligned.
- Before acting, make sure you are in a calm and centered place. Listen to your inner voice and let what you need guide you.
- Take time for yourself before committing to actions, and remain open and flexible if you need to revise your plans.

Physical/Biological World
Channel 5-15 *(Sagittarius-Gemini/Cancer)*

Keywords: Being in the Flow, Multidimensionality, Rhythm, Transcendence, Assuredness, Wisdom, Wavelength

You align with energy that feels right for you and have a good sense of timing.

Your multidimensional awareness may set you apart from others who do not recognize energy and how it flows. You know you are part of a greater consciousness and trust your inner integration of knowing. You recognize that you exist in Four Worlds, and you often feel tuned into high-frequency consciousness and think outside of the ordinary ways people around you think. You sense when patterns and rhythms align and resonate with your body chemistry. When something physically misaligns with your frequency, you instinctively sense it and want to move away from that person or situation. It is imperative for your health and peace of mind to honor your instinctive sensibilities and timing for acting if that is an option for you. Pay attention to patterns in your life and discern which uplifts you and which ones may be best eliminated. Take time for Self-Care and especially balance it in all Four Worlds.

Your Keys to Empowerment
- You recognize your multidimensional nature and honor it.
- Wait until you know in your "gut" that your energy is balanced and aligned with any considered actions.
- Your wisdom and knowing guide your life and its timing.
- You are confident and self-assured when you are "in the flow."

Action Points for Manifesting Your Dreams
- Only act when you feel aligned in all Four Worlds: the Mental, Emotional, Spiritual, and Physical.
- Your integrity is crucial to you. Do not compromise when you know you are internally aligned.
- Breathe and center before you commit to actions to be certain that you are acting from a place of strength and inner alignment.
- Take time for yourself before you commit to actions, and remain open and flexible if you sense you need to revise your plans.

Channel 6-59

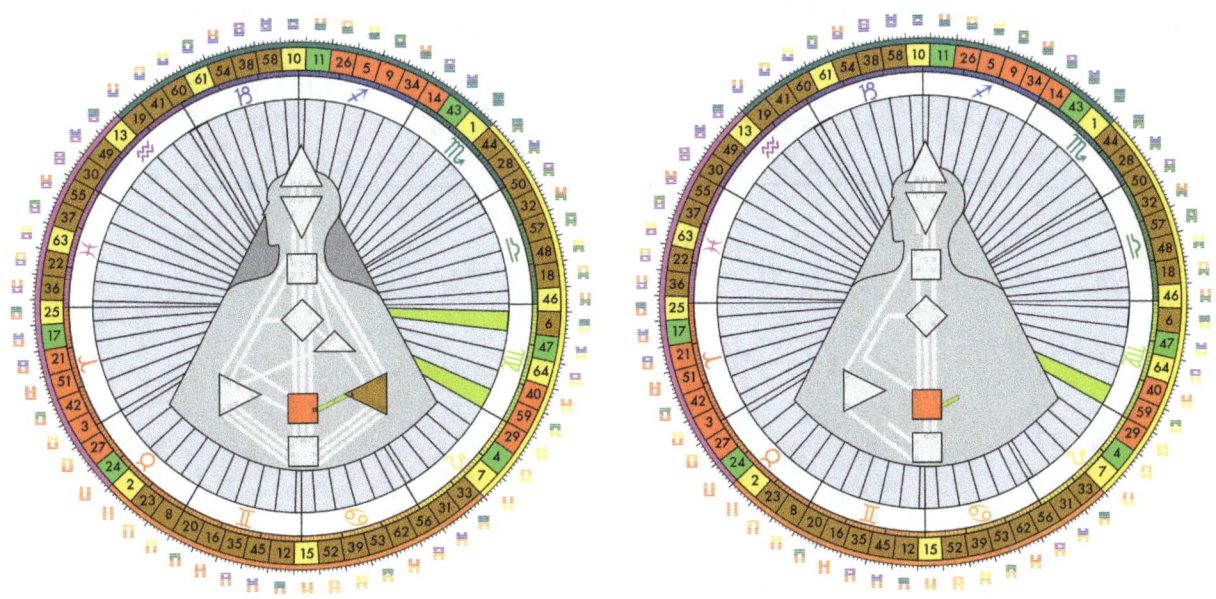

Mental World

Emotional World

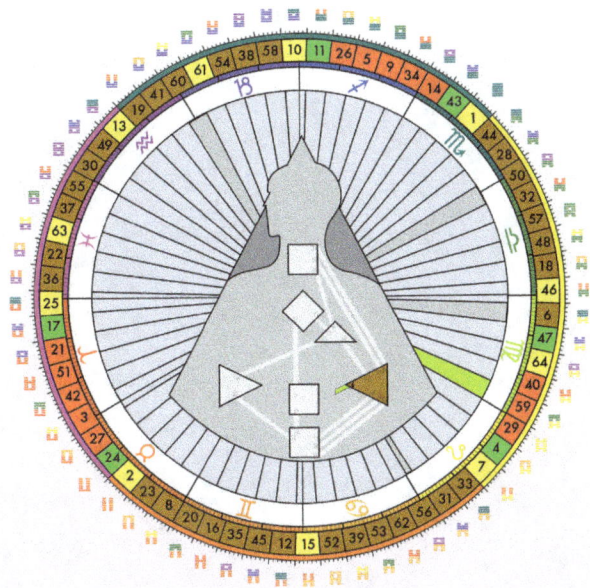

Physical World

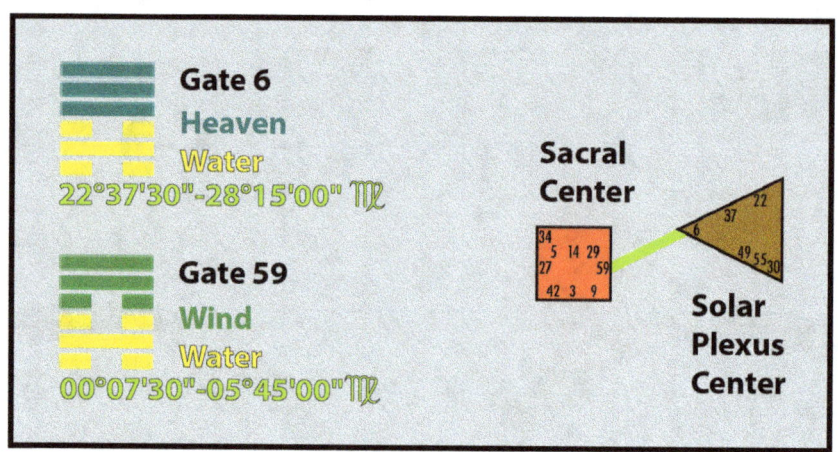

Channel 6-59

Integrated Mental World and Emotional/Angelic and Physical/Biological World Portals
Channel 6-59 *(Virgo-Virgo)*

Keywords: Regulation, Relating, Mating, Chemistry

Relationships are important to you; transform emotional reactivity through meditation, communication, and compassion.

When you are emotionally triggered positively or negatively, you will likely experience intense feelings that impact you physically. Although emotional reactivity is instinctive and self-protective, it never defines you. Because you experience life through your emotional filters, you like to connect with others, value all your relationships, and like to maintain them. Use breathing to monitor your emotional reactivity; by changing the rhythm of your breathing, you can change how you feel. When you find yourself emotionally reactive or physically stressed, breathe and take all the time you need to rebalance and realign.

You have gut experiences about people you meet and feel part of your life mission is connecting people. Your intense energy has a significant impact, so pay attention, especially if you are outgoing and engaging.

Your relationships are multifaceted, and you enjoy those relationships that have depth and meaning to you spiritually. You also know that your relationships impact you physically because your body chemistry affects your feelings and moods. You know that your body chemistry is involved in your feelings and moods. Thus, continually realign your emotions with your assessment of your situation and determine what you want to have happen before you react physically and in a way that puts stress on your body. If you are mindful and always work with the Four Integrative Worlds, you will find that relationships and the issues you confront in them deepen your consciousness.

Your Keys to Empowerment
- Relationships are important to you; know your boundaries and honor them.
- Use discernment in your relationships so you honor yourself and the other person.
- Transform emotional reactivity into awareness through breathing, meditation, and communication.
- You are confident and self-assured when you communicate well with others. Your sensitivity puts stress on you physically. Be diligent about self-care.

Action Points for Manifesting Your Dreams
- When relationships deplete your energy, back away and take time for yourself.
- You can transform emotional reactivity into conscious awareness. Pay attention and avoid emotional volatility.
- Breathe and center before committing to helping someone else.
- Self-awareness allows you to self-regulate emotionally when you are stressed. Pause and realign internally when you are emotionally triggered.
- Be mindful about your needs and make sure you maintain balance in relationships

Integrated Mental World and Physical/Biological World Portals
Channel 6-59 *(Virgo-Virgo)*

Keywords: Regulation, Relating, Mating, Chemistry

Relationships are important to you; transform emotional reactivity through meditation, communication, and compassion.

When you are emotionally triggered positively or negatively, you will likely experience intense feelings. Because you experience life through your emotional filters, you like to connect with others, value all your relationships, and like to maintain them. Use your breathing to monitor your emotional reactivity; by changing the rhythm of your breathing, you can change how you feel.

Be mindful of your impact on others. You have gut experiences about people you meet. You feel part of your life mission is connecting people. Your intense energy has a significant impact, so pay attention, especially if you are outgoing and engaging.

Your body chemistry is involved in your feelings and moods. Thus, continually realign your emotions with your assessment of your situation and determine what you want to have happen before you react physically in ways that stress your body. If you are mindful and always work with the Four Integrative Worlds, you will find this channel as a portal to consciousness compelling.

Your Keys to Empowerment
- You value your relationships and feel your best when you nurture them.
- Use discernment in your relationships so you honor yourself and the other person.
- You can transform emotional reactivity into awareness using appropriate communication skills.
- You are confident and self-assured when you communicate well with others.

Action Points for Manifesting Your Dreams
- When relationships deplete your energy, back away and take time for yourself.
- You can transform emotional reactivity into conscious awareness. Pay attention and avoid emotional volatility.
- Breathe and center before committing to a problem for someone else.
- Take time before committing to actions, and remain open and flexible if you need to revise your plans.

Integrated Emotional/Angelic and Physical/Biological World Portals
Channel 6-59 *(Virgo-Virgo)*

Keywords: Regulation, Relating, Mating, Chemistry

Relationships are important to you; transform emotional reactivity through meditation, communication, and compassion.

When you are emotionally triggered positively or negatively, you will likely experience intense feelings. Because you experience life through your emotional filters, you like to connect with others, value all your relationships, and like to maintain them. Use your breathing to monitor your emotional reactivity; by changing the rhythm of your breathing, you can change how you feel.

You have gut experiences about people you meet and feel part of your life mission is connecting people. Your intense energy has a significant impact, so pay attention, especially if you are outgoing and engaging.

Your relationships are multifaceted, and you enjoy those relationships that have depth and meaning to you spiritually. You also know that your relationships impact you physically because your body chemistry affects your feelings and moods. You know that your body chemistry is involved in your feelings and moods. Thus, continually realign your emotions with your assessment of your situation and determine what you want to have happen before you react physically and in a way that puts stress on your body. If you are mindful and always work with the Four Integrative Worlds, you will find that relationships and the issues you confront in them deepen your consciousness.

Your Keys to Empowerment
- Relationships are important to you; know your boundaries and honor them.
- Use discernment in your relationships so you honor yourself and the other person.
- Transform emotional reactivity into awareness through meditation and communication.
- You are confident and self-assured when you communicate well with others.

Action Points for Manifesting Your Dreams
- When relationships deplete your energy, back away and take time for yourself.
- You can transform emotional reactivity into conscious awareness. Pay attention and avoid emotional volatility.
- Breathe and center before committing to a problem for someone else.
- Self-awareness allows you to self-regulate emotionally when you are stressed.
- Pause and realign internally when you are emotionally triggered.

Mental World
Channel 6-59 *(Virgo-Virgo)*

Keywords: Regulation, Relating, Mating, Chemistry

Relationships are important to you; transform emotional reactivity through meditation, communication, and compassion.

When you are emotionally triggered positively or negatively, you will likely experience intense feelings that impact you physically. Although emotional reactivity is instinctive and self-protective, it never defines you. Be aware that emotional reactivity exists only in the Mental World, the world of your day-to-day functioning. In this world, you will likely, at times, experience challenges that cause you stress. Use breathing to monitor your emotional reactivity; by changing the rhythm of your breathing, you can change how you feel. When you find yourself emotionally reactive or physically stressed, breathe and take all the time you need to rebalance and realign. In order to transform emotions into a higher frequency energy, you need to align spiritually with your higher spiritual self.

Your Keys to Empowerment
- Relationships are meaningful to you; know your boundaries and honor them.
- Use discernment in your relationships so you honor yourself and the other person.
- Transform emotional reactivity into awareness through breathing, meditation, and communication.
- Make sure to be disciplined about self-care that aligns you and balances you emotionally.

Action Points for Manifesting Your Dreams
- Back away from stressful situations by taking time for yourself so you can rebalance.
- Pay attention to situations that trigger you to avoid emotional volatility.
- Breathe and center before committing to helping someone else.
- Self-awareness allows you to self-regulate emotionally when you are stressed. Pause and realign internally when you are emotionally triggered.

Channel 7-31

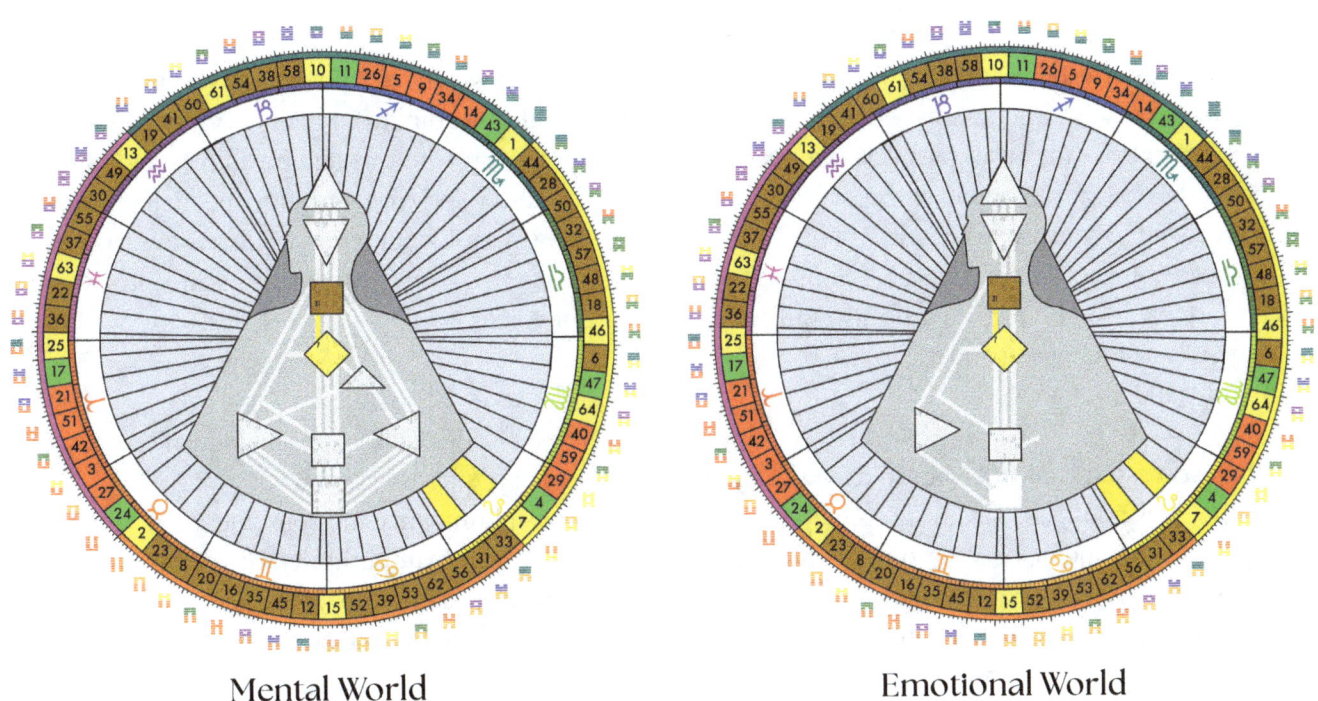

Mental World　　　　　　　　　　Emotional World

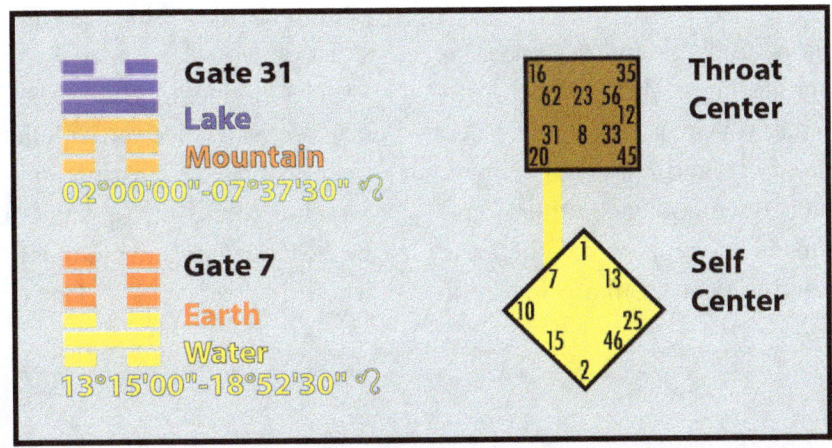

Channel 7-31

Integrated Mental and Emotional/Angelic Worlds
Channel 7-31 *(Leo-Leo)*

Keywords: Leadership, The Alpha, Responsibility, Legitimate Authority

You are a natural leader who uses your position to empower others and leads with integrity.

Your role as a leader carries significant influence. You like to take charge and have things go as you envision them. You use past experiences and knowledge to lead a group in an effective and well-received way. You use your authority efficiently, as a leadership position is natural. You are more comfortable in a position of authority than as a follower. Claim your power and use it with responsible integrity and consciousness.

When you assume a leadership role, you carry the group's consciousness. This responsibility requires that you be mindful of your power and authority and only use it to benefit those you serve. If, at any time, you become ego-inflated and operate for your benefit at the expense of those you lead, you are abusing your power, and there are likely to be consequences.

Be cautious and show kindness and compassionate understanding at all times. Always check with yourself to confirm that you are acting from a place of love and not one of ego and self-enhancement. Power used legitimately empowers others, and power used illegitimately disempowers others. As a leader, your role and mission from a position of consciousness is to empower others and, thus, to be rewarded by leading your team toward growth and awareness. Breathe through any stress and always take time for self-care and introspective examination. Always use your ability to listen to those you serve, and make sure you communicate clearly and in your voice.

Your Keys to Empowerment
- You are a leader with significant influence.
- Use your positions of power with responsible integrity and consciousness.
- Use only legitimate authority with compassion.
- Only take on leadership roles when you feel competent and envision what you want to have happen.

Action Points for Manifesting Your Dreams
- Commit to leadership roles in situations you feel drawn to.
- Express kindness and compassion to others because your voice carries influence.
- Breathe through any stress and always take time for self-care and introspective examination.
- Be clear on your expectations from others when in a position of leadership.

Mental World
Channel 7-31 *(Leo-Leo)*

Keywords: Leadership, The Alpha, Responsibility, Legitimate Authority

You are a natural leader who uses your position to empower others and leads with integrity.

You are a leader and influential in a group. You like to take charge and have things go how you envision them. You use past experiences and knowledge to lead a group in an effective and well-received way. You use your authority efficiently, as a leadership position is natural. You are more comfortable in a position of authority than as a follower. Claim your power and use it with responsible integrity and consciousness. The danger for you is to involve your ego in your role. Be cautious to use kindness and compassionate understanding when in a position of authority. Always check with yourself to confirm that you are acting from a place of love and not one of ego and self-enhancement. Power used legitimately empowers others, and power used illegitimately disempowers others. As a leader, your role and mission from a position of consciousness is to empower others and, thus, to be rewarded by leading your team toward growth and awareness. Breathe through any stress and always take time for self-care and introspective examination.

Your Keys to Empowerment
- You are an influential leader.
- Use your positions of power with responsible integrity and consciousness.
- Use only legitimate authority with compassion.
- When in a leadership role, make sure you take time for yourself to replenish your energy and set your course of action.

Action Points for Manifesting Your Dreams
- Only commit to leadership roles when you have the inner resources to do so.
- Express kindness and compassion to others because your voice carries influence.
- Breathe through any stress and always take time for self-care and introspective examination.
- Know what is involved in a leadership position before you commit to it.

Emotional/Angelic World
Channel 7-31 *(Leo-Leo)*

Keywords: Leadership, The Alpha, Responsibility, Legitimate Authority

You are a natural leader who uses your position to empower others and leads with integrity.

Your role as a leader carries significant influence. You like to take charge and have things go as you envision them. You use past experiences and knowledge to lead a group in an effective and well-received way. You use your authority efficiently, as a leadership position is natural. You are more comfortable in a position of authority than as a follower. When you assume a leadership role, you carry the group's consciousness. This responsibility requires that you be mindful of your power and authority and only use it to benefit those you serve. If, at any time, you become ego-inflated and operate for your benefit at the expense of those you lead, you are abusing your power, and there are likely to be consequences. Be cautious and show kindness and compassionate understanding at all times. Always check with yourself to confirm that you are acting from a place of love and not one of ego and self-enhancement. Power used legitimately empowers others, and power used illegitimately disempowers others. As a leader, your role and mission from a position of consciousness is to empower others and, thus, to be rewarded by leading your team toward growth and awareness. Breathe through any stress and always take time for self-care and introspective examination. Always use your ability to listen to those you serve, and make sure you communicate clearly and in your voice.

Your Keys to Empowerment
- You are a significantly influential leader.
- Use your positions of power with responsible integrity and consciousness.
- Recognize that your presence commands respect. Be worthy of respect.
- Only take on leadership roles when you feel competent and have the inner resources to do so.

Action Points for Manifesting Your Dreams
- Commit to leadership roles in situations you feel you can contribute to well.
- Express kindness and compassion to others because your voice carries influence.
- Breathe through any stress and always take time for self-care and introspective examination.
- Empower those who look to you for guidance.

Channel 9-52

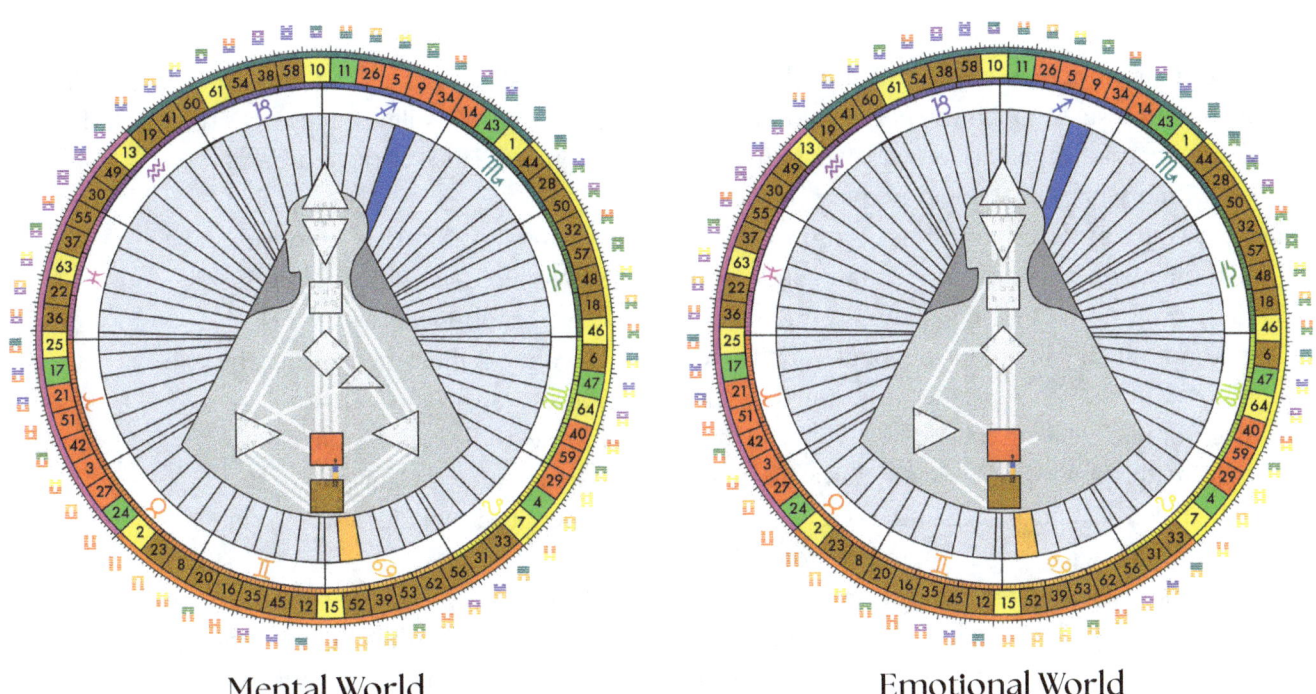

Mental World

Emotional World

Gate 9	Sacral Center
Wind	
Heaven	
05°45'00"-11°22'30" ♐	

Gate 52	Root Center
Mountain	
Mountain	
03°52'30"-09°30'00" ♋	

Channel 9-52

Integrated Mental and Emotional/Angelic Worlds
Channel 9-52 *(Sagittarius-Cancer)*

Keywords: Concentration, Determination, Focused Clarity, Inner Stillness

When you are centered in yourself, you are at peace and focus on what aligns with your values.

At your Core, you feel still and quiet, and you can maintain this sense of inner peace and stillness despite what is happening around you. You know deep within who you are, and nothing happening around you can shake your inner sense of peace. When needed, you can concentrate and focus entirely on what you must accomplish, and you do so without much talk or fanfare about your agenda and how you will achieve it. Because your activities derive from that still internal place in you, you must recognize this inner gut knowing. Knowing when you are balanced and aligned and when you are not comes from inner observation and contemplation. Thus, make sure you take time daily to meditate and be still. Breathing is a good help for balance and inner clarity. The Microcosmic Orbit is a powerful mediation that will keep your yang and yin energy balanced and grounded. In addition, Tai Chi Gung warm-ups and standing exercises would be extraordinarily balancing and growth-enhancing for you. You are here to help others with your calm presence when they are agitated or out of alignment. Bring your strength of stillness to every situation and be a beacon of balance to those around you.

Your Keys to Empowerment
- Stay focused on your goals and take time to gain inner clarity.
- Take time daily to meditate and be still.
- You know who you are, do not let anyone "ruffle your feathers."
- When you have a "gut" feeling that something is right for you, trust it.

Action Points for Manifesting Your Dreams
- You are a beacon of light who attracts others with your energy. Radiate love.
- Keep notes to yourself for what you want to manifest.
- Meditate Daily.
- Movement is essential for you daily.

Mental World
Channel 9-52 *(Sagittarius-Cancer)*

Keywords: Concentration, Determination, Focused Clarity, Inner Stillness

When you are centered in yourself, you are at peace and focus on what aligns with your values.

At your Core, you feel still and quiet, and you can maintain this sense of inner peace and stillness despite what is happening around you. You know deep within who you are, and nothing happening around you can shake your inner sense of peace. When needed, you can concentrate and focus entirely on what you must accomplish, and you do so without much talk or fanfare about your agenda and how you will achieve it. Because your activities derive from that still internal place in you, you must recognize this inner gut knowing. Knowing when you are balanced and aligned and when you are not comes from inner observation and contemplation. Thus, make sure you take time daily to meditate and be still. Breathing is a good help for balance and inner clarity. The Microcosmic Orbit is a powerful mediation that will keep your yang and yin energy balanced and grounded. In addition, Tai Chi Gung warm-ups and standing exercises would be extraordinarily balancing and growth-enhancing for you.

Your Keys to Empowerment
- Stay focused on your goals and take time to gain inner clarity.
- Take time daily to meditate and be still.
- You know who you are, do not let anyone "ruffle your feathers."
- When you have a "gut" feeling that something is right for you, trust it.

Action Points for Manifesting Your Dreams
- Meditate daily.
- Keep a journal handy and write down your inspired ideas.
- Dialogue with your Higher Self
- Movement is essential for you daily.

Emotional/Angelic World
Channel 9-52 *(Sagittarius-Cancer)*

Keywords: Concentration, Determination, Focused Clarity, Inner Stillness

When you are centered in yourself, you are at peace and focus on what aligns with your values.

Recognize that your Core remains still and quiet and that you can maintain this inner peace and stillness despite what is happening around you. You know deep within who you are, and nothing happening around you can shake your inner sense of peace. When needed, you can concentrate and focus entirely on what you must accomplish, and you do so without much talk or fanfare about your agenda and how you will achieve it. Because your activities derive from that still internal place in you, you must recognize this inner gut knowing. Knowing when you are balanced and aligned and when you are not coming from inner observation and contemplation. Thus, make sure you take time daily to meditate and be still. Breathing is a good help for balance and inner clarity. The Microcosmic Orbit is a powerful mediation that will keep your yang and yin energy balanced and grounded. In addition, Tai Chi Gung warm-ups and standing exercises would be highly balancing and growth-enhancing for you. Because this Channel is active in your Emotional/Angelic World, you are here to help others with your calm presence when they are agitated or out of alignment. Bring your strength of stillness to every situation and be a beacon of balance to those around you.

Your Keys to Empowerment
- Stay focused on your goals and take time to gain inner clarity.
- Take time daily to meditate and be still.
- You know who you are, do not let anyone "ruffle your feathers."
- When you have a "gut" feeling that something is right for you, trust it.

Action Points for Manifesting Your Dreams
- Meditate daily.
- Keep a journal handy and write down your inspired ideas.
- Dialogue with your Higher Self
- Movement is essential for you daily.

Channel 10-20

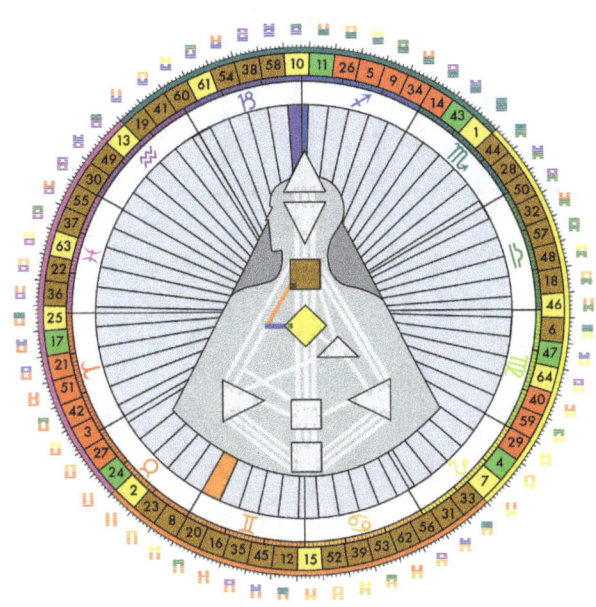

Mental World

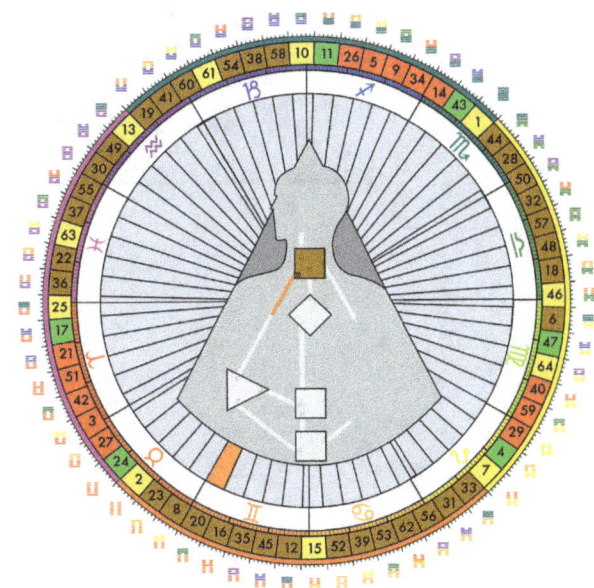

Spiritual World

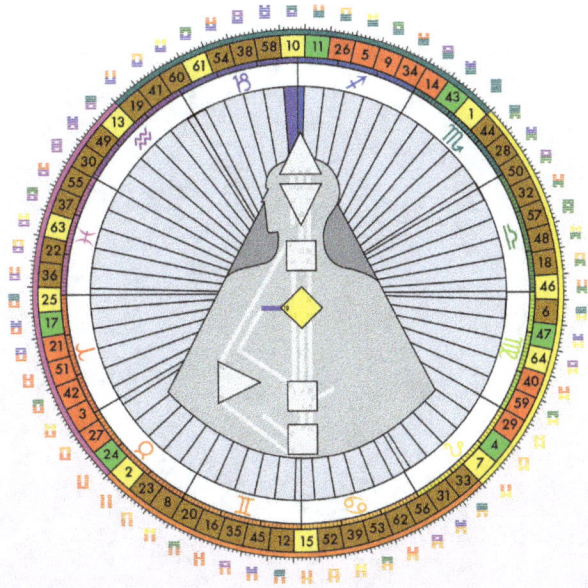

Emotional World

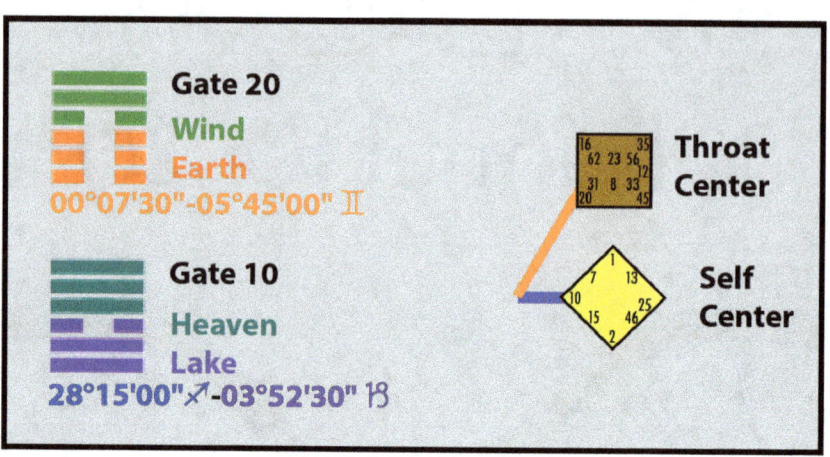

Channel 10-20

Integrated Mental World, Spiritual/Archetypal, and Emotional/Angelic Portals
Channel 10-20 *(Sagittarius/Capricorn-Gemini)*

Keywords: Watchfulness, Awakening, Self-Clarity

Because you acutely sense how you are perceived, you are at your best when clear about your role.

You feel a sense of purpose when you find yourself in a situation that warrants your taking a role and communicating that to those around you. You observe what is around you and notice other people's behavior. You know when energy aligns for action or communication and when it is best to "stand down." When you know that you are standing up for your most profound principles and feel good about what you stand for, you are confident and willing to be visible and vocal. Your timing is impeccable in this situation, so when you know it is right for you to act, do not hesitate. Act with confidence and authority. Be clear about the role you want to take on in any situation; take all the time you need to ask yourself, "Am I in the right place, in the right role?" "Am I at ease and honoring my deepest values?" These two questions mindfully realign you and may clarify your life direction. Only take on a role that aligns with your inner sense of self and brings you a sense of fulfillment.

Your Keys to Empowerment
- You are observant of what is around you and perceive nuances in people.
- When you can contribute to the consciousness of someone you care about, you can be a guiding force.
- Inner clarity requires asking: "Am I in the right place and right role"?
- Only take on roles that bring you fulfillment.

Action Points for Manifesting Your Dreams
- Use "Clean Language" meditations for self-direction.
- Before you take on a role, take time to self-reflect so you are confident that your action aligns with your goals.
- Are you clear about the role you are in and whether it honors you as well as others?
- Keep a journal to document your perceptions and consequent actions.

Integrated Mental World and Spiritual/Archetypal Portal
Channel 10-20 *(Sagittarius/Capricorn-Gemini)*

Keywords: Watchfulness, Awakening, Self-Clarity

Because you acutely sense how you are perceived, you are at your best when clear about your role.

You feel a sense of purpose when you find yourself in a situation that warrants your taking a role and communicating that to those around you. You observe what is around you and notice other people's behavior. You know when energy aligns for action or communication and when it is best to "stand down." When you know that you are standing up for your most profound principles and feel good about what you stand for, you are confident and willing to be visible and vocal. Your timing is impeccable in this situation, so when you know it is right for you to act, do not hesitate. Act with confidence and authority. Be clear about the role you want to take on in any situation; take all the time you need to ask yourself, "Am I in the right place, in the right role?" "Am I at ease and honoring my deepest values?" These two questions do mindfully realign you and may clarify your life direction. Only take on a role that aligns with your inner sense of self and brings you a sense of fulfillment.

Your Keys to Empowerment
- You are observant of what is around you and perceive nuances in people.
- When you can contribute to the consciousness of someone you care about, you can be a guiding force.
- Inner clarity requires asking: "Am I in the right place and right role"?
- Only take on roles that bring you fulfillment.

Action Points for Manifesting Your Dreams
- Use "Clean Language" meditations for self-direction.
- When you take on a role, be confident and assume authority.
- Wait for the right time to act.
- Keep a journal to document your perceptions and consequent actions.

Integrated Spiritual/Archetypal and Emotional/Angelic Portals
Channel 10-20 *(Sagittarius/Capricorn-Gemini)*

Keywords: Watchfulness, Awakening, Self-Clarity

Because you acutely sense how you are perceived, you are at your best when clear about your role.

You feel a sense of purpose when you find yourself in a situation that warrants your taking a role and communicating that to those around you. You observe what is around you and notice other people's behavior. You know when energy aligns for action or communication and when it is best to "stand down." When you know that you are standing up for your most profound principles and feel good about what you stand for, you are confident and willing to be visible and vocal. Your timing is impeccable in this situation, so when you know it is right for you to act, do not hesitate. Act with confidence and authority. To be clear about the role you want to take on in any situation, take all the time you need to ask yourself, "Am I in the right place, in the right role?" "Am I at ease and honoring my deepest values?" These two questions do mindfully realign you and may clarify your life direction.

Your Keys to Empowerment
- You are observant of what is around you and perceive nuances in people.
- When you can contribute to the consciousness of someone you care about, you can be a guiding force.
- Inner clarity requires asking: "Am I in the right place and right role"?
- Only take on roles that bring you fulfillment.

Action Points for Manifesting Your Dreams
- Use "Clean Language" meditations for self-direction.
- When you take on a role, be confident and assume authority.
- Wait for the right time to act.
- Keep a journal to document your perceptions and consequent actions.

Mental World
Channel 10-20 *(Sagittarius/Capricorn-Gemini)*

Keywords: Watchfulness, Awakening, Self-Clarity

Because you acutely sense how you are perceived, you are at your best when clear about your role.

You are exceptionally watchful of what is around you and notice other people and how they behave. You often take a position as a role model and believe deeply in what you know to be your proper direction. When you know that you are standing up for your most profound principles and feel good about what you stand for, you are confident and willing to be visible and vocal. Your timing is impeccable in this situation, so when you know it is right for you to act, do not hesitate. Act with confidence and authority. Be clear about the role you want to take on in any situation. Take all the time you need to ask yourself, "Am I in the right place, in the right role?" "Am I at ease and honoring my deepest values?" These two questions mindfully realign you and may clarify your life direction.

Your Keys to Empowerment
- You are observant of what is around you and perceive nuances in people.
- When you can contribute to the consciousness of someone you care about, you can be a guiding force.
- Inner clarity requires asking: "Am I in the right place and right role"?
- Only take on roles that bring you fulfillment.

Action Points for Manifesting Your Dreams
- Use "Clean Language" meditations for self-direction.
- When you take on a role, be confident and assume authority.
- Wait for the right time to act.
- Keep a journal to document your perceptions and consequent.

Channel 10-57

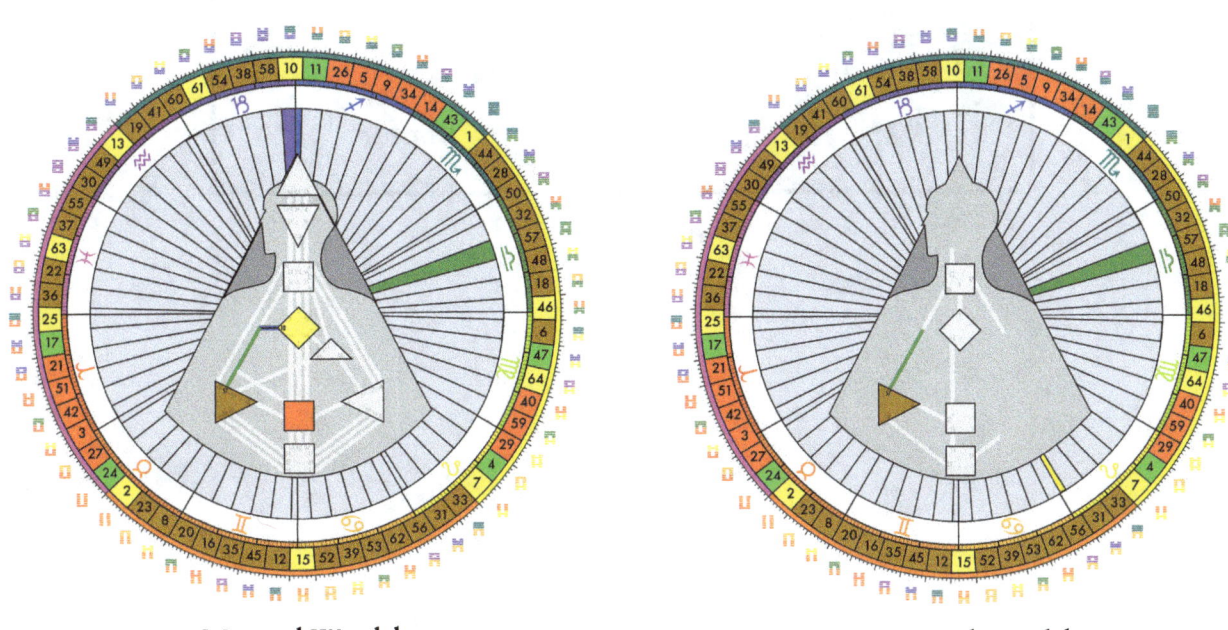

Mental World

Spiritual World

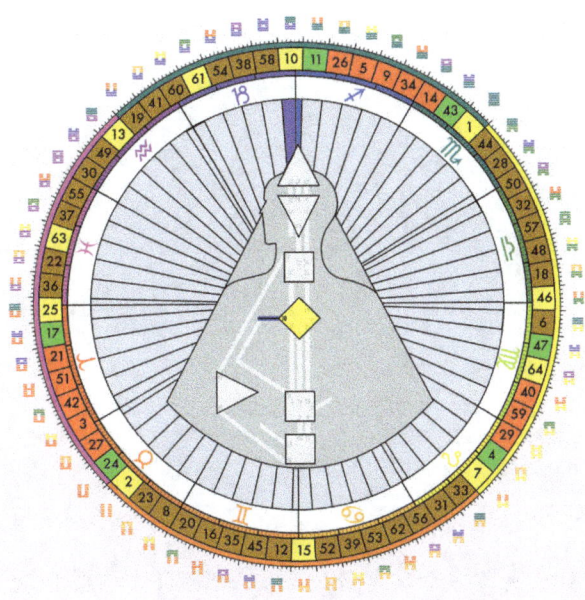

Emotional World

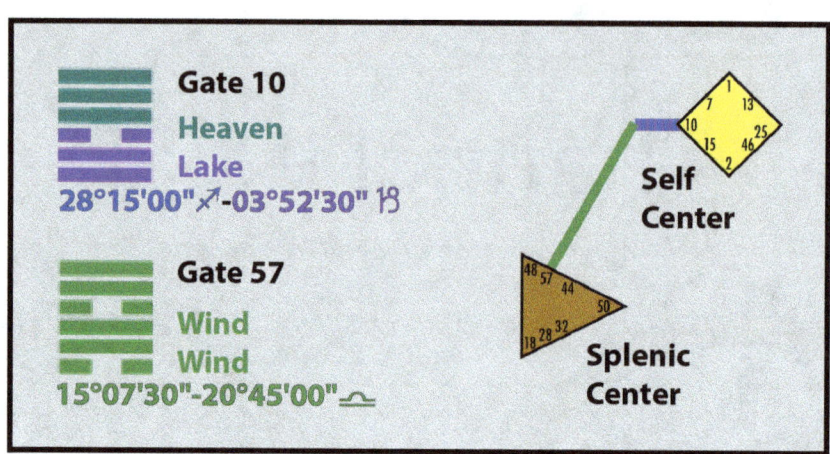

Channel 10-57

Integrated Mental World and Spiritual/Archetypal and Emotional/Angelic Portals
Channel 10-57 *(Capricorn/Libra-Sagittarius)*

Keywords: Intuitive Knowing, Sensitivity, Perfected Form

You are highly sensitive to people and your environment. Honor your knowing and be courageous in being visible.

You are highly intuitive and sensitive to the environment and people around you. When you tune in to your inner knowing, you feel guided from within, are usually accurate, and can trust yourself and what you know because it carries a specific energy you recognize. You access two Worlds working together to advance your consciousness and inner sense of depth. Intuition and sensitivity to the environment and people around you may influence your life mission and circumstances.

Your sensitivity can be acute to the point that you know if your environment is healthy for you and what you need to do to stay healthy and function at your best. Rest is always essential for you because you are likely to get messages in your dreams, and they are often reliable in terms of what you need to know for your inner process and clarity. Be sure to keep a journal by your bedside for your dreams and give yourself suggestions before you go to sleep so that you will remember your dreams.

You are sensitive to other people and their energy, and you might feel pulled toward being a help agent when you think you can make a difference for them. Understanding energy shifts makes you sensitive in ways not everyone can understand. It is wise to trust your perceptions to verify them in your own way rather than trusting others before you trust yourself. You must meditate in your own space and do a meditation where you listen for your inner voice of wisdom. Transcendental Meditation, Tai Chi Gung, Prayer, and being alone in nature are empowering practices to consider because they will enhance and expand your natural perceptiveness.

Your Keys to Empowerment
- You have strong, intuitive inner guidance. Pay attention to it.
- You are environmentally sensitive. Listen to your intuition about all your needs.
- Inner clarity requires asking: "What do I know now"?
- You lean toward being a caretaker. Always take care of yourself first.

Action Points for Manifesting Your Dreams
- Meditate daily using Transcendental Meditation, Prayer, or another deepening meditation.
- Pay attention to your inner voice of wisdom.
- Value your sensitivity and protect it.
- Keep a dream journal and work with your dreams.

Integrated Mental World and Spiritual/Archetypal Portal
Channel 10-57 *(Capricorn/Libra-Sagittarius)*

Keywords: Intuitive Knowing, Sensitivity, Perfected Form

You are highly sensitive to people and your environment. Honor your knowing and be courageous in being visible.

You are highly intuitive, and your sensitivity and sense of self give you a deep sense of knowing what you know. When you tune in to your inner knowing, you feel guided from within, are usually accurate, and can trust yourself and what you know because it carries a specific energy you recognize. Always consider the role you play in your relationships. What another person projects onto you may or may not be a good fit for aligning with who you perceive yourself to be. Make sure you are clear before you make commitments so you do not find yourself taking on a role you feel uncomfortable in.

Your sensitivity can be acute to the point that you know if your environment is healthy for you and what you need to do to stay healthy and function at your best. Rest is always essential for you because you are likely to get messages in your dreams, and they are often reliable in terms of what you need to know for your inner process and clarity. Understanding energy shifts makes you sensitive in ways not everyone can understand. It is wise to trust your perceptions to verify them in your own way rather than trusting others before you trust yourself.

Meditate in your own space (with your pets if possible) and do a meditation where you listen for your inner voice of wisdom. Transcendental Meditation, Tai Chi Gung, Prayer, and being alone in nature are empowering practices to consider because they will enhance and expand your natural perceptiveness.

Your Keys to Empowerment
- You have strong, intuitive inner guidance. Pay attention to it.
- You are environmentally sensitive. Listen to your intuition about all your needs.
- Only take on new commitments about which you feel at ease and excited.
- You lean toward being a caretaker. Always take care of yourself first.

Action Points for Manifesting Your Dreams
- Meditate daily using Transcendental Meditation, Prayer, or another deepening meditation.
- Pay attention to your inner voice of wisdom.
- Value your sensitivity, listen to it, and protect it.
- Keep a dream journal and work with your dreams

Integrated Mental World and Emotional/Angelic Portal
Channel 10-57 *(Capricorn/Libra-Sagittarius)*

Keywords: Intuitive Knowing, Sensitivity, Perfected Form

You are highly sensitive to people and your environment. Honor your knowing and be courageous in being visible.

You are highly intuitive, and your sensitivity and sense of self give you a deep sense of knowing what you know. When you tune in to your inner knowing, you feel guided from within, are usually accurate, and can trust yourself and what you know because it carries a specific energy you recognize. Always consider the role you play in your relationships. What another person projects onto you may or may not be a good fit for aligning with who you perceive yourself to be. Make sure you are clear before you make commitments so you do not find yourself taking on a role you feel uncomfortable in.

You are sensitive to other people and their energy, and you might feel pulled toward being a help agent when you think you can make a difference for them. Understanding energy shifts makes you sensitive in ways not everyone can understand. It is wise to trust your perceptions to verify them in your own way rather than trusting others before you trust yourself. You must meditate in your own space and do a meditation where you listen for your inner voice of wisdom. Transcendental Meditation, Tai Chi Gung, Prayer, and being alone in nature are empowering practices to consider because they will enhance and expand your natural perceptiveness.

Your Keys to Empowerment
- You have strong, intuitive inner guidance. Pay attention to it.
- You are environmentally sensitive. Listen to your intuition about all your needs.
- Only take on new commitments about which you feel at ease and excited.
- You lean toward being a caretaker. Always take care of yourself first.

Action Points for Manifesting Your Dreams
- Meditate daily using Transcendental Meditation, Prayer, or another deepening meditation.
- Pay attention to your inner voice of wisdom.
- Value your sensitivity, listen to it, and protect it.
- Keep a dream journal and work with your dreams

Mental World
Channel 10-57 *(Capricorn/Libra-Sagittarius)*

Keywords: Intuitive Knowing, Sensitivity, Perfected Form

You are highly sensitive to people and your environment. Honor your knowing and be courageous in being visible.

You are highly intuitive, and your sensitivity and sense of self give you a deep sense of knowing what you know. When you tune in to your inner knowing, you feel guided from within, are usually accurate, and can trust yourself and what you know because it carries a specific energy you recognize. Your sensitivity can be acute to the point that you know if your environment is healthy for you and what you need to do to stay healthy and function at your best. Rest is always essential for you because you are likely to get messages in your dreams, and they are often reliable in terms of what you need to know for your inner process and clarity. You are sensitive to other people and their energy, and you might feel pulled toward being a help agent when you think you can make a difference for them. Understanding energy shifts makes you sensitive in ways not everyone can understand. It is wise to trust your perceptions to verify them in your way rather than trusting others before you trust yourself. You must meditate in your own space and do a form of meditation where you listen for your inner voice of wisdom. Transcendental Meditation, Tai Chi Gung, Prayer, and being alone in nature are empowering practices for you to consider because they will enhance and expand your natural perceptiveness.

Your Keys to Empowerment
- You have strong, intuitive inner guidance. Pay attention to it.
- You are environmentally sensitive. Listen to your intuition about all your needs.
- Inner clarity requires asking: "What do I know now"?
- You lean toward being a caretaker. Always take care of yourself first.

Action Points for Manifesting Your Dreams
- Meditate daily using Transcendental Meditation, Prayer, or another deepening meditation.
- Pay attention to your inner voice of wisdom.
- Value your sensitivity and protect it.
- Keep a dream journal and work with your dreams.

Emotional/Angelic World Portal to the Spiritual/Archetypal World Portal
Channel 10-57 *(Capricorn/Libra-Sagittarius)*

Keywords: Intuitive Knowing, Sensitivity, Perfected Form

You are highly sensitive to people and your environment. Honor your knowing and be courageous in being visible.

You access two Worlds working together to advance your consciousness and inner sense of depth. Your intuition and sensitivity to the environment and people around you may influence your life mission and life circumstances. When you tune in to your inner knowing, you feel guided by a higher force and are usually accurate. Trust yourself and what you know because it carries a specific energy you recognize. Your sensitivity can be acute to the point that you know if your environment is healthy for you and what you need to do to stay healthy and function at your best. Rest is always essential for you because you are likely to get messages in your dreams, and they are often reliable in terms of what you need to know for your inner process and clarity. Be sure to keep a journal by your bedside for your dreams and give yourself suggestions before you go to sleep so that you will remember your dreams.

You are sensitive to other people and their energy, and you might feel pulled toward being a help agent when you think you can make a difference for them. Understanding energy shifts makes you sensitive in ways not everyone can understand. It is wise to trust your perceptions to verify them in your own way rather than trusting others before you trust yourself. You must meditate in your own space and do a form of meditation where you listen for your inner voice of wisdom. Transcendental Meditation, Tai Chi Gung, Prayer, and being alone in nature are empowering practices for you to consider because they will enhance and expand your natural perceptiveness.

Your Keys to Empowerment
- You have strong, intuitive inner guidance. Pay attention to it.
- You are environmentally sensitive. Listen to your intuition about all your needs.
- Inner clarity requires asking: "What do I know now"?
- You lean toward being a caretaker. Always take care of yourself first.

Action Points for Manifesting Your Dreams
- Meditate daily using Transcendental Meditation, Prayer, or another deepening meditation.
- Pay attention to your inner voice of wisdom.
- Value your sensitivity and protect it.
- Keep a dream journal and work with your dreams.

Channel 10-34

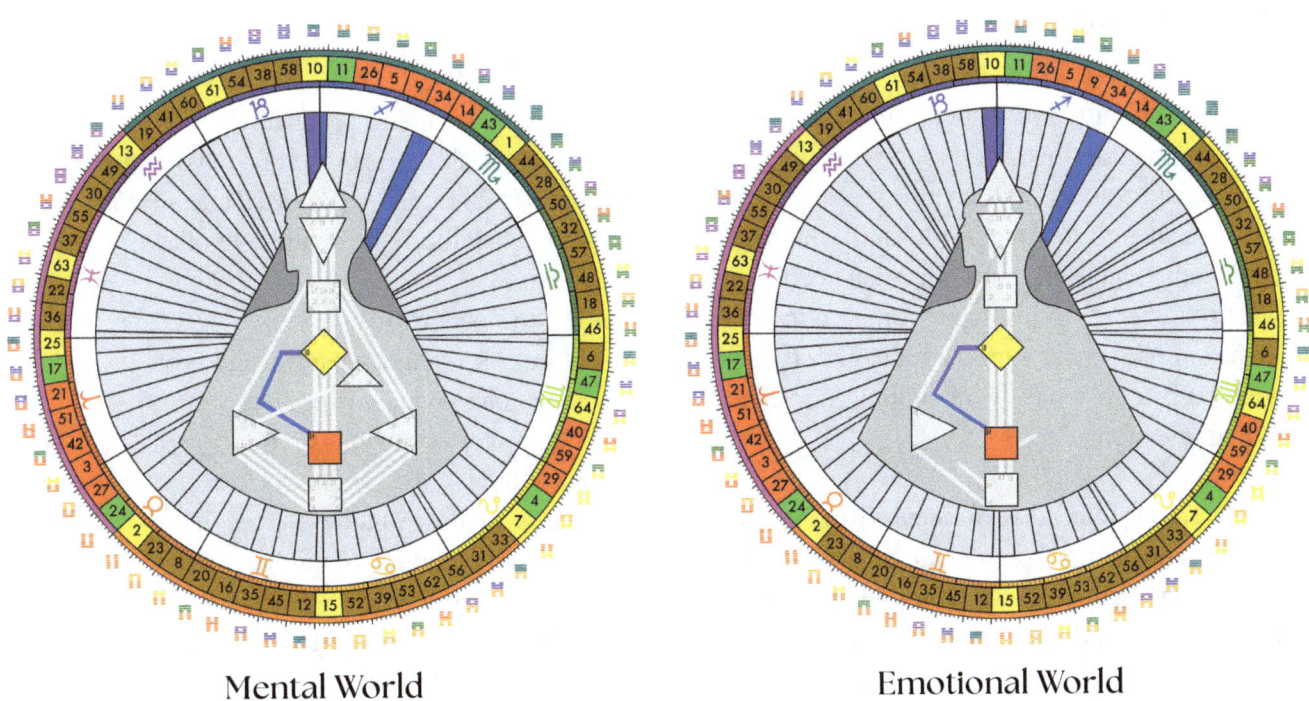

Mental World　　　　　　　　Emotional World

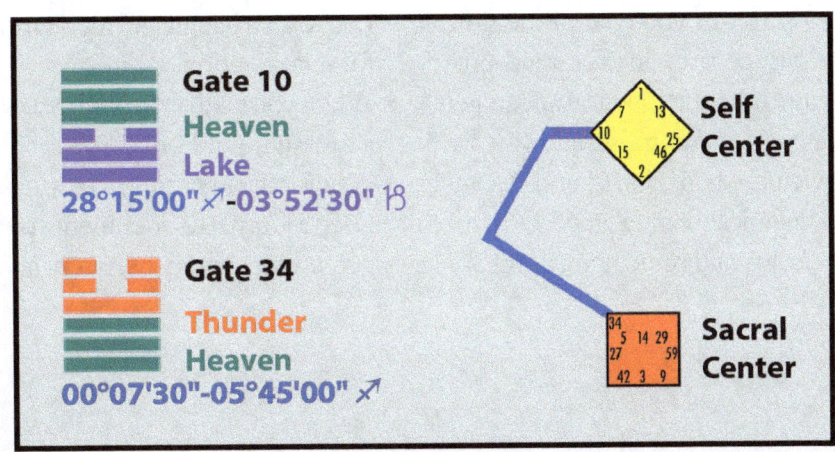

Channel 10-34

Integrated Mental and Emotional/Angelic Worlds
Channel 10-34 *(Sagittarius/Capricorn-Sagittarius)*

Keywords: Trust, Exploration, Self-Responsiveness, Energy, Empowerment

You know when to trust yourself and when to explore new possibilities. Go slow to align with your values.

You feel committed to higher values and principles that tend to push you toward action because you feel empowered to serve the greater whole. Nevertheless, you "march to your own drum," which means that when you clearly know what you need to do or what role you want to assume, you have the energy to make what you know you want to have to happen manifest by envisioning it and putting yourself in the right frame of mind.

You feel a deep inner drive to act; it is hard sometimes to wait until you are confident that what you are contemplating doing is the right thing for you to do. Explore your options thoroughly before you make any commitments, trust your connection to the Divine, and follow your inner guidance. It is always beneficial to pay attention to your instinctive pressure to act and to be sure that you take all the time you need to play various scenarios in your mind, projecting what you want to have happen. You can get deeply into your life goals and purpose, and you are likely to feel empowered when aligned and disempowered when your energies are misaligned. Do your inner work to gain clarity, and remember, you have plenty of time. Acting prematurely often backfires. Meditate, visualize, and be certain of your instinctive imperatives before you act. Meditate in your own space and breathe in the divine light of love.

Your Keys to Empowerment
- You are observant of what is around you and perceive nuances in people.
- When you can contribute to the consciousness of someone you care about, you can be a guiding force.
- Inner clarity requires asking: "Am I in the right place and right role"?
- You "march to your own drum." Do not compromise who you are to please others.

Action Points for Manifesting Your Dreams
- Use "Clean Language" meditations for self-direction.
- When you take on a role, be confident and assume authority.
- Wait for the right time to act.
- Keep a journal to document your perceptions and consequent actions.

Mental World
Channel 10-34 *(Sagittarius/Capricorn-Sagittarius)*

Keywords: Trust, Exploration, Self-Responsiveness, Energy, Empowerment

You know when to trust yourself and when to explore new possibilities. Go slow to align with your values.

You feel committed to higher values and principles that tend to push you toward action because you feel empowered to serve the greater whole. When you feel a deep inner drive to act, it is hard sometimes to wait until you are confident that what you are contemplating doing is the right thing for you to do. Explore your options thoroughly before you make any commitments, trust your connection to the Divine, and follow your inner guidance. It is always beneficial to pay attention to your instinctive pressure to act and to be sure that you take all the time you need to play various scenarios in your mind, projecting what you want to have happen. You can get deeply into your life goals and purpose through this Channel, and you are likely to feel empowered when aligned and disempowered when your energies are misaligned. Do your inner work to gain clarity, and remember, you have plenty of time. Acting prematurely often backfires. Meditate, visualize, and be certain of your instinctive imperatives before you act. Meditate in your own space and breathe in the divine light of love.

Your Keys to Empowerment
- You are observant of what is around you and perceive nuances in people.
- When you can contribute to the consciousness of someone you care about, you can be a guiding force.
- Inner clarity requires asking: "Am I in the right place and right role"?
- You "march to your own drum." Do not compromise who you are to please others.

Action Points for Manifesting Your Dreams
- Use "Clean Language" meditations for self-direction.
- When you take on a role, be confident and assume authority.
- Wait for the right time to act.
- Keep a journal to document your perceptions and consequent actions

Emotional/Angelic World
Channel 10-34 *(Sagittarius/Capricorn-Sagittarius)*

Keywords: Trust, Exploration, Self-Responsiveness, Energy, Empowerment

You know when to trust yourself and when to explore new possibilities. Go slow to align with your values.

You feel a sense of purpose, although you may not always be clear on what it is. You "march to your own drum," which means that when you know clearly what you need to do or what role you want to assume, you have the energy to make what you want to have happen manifest when you project it forward and put yourself in the right frame of mind. You feel empowered in service of the greater whole and committed to higher values and principles that tend to push you toward action. When you feel a deep inner drive to act, it is hard sometimes to wait until you are confident that what you are contemplating is the right thing for you to do. Explore your options thoroughly before you make any commitments, trust your connection to the Divine, and follow your inner guidance. It is always beneficial with this activated Channel to pay attention to your instinctive pressure to act and to be certain that you take all the time you need to play various scenarios in your mind, projecting what you want to have happen. You can get deeply into your life goals and purpose, and you are likely to feel empowered when aligned and disempowered when your energies are misaligned. Do your inner work to gain clarity, and remember, you have plenty of time.

Acting prematurely often backfires. Take time to meditate, visualize, and be certain of your instinctive imperatives before you act. Meditate in your own space and breathe in the divine light of love.

Your Keys to Empowerment
- You are observant of what is around you and perceive nuances in people.
- When you can contribute to the consciousness of someone you care about, you can be a guiding force.
- Inner clarity requires asking: "Am I in the right place and right role"?
- You "march to your own drum." Do not compromise who you are to please others.

Action Points for Manifesting Your Dreams
- Use "Clean Language" meditations for self-direction.
- When you take on a role, be confident and assume authority.
- Wait for the right time to act.
- Keep a journal to document your perceptions and consequent actions.

Channel 10-34-57

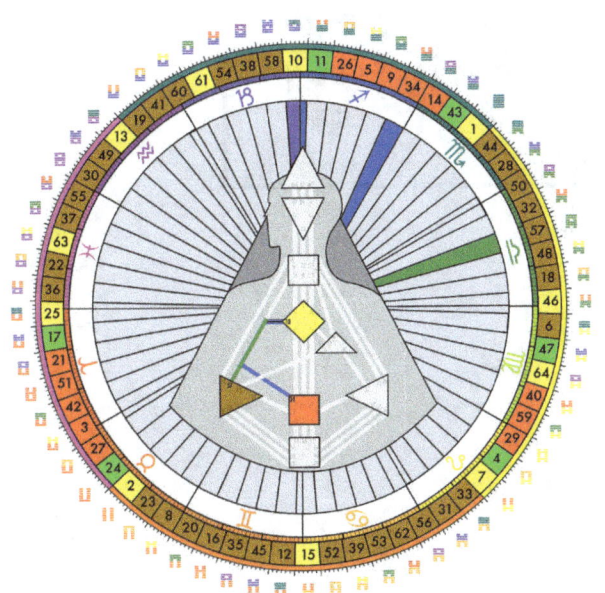

Mental World

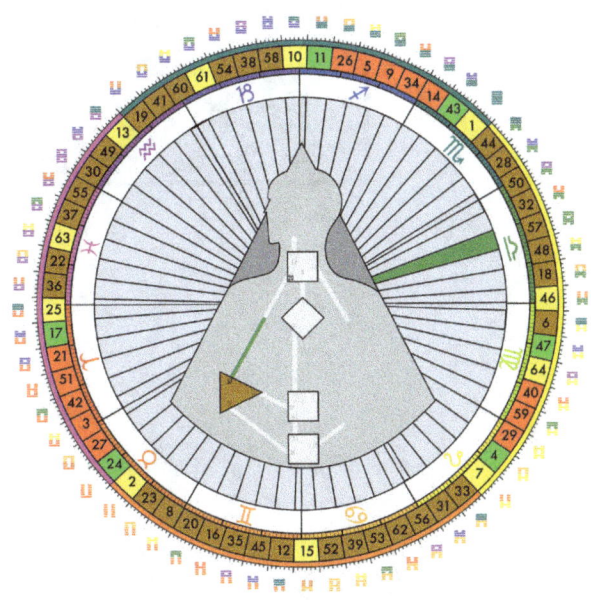

Spiritual World

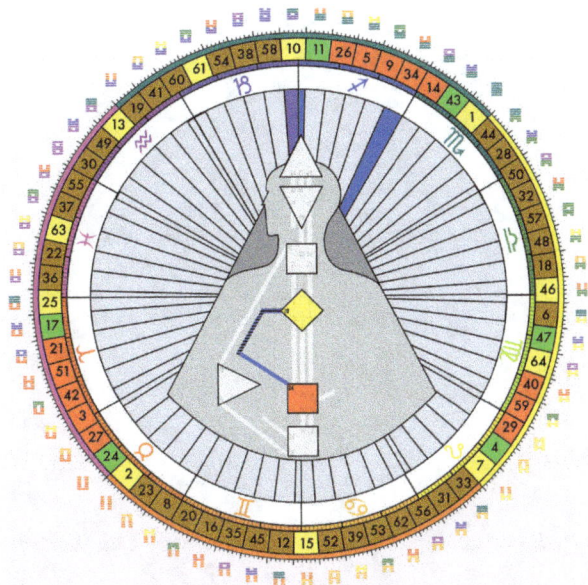

Emotional World

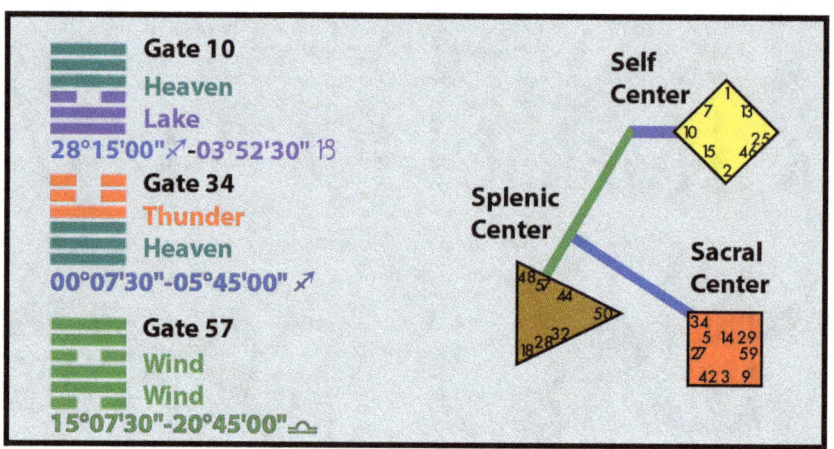

Channel 10-34-57

Integrated Mental, Spiritual/Archetypal Portal and Emotional/Angelic Portal
Channel 10-34-57 *(Sagittarius/Capricorn-Sagittarius-Libra)*

Keywords: Potential, Power, Intuitive Knowing, Trust, Exploration, Self-Responsiveness, Energy, Empowerment

You know when to trust yourself and when to explore new possibilities. Although your strong intuition drives you toward action, waiting until the timing is right to do so serves you well. Go slow to align with your values.

You feel committed to higher values and principles that tend to push you toward action because you feel empowered to serve the greater whole. Nevertheless, you "march to your own drum," which means that when you know clearly what you need to do or what role you want to assume, you have the energy to make what you know you want to have to happen manifest by envisioning it and putting yourself in the right frame of mind.

You feel a deep inner drive to act; it is hard sometimes to wait until you are confident that what you are contemplating doing is the right thing for you to do. Explore your options thoroughly before you make any commitments, trust your connection to the Divine, and follow your inner guidance. It is always beneficial to pay attention to your instinctive pressure to act and to be sure that you take all the time you need to play various scenarios in your mind, projecting what you want to have happen. You can get deeply into your life goals and purpose, and you are likely to feel empowered when aligned and disempowered when your energies are misaligned.

You are highly perceptive and intuitive. You tune in to the energy around you, and you know things that are not available to those not sensitive at that level of awareness. Your strong intuition and instinct drive you to manifest whatever you feel warrants your energy. However, because of your instinctive drive to manifest what comes into your awareness, you must intervene on behalf of your highest consciousness and make choices that optimize your energy.

Hence, you focus on what you truly value. Take time to process your internal direction of Self and make sure you align your inner Self with current considered actions. Go Slow. You have plenty of time. Knowing what aligns with your goals and life purpose requires you to wait until you know the appropriate timing for the best outcome. Patience and mindful attention benefit you by allowing your perceptions to go deep within and anchor your actions in what aligns with your highest purpose. Make sure you meditate daily in your own space, with your pets, if you have them, so you listen for the voice of wisdom that guides your truth.

Use the Four Worlds Clarity Worksheet to review factors you consider about any major decisions to ensure you are balanced and aligned in all worlds before acting. In addition, meditate daily in your own space, allowing your pets to be with you so you listen for the voice of wisdom that guides your truth.

Your Keys to Empowerment

- Your intuitive gut instincts drive you toward manifesting. Wait for the right time. You are observant of what is around you and perceive nuances in people.
- When you can contribute to the consciousness of someone you care about, you can be a guiding force.
- Inner clarity requires asking: "Am I in the right place and right role"?
- You "march to your own drum." Do not compromise who you are to please others.
- You know more than you think you know. Wait for clarity and be patient.

Action Points for Manifesting Your Dreams

- Use "Clean Language" meditations for self-direction.
- When you take on a role, be confident and assume authority.
- Wait for the right time to act.
- Use the Four Worlds Clarity Worksheets to review factors you consider about any significant decisions.
- When you know what you know and no one can tell you otherwise, wait for an opportunity to speak or act. Be patient and strategic.

Integrated Mental, Spiritual/Archetypal and Emotional/Angelic Portals
Channel 10-34-57 *(Sagittarius/Capricorn-Sagittarius-Libra)*

Keywords: Potential, Power, Empowerment, Intuitive Knowing, Trust, Exploration, Self-Responsiveness, Energy.

You know when to trust yourself and when to explore new possibilities. Although your strong intuition drives you toward action, waiting until the timing is right to do so serves you well. Go slow to align with your values.

You feel committed to higher values and principles that tend to push you toward action because you feel empowered to serve the greater whole. Nevertheless, you "march to your own drum," which means that when you know clearly what you need to do or what role you want to assume, you have the energy to make what you know you want to have to happen manifest by envisioning it and putting yourself in the right frame of mind.

You feel a deep inner drive to act; it is hard sometimes to wait until you are confident that what you are contemplating doing is the right thing for you to do. Explore your options thoroughly before you make any commitments, trust your connection to the Divine, and follow your inner guidance. It is always beneficial to pay attention to your instinctive pressure to act and to be sure that you take all the time you need to play various scenarios in your mind, projecting what you want to have happen. You can get deeply into your life goals and purpose, and you are likely to feel empowered when aligned and disempowered when your energies are misaligned.

You are highly perceptive and intuitive. You tune in to the energy around you, and you know things that are not available to those not sensitive at that level of awareness. Your strong intuition and instinct drive you to manifest whatever you feel warrants your energy. However, because of your instinctive drive to manifest what comes into your awareness, you must intervene on behalf of your highest consciousness and make choices that optimize your energy.

Hence, you focus on what you truly value. Take time to process your internal direction of Self and make sure you align your inner Self with current considered actions. Go Slow. You have plenty of time. Knowing what aligns with your goals and life purpose requires you to wait until you know the appropriate timing for the best outcome. Patience and mindful attention benefit you by allowing your perceptions to go deep within and anchor your actions in what aligns with your highest purpose. Make sure you meditate daily in your own space, with your pets, if you have them, so you listen for the voice of wisdom that guides your truth.

Use the Four Worlds Clarity Worksheet to review factors you consider about any major decisions to ensure you are balanced and aligned in all worlds before acting. In addition, meditate daily in your own space, allowing your pets to be with you so you listen for the voice of wisdom that guides your truth.

Your Keys to Empowerment
- Your intuitive gut instincts drive you toward manifesting. Wait for the right time. You are observant of what is around you and perceive nuances in people.
- When you can contribute to the consciousness of someone you care about, you can be a guiding force.
- Inner clarity requires asking: "Am I in the right place and right role"?
- You "march to your own drum." Do not compromise who you are to please others.
- You know more than you think you know. Wait for clarity and be patient.

Action Points for Manifesting Your Dreams
- Use "Clean Language" meditations for self-direction.
- When you take on a role, be confident and assume authority.
- Wait for the right time to act.
- Use the Four Worlds Clarity Worksheets to review factors you consider about any significant decisions.
- When you know what you know and no one can tell you otherwise, wait for an opportunity to speak or act. Be patient and strategic.

Channel 10-20-34

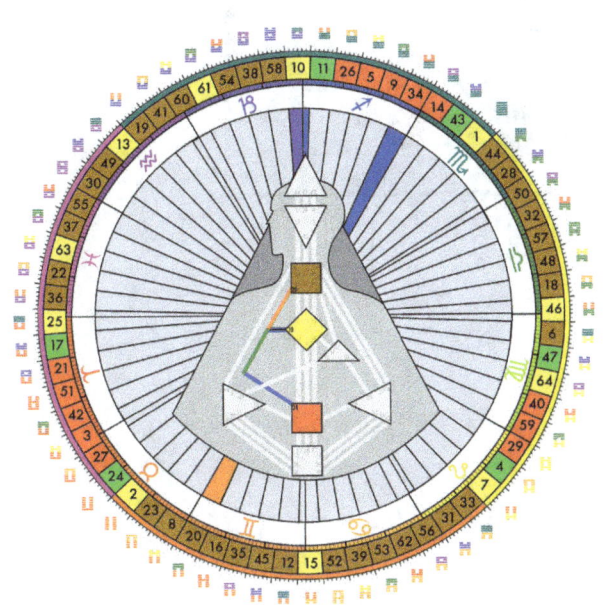

Mental World

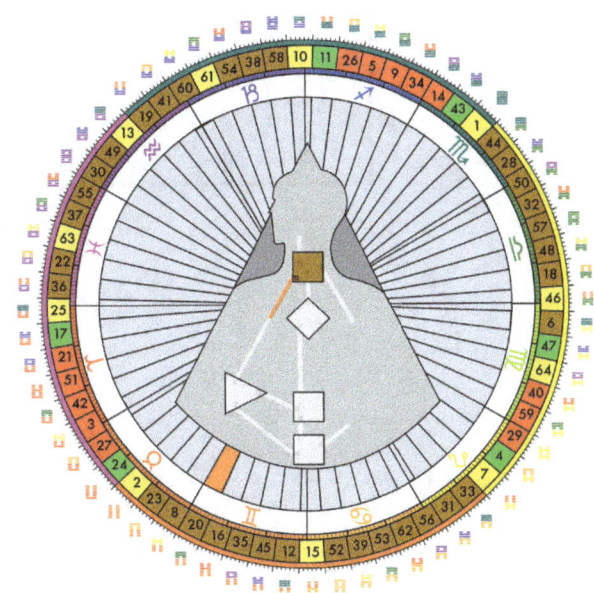

Spiritual World

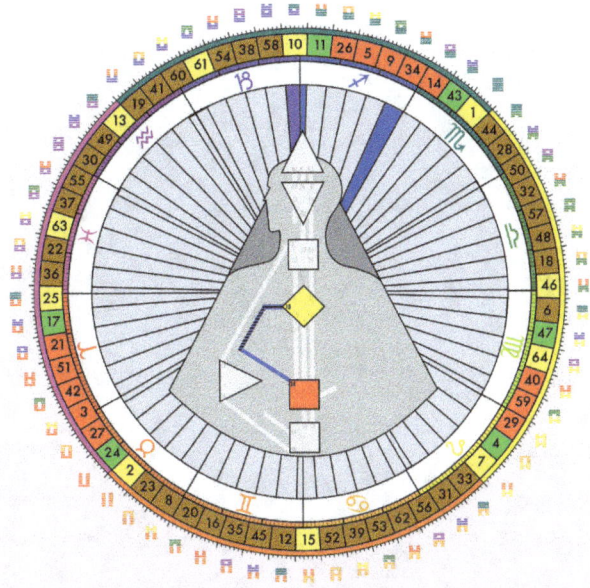

Emotional World

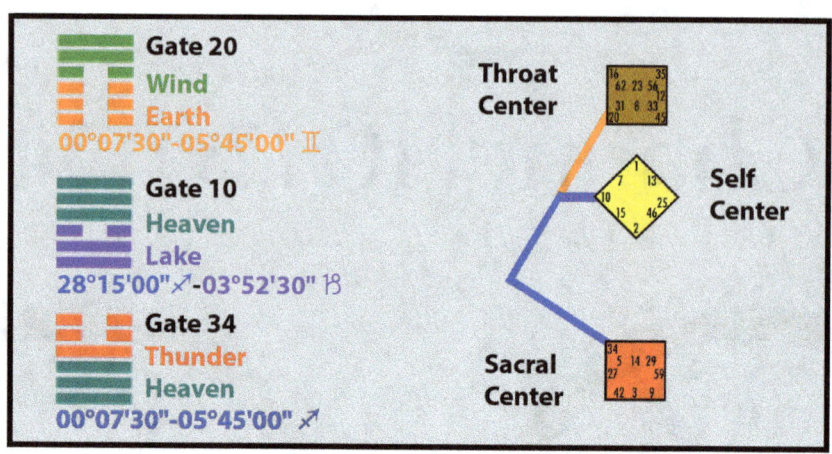

Channel 10-20-34

Integrated Mental World, Spiritual/Archetypal, and Emotional/Angelic Portals
Channel 10-20-34 *(Sagittarius/Capricorn-Gemini/Sagittarius)*

Keywords: Watchfulness, Awakening, Self-Clarity, Trust, Exploration, Self-Responsiveness, Energy, Empowerment

You know when to trust yourself and when to explore new possibilities, and you acutely sense how you are perceived. Thus, you are at your best when clear about your role. Go slow to align with your values.

You feel committed to higher values and principles that tend to push you toward action because you feel empowered to serve the greater whole. Nevertheless, you "march to your drum," which means that when you know what you need to do or what role you want to assume, you have the energy to make what you know you want to have to happen manifest by envisioning it and putting yourself in the right frame of mind.

You feel a deep inner drive to act; it is hard sometimes to wait until you are confident that what you are contemplating doing is the right thing for you to do. Explore your options thoroughly before you make any commitments, trust your connection to the Divine, and follow your inner guidance. It is always beneficial to pay attention to your intuitive pressure to act and to be sure that you take all the time you need to play various scenarios in your mind, projecting what you want to have happen.

You feel a sense of purpose when you find yourself in a situation that warrants your taking a role and communicating that to those around you. You observe what is around you and notice other people's behavior. You know when energy aligns for action or communication and when it is best to "stand down." When you know that you are standing up for your most profound principles and feel good about what you stand for, you are confident and willing to be visible and vocal. Your timing is impeccable in this situation, so when you know it is right for you to act, do not hesitate. Act with confidence and authority.

You can get deeply into your life goals and purpose, and you are likely to feel empowered when aligned and disempowered when your energies are misaligned. Do your inner work to gain clarity, and remember, you have plenty of time. Acting prematurely often backfires. Meditate, visualize, and be sure of your instinctive imperatives before you act. Meditate in your own space and breathe in the divine light of love.

Be clear about the role you want to take on in any situation. Take all the time you need to ask yourself, "Am I in the right place, in the right role?" "Am I at ease and honoring my deepest values?" These two questions will mindfully realign you and may clarify your life direction. Only take on a role that aligns with your inner sense of self and brings you a sense of fulfillment.

Your Keys to Empowerment

- You are observant of what is around you and perceive nuances in people.
- When you can contribute to the consciousness of someone you care about, you can be a guiding force.
- Inner clarity requires asking: "Am I in the right place and role"?
- Only take on roles that bring you fulfillment.
- You "march to your own drum." Do not compromise who you are to please others.

Action Points for Manifesting Your Dreams

- Use "Clean Language" meditations for self-direction.
- When you take on a role, be confident and assume authority.
- Wait for the right time to act.
- Keep a journal to document your perceptions and consequent actions.

Channel 10-20-57

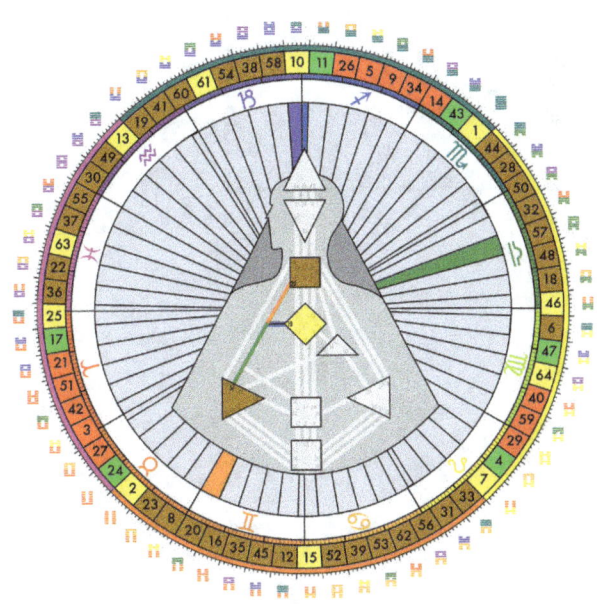

Mental World

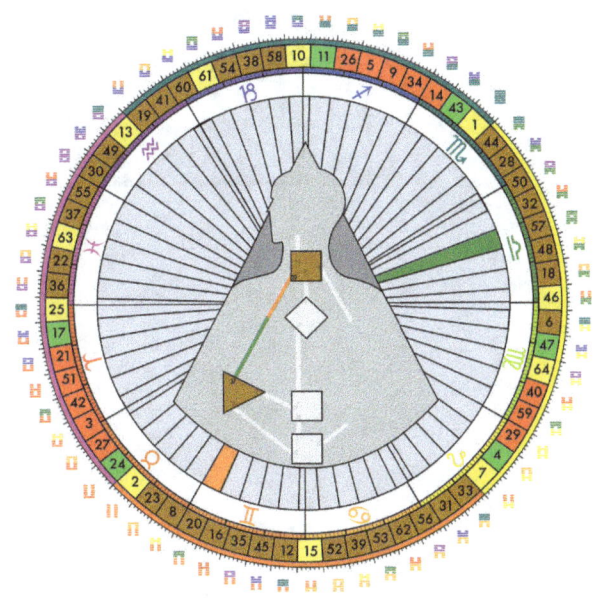

Spiritual World

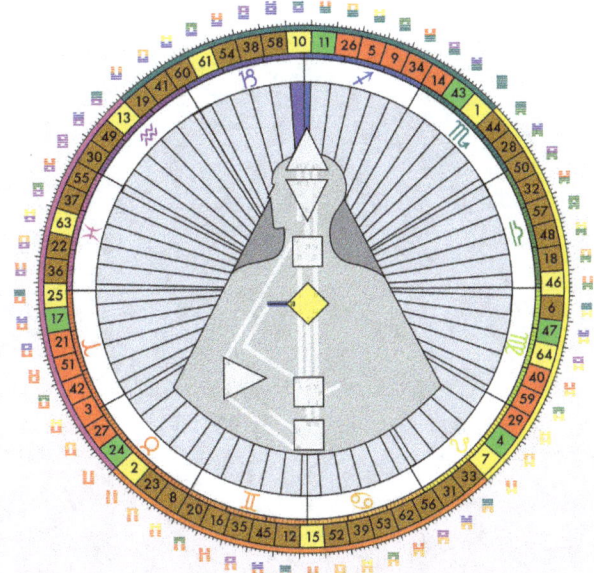

Emotional World

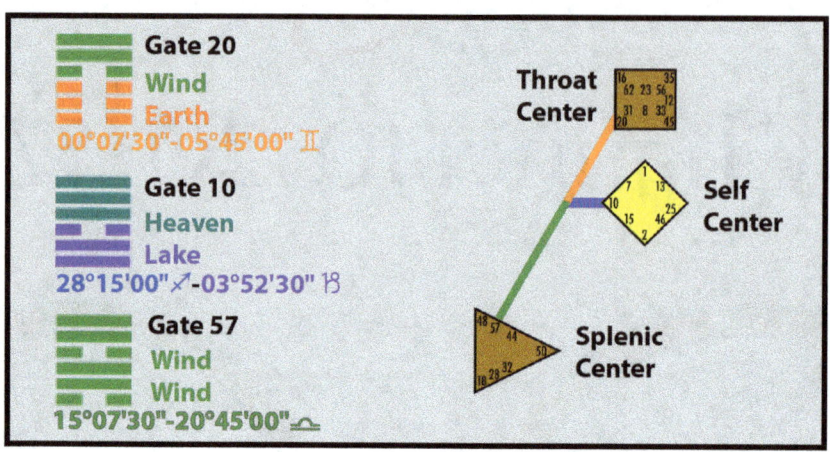

Channel 10-20-57

Integrated Mental World and Spiritual/Archetypal and Emotional/Angelic Portals
Channel 10-20-57 *(Sagittarius/Capricorn-Gemini/Sagittarius-Libra)*

Keywords: Keywords Watchfulness, Awakening, Self-Clarity, Trust, Exploration, Self-Responsiveness, Intuitive Knowing, Sensitivity, Perfected Form

You are highly sensitive to people and your environment and acutely sense how you are perceived. Honor your knowing and be courageous in being visible. You are at your best when clear about your role and your perceptions.

You are highly intuitive and sensitive to the environment and people around you. You feel a sense of purpose when you find yourself in a situation that warrants your taking a role and communicating that. You observe what is around you and notice other people's behavior. You know when energy aligns for action or communication and when it is best to "stand down." When you know that you are standing up for your most profound principles and feel good about what you stand for, you are confident and willing to be visible and vocal. Your timing is impeccable in this situation, so when you know it is right for you to act, do not hesitate. Act with confidence and authority. Be clear about the role you want to take on in any situation; take all the time you need to ask yourself, "Am I in the right place, in the right role?" "Am I at ease and honoring my deepest values?" These two questions do mindfully realign you and may clarify your life direction. Only take on a role that aligns with your inner sense of self and brings you a sense of fulfillment.

When you tune in to your inner knowing, you feel guided from within, are usually accurate, and can trust yourself and what you know because it carries a specific energy you recognize. You access three Worlds working together to advance your consciousness and inner sense of depth. Intuition and sensitivity to the environment and people around you may influence your life mission, your circumstances, and the role you choose to play.

Your sensitivity can be acute to the point that you know if your environment is healthy for you and what you need to do to stay healthy and function at your best. Rest is always essential for you because you are likely to get messages in your dreams, and they are often reliable in terms of what you need to know for your inner process and clarity. Be sure to keep a journal by your bedside for your dreams and give yourself suggestions before you go to sleep so that you will remember your dreams.

You are sensitive to other people and their energy, and you might feel pulled toward being a help agent when you think you can make a difference for them. Understanding energy shifts makes you sensitive in ways not everyone can understand. It is wise to trust your perceptions to verify them rather than trusting others before you trust yourself. You must meditate in your own space and do a meditation where you listen for your inner voice of wisdom. Transcendental Meditation, Tai Chi Gung, Prayer, and being alone in nature are empowering practices.

Your Keys to Empowerment
- When you can contribute to the consciousness of someone you care about, you can be a guiding force.
- Inner clarity requires asking: "Am I in the right place and role"?
- You have strong, intuitive inner guidance. Pay attention to it.
- Inner clarity requires asking: "What do I know now"?
- You are environmentally sensitive. Listen to your intuition about all your needs.

Action Points for Manifesting Your Dreams
- Use "Clean Language" meditations for self-direction.
- When you take on a role, be confident and assume authority.
- Meditate daily using Transcendental Meditation, Prayer, or another deepening meditation.
- Value your sensitivity and protect it.
- Keep a dream journal and work on your dreams.
- Keep a journal to document your perceptions and consequent actions.

Channel 10-20-34-57

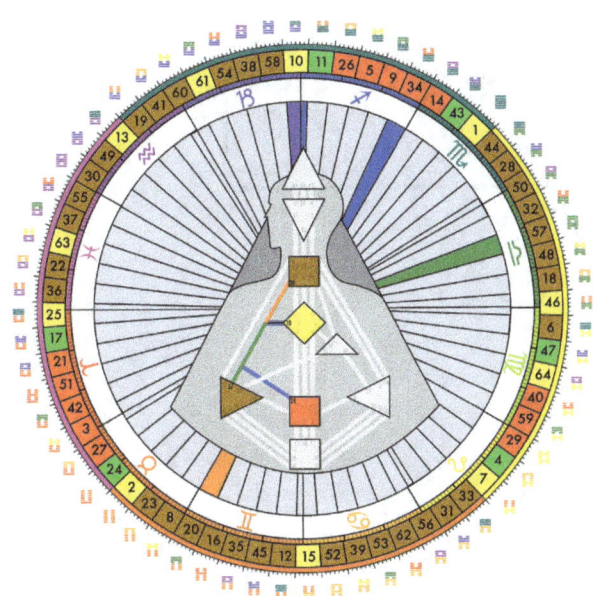

Mental World

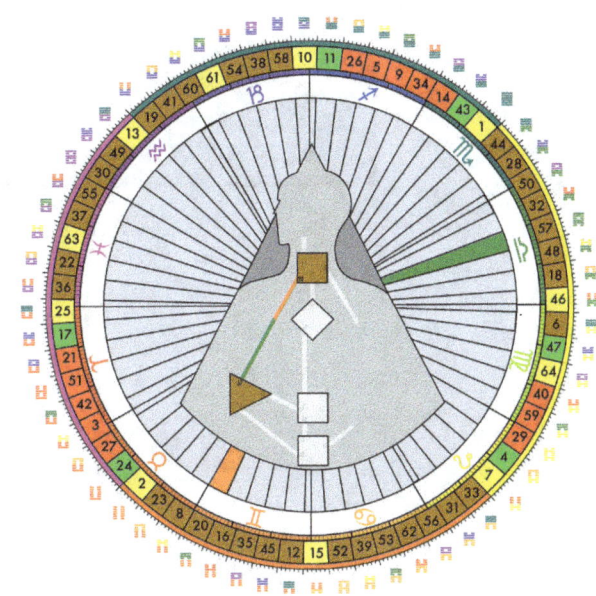

Spiritual World

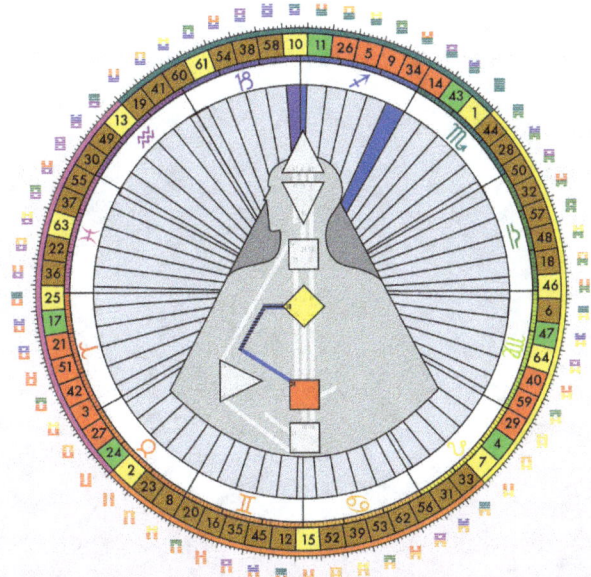

Emotional World

CHANNEL 10-20-34-57

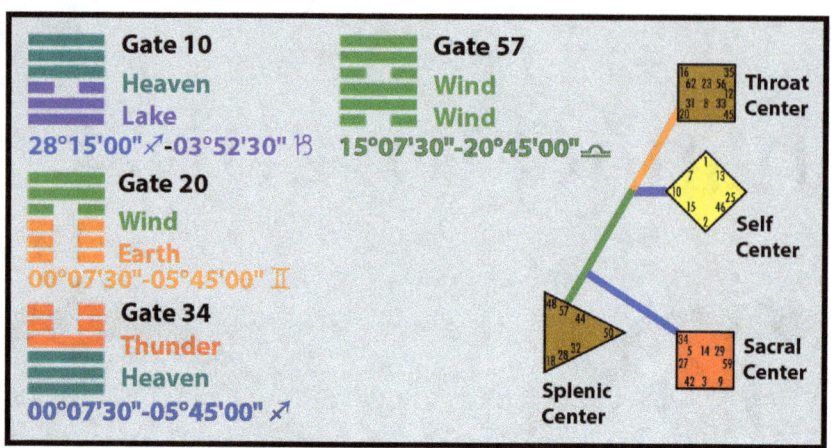

Channel 10-20-34-57

Integrated Mental World, Spiritual/Archetypal, and Emotional/Angelic Portals
Channel 10-20-34-57 *(Sagittarius/Capricorn-Gemini/Sagittarius-Libra)*

Keywords: Watchfulness, Awakening, Self-Clarity, Trust, Exploration, Self-Responsiveness, Energy, Empowerment, Intuitive Knowing, Sensitivity, Perfected Form.

You are highly sensitive to people and your environment. You know when to trust yourself and when to explore new possibilities, and you acutely sense how you are perceived. Thus, you are at your best when clear about your role. Honor your knowing and be courageous in being visible. Go slow to align with your values.

You are highly intuitive and sensitive to the environment and people around you. When you tune in to your inner knowing, you feel guided from within, are usually accurate, and can trust yourself and what you know because it carries a specific energy you recognize. You access multiple Worlds working together to advance your consciousness and inner sense of depth. Intuition and sensitivity to the environment and people around you may influence your life mission and circumstances.

Your sensitivity can be acute to the point that you know if your environment is healthy for you and what you need to do to stay healthy and function at your best. Rest is always essential for you because you are likely to get messages in your dreams, and they are often reliable in terms of what you need to know for your inner process and clarity. Be sure to keep a journal by your bedside for your dreams and give yourself suggestions before you go to sleep so that you will remember your dreams.

Because you are so sensitive to other people and their energy, you might feel pulled toward being a help agent when you think you can make a difference for them. Understanding energy shifts makes you sensitive in ways not everyone can understand. It is wise to trust your perceptions and to verify them rather than trusting others before you trust yourself.

You are committed to higher values and principles that tend to push you toward action because you feel empowered to serve the greater whole. Nevertheless, you "march to your drum," which means that when you know what you need to do or what role you want to assume, you have the energy to make what you know you want to have happen manifest by envisioning it and putting yourself in the right frame of mind.

You feel a deep inner drive to act; it is hard sometimes to wait until you are confident that what you are contemplating doing is the right thing for you to do. Explore your options thoroughly before you make any commitments, trust your connection to the Divine, and follow your inner guidance. It is always beneficial to pay attention to your intuitive pressure to act and to be sure that you take all the time you need to play various scenarios in your mind, projecting what you want to have happen.

You feel a sense of purpose when you find yourself in a situation that warrants your taking a role and communicating that to those around you. You observe what is around you and notice other people's behavior. You know when energy aligns for action or communication and when it is best to "stand down." When you know that you are standing up for your most profound principles and feel good about what you stand for, you are confident and willing to be visible and vocal. Your timing is impeccable in this situation, so when you know it is right for you to act, do not hesitate. Act with confidence and authority.

Do inner work to gain clarity; remember, you have plenty of time. Acting prematurely often backfires. Meditate, visualize, and be sure of your instinctive imperatives before you act. Meditate in your own space and breathe in the divine light of love.

Be clear about the role you want to take on in any situation; take all the time you need to ask yourself, "Am I in the right place, in the right role?" "Am I at ease and honoring my deepest values?" These two questions do mindfully realign you and may clarify your life direction. Only take on a role that aligns with your inner sense of self and brings you a sense of fulfillment.

You must meditate in your own space and do a meditation where you listen for your inner voice of wisdom. Transcendental Meditation, Tai Chi Gung, Prayer, and being alone in nature are empowering practices to consider because they will enhance and expand your natural perceptiveness.

Your Keys to Empowerment
- You are observant of what is around you and perceive nuances in people.
- When you can contribute to the consciousness of someone you care about, you can be a guiding force.
- Inner clarity requires asking: "Am I in the right place and role"?
- Only take on roles that bring you fulfillment.
- You "march to your own drum." Do not compromise who you are to please others.
- You are highly sensitive and intuitive. Honor your perceptions and what you know that you know.

Action Points for Manifesting Your Dreams
- Use "Clean Language" meditations for self-direction.
- When you take on a role, be confident and assume authority.
- Wait for the right time to act.
- Keep a journal to document your perceptions and consequent actions.
- Use your intuition.

Channel 11-56

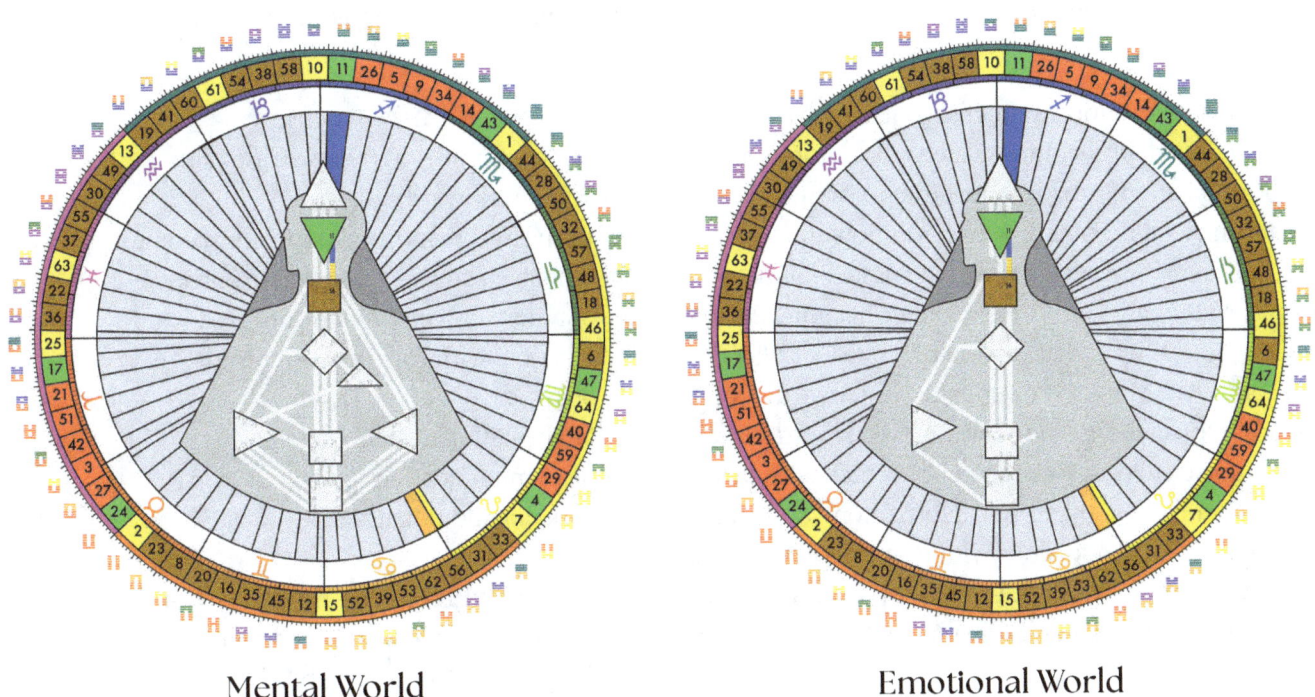

Mental World　　　　　　　　　Emotional World

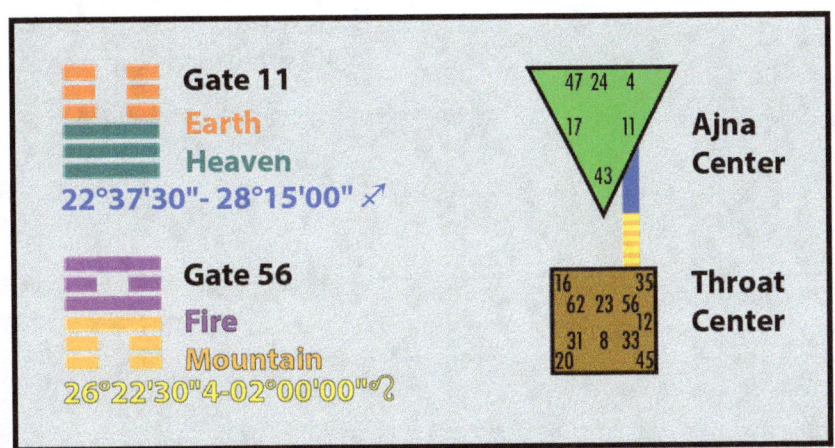

Channel 11-56

Integrated Mental and Emotional/Angelic Worlds
Channel 11-56 *(Sagittarius-Cancer/Leo)*

Keywords: Stories, Curiosity, Exploration, Understanding

You are an acute observer of everyone and everything around you, and you put threads of information together in a way that creates a story for you. Use your skills wisely.

Your active curiosity keeps your mind busy, and your visual observations keep you curious about organizing information regarding events, people, and history that make sense and flow into a story. You enjoy communicating your understanding on all levels of awareness, expanding what you perceive in practical ways that may help the wider collective. You always want to communicate in ways that push consciousness, moving awareness forward toward empowerment. You acutely perceive nuances energetically and can put information sequentially to understand and work with it in transformational ways. Time is your friend in comprehending complexity. Be patient and remain observant for clarity to emerge.

Your Keys to Empowerment
- Your mind is very active; use discipline to guide it toward your goals.
- Putting information into story form comes naturally to you. Use that skill to enhance your memory and expand your creativity.
- Be patient with your process; time is your friend while you wait for all pieces of information to take shape.
- Use communication specific to each World for additional clarity.

Action Points for Manifesting Your Dreams
- Keep a journal and write observations daily.
- Always think "outside the box".
- Learn which communication skills have power in each World.
- Keep a journal for your dreams and look for the storyline in them.

Mental World
Channel 11-56 *(Sagittarius-Cancer/Leo)*

Keywords: Stories, Curiosity, Exploration, Understanding

You are an acute observer of everyone and everything around you, and you put threads of information together in a way that creates a story for you. Use your skills wisely.

Your active curiosity keeps your mind busy looking for how to put together information about events, people, and history that make sense and flow into a story. You enjoy communicating your understanding on all levels of awareness, expanding what you perceive in practical ways that may help the wider collective. You always seek to share in ways that push consciousness and move attention toward empowerment. When you do not understand the flow of communication and its impact, you feel compelled to push through for more information so you understand how things come together.

Your Keys to Empowerment
- Your mind is very active; use discipline to guide it toward your goals.
- Putting information into story form comes naturally to you. Use that skill to enhance your memory and expand your creativity.
- Be patient with your process; time is your friend while you wait for all pieces of information to take shape.
- Use communication specific to each World for additional clarity.

Action Points for Manifesting Your Dreams
- Keep a journal and write observations daily.
- Always think "outside the box".
- Learn which communication skills have power in each World.
- Keep a journal for your dreams and look for the storyline in them.

Emotional/Angelic World
Channel 11-56 *(Sagittarius-Cancer/Leo)*

Keywords: Stories, Curiosity, Exploration, Understanding

You are an acute observer of everyone and everything around you, and you put threads of information together in a way that creates a story for you. Use your skills wisely.

Your visual observations keep you curious about how you can put together pieces of information about events, people, and history that make sense so you can weave them into a story. You always want to communicate in ways that push consciousness, moving awareness forward toward empowerment. When you do not understand the flow of communication and its impact, you feel compelled to push through for more information to understand how things come together cohesively. You acutely perceive nuances energetically and can put information sequentially to understand and work with it in transformational ways. Time is your friend in comprehending complexity. Be patient and remain observant for clarity to emerge.

Your Keys to Empowerment
- Your mind is very active; use discipline to guide it toward your goals.
- Putting information into story form comes naturally to you. Use that skill to enhance your memory and expand your creativity.
- Be patient with your process; time is your friend while you wait for all pieces of information to take shape.
- Use communication specific to each World for additional clarity.

Action Points for Manifesting Your Dreams
- Keep a journal and write observations daily.
- Always think "outside the box".
- Learn which communication skills have power in each World.
- Keep a journal for your dreams and look for the storyline in them.

Channel 12-22

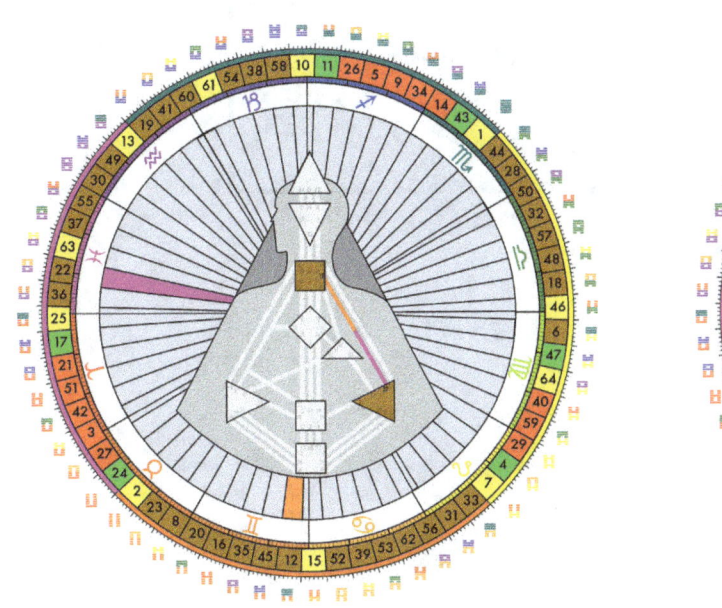

Mental World

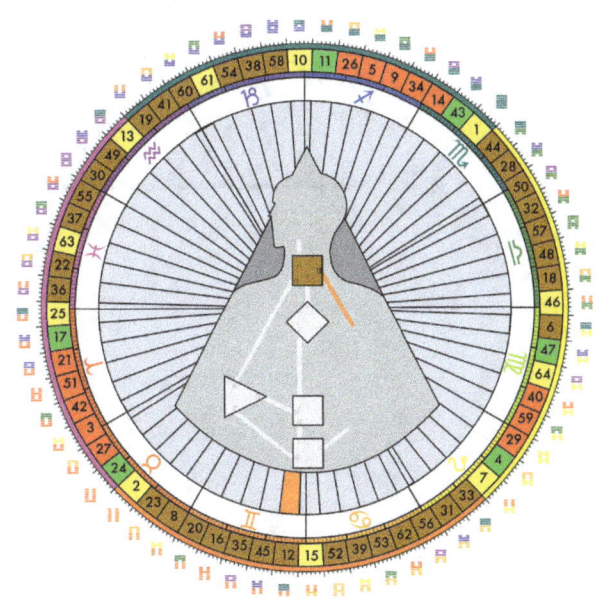

Spiritual World

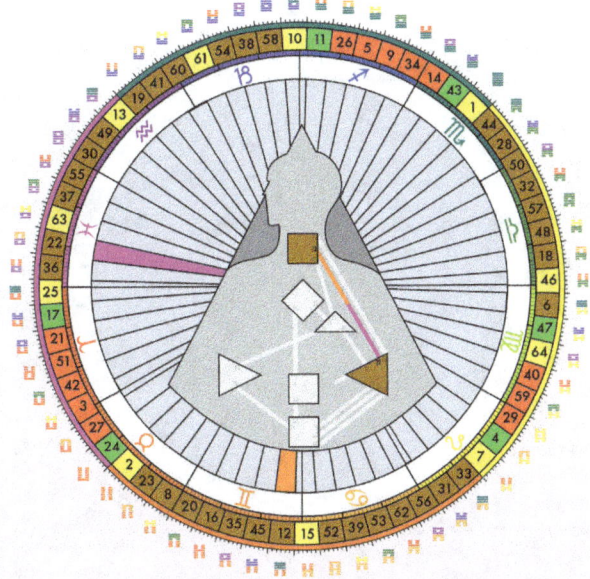

Physical World

Channel 12-22

Integrated Mental World, the Physical/Biological World, and The Spiritual/Archetypal World Portal
Channel 12-22 *(Gemini-Pisces)*

Keywords: Communication, Openness, Translation, Elusiveness

You are sensitive to the energy around you and read people's energy. Your breathing is key to your unconscious perceptions. Pay attention.

You sense a solid connection to your physical perceptions that activates a relationship between the Physical and Spiritual/Archetypal Worlds, giving you an energetic way of knowing that defies description. Thus, your sensitivity to energetic perceptions maximizes your physical consciousness.

The Spiritual/Archetypal World brings the energy of dreams, and you can understand instinctively toned language through voice frequencies. Pay attention to your breath and breathing because it reveals your stress level at any given moment. You are a highly social being who likes to engage with others, and you can, and often are, a person who influences others, especially with something you do. You have a talent for using powerful words and language that carry impact, and you can change someone's course of action based on your influence. Pay attention to your breathing to monitor your stress levels and gauge where and when you want to be social based on your unique chemistry and emotional state. You like to take time alone to clarify where and when you want to be social.

When you sleep, you lay down horizontally to rest, and your energy field shifts, as does how energy impacts your body. Because of your spiritual connection to your physical body, you are very in tune with what is healthy for you or not. Use your voice to express your deep spiritual knowing rather than repressing it. Speaking up frees your energy, whereas "holding your tongue" may put you under stress. Be strategic.

Use your words carefully, remembering your power of influence through language. Do the Microcosmic Orbit, Chant, or Sing. Any use of your voice can release debris from your energy field. Take time to be with yourself.

Your Keys to Empowerment
- Pay attention to your breathing. Changes in your breathing pattern indicate stress; use your Mind to regulate your breathing for optimal HRV (Heart Rate Variability).
- Your words are powerful. Use them with discretion, always being kind and compassionate.
- Speak your truth courageously and wisely to prevent throat issues.
- Using the Microcosmic Orbit Meditation can keep your energy clear.

Action Points for Manifesting Your Dreams
- Be strategic in your relationships and vet the people you call friends.
- Use your words auspiciously and powerfully.
- Learn which communication skills have power in each World.
- Pay attention to your body's signals and commit to self-care.

Integrated Mental World and Portal of the Spiritual/Archetypal World
Channel 12-22 *(Gemini-Pisces)*

Keywords: Communication, Openness, Translation, Elusiveness

You are sensitive to the energy around you and read people's energy. Your breathing is key to your unconscious perceptions. Pay attention.

You sense a solid connection to your physical perceptions that activates a relationship between the Physical and Spiritual/Archetypal Worlds. The Spiritual/Archetypal World brings the energy of dreams, and you can understand instinctively toned language through voice frequencies. Pay attention to your breath and breathing because it reveals your stress level at any given moment. You are a highly social being who likes to engage with others, and you can, and often are, a person who influences others, especially with something you do. You have a talent for using powerful words and language that carry impact, and you can change someone's course of action based on your influence. Pay attention to your breathing to monitor your stress levels and gauge where and when you want to be social based on your unique chemistry and emotional state. You like to take time alone to clarify where and when you want to be social.

When you sleep, you lay down horizontally to rest, and your energy field shifts, as does how energy impacts your body. Because of your spiritual connection to your physical body, you are very in tune with what is healthy for you or not. Use your voice to express your deep spiritual knowing rather than repressing it. Speaking up frees your energy, whereas "holding your tongue" may put you under stress. Be strategic.

Use your words carefully, remembering your power of influence through language. Do the Microcosmic Orbit, chant, or sing. Any use of your voice can release debris from your energy field. Take time to be with yourself.

Your Keys to Empowerment
- Pay attention to your breathing. Changes in your breathing pattern indicate stress; use your Mind to regulate your breathing for optimal HRV (Heart Rate Variability).
- Your words are powerful. Use them with discretion, always being kind and compassionate.
- Speak your truth courageously and wisely to prevent throat issues.
- Using the Microcosmic Orbit Meditation can keep your energy clear.

Action Points for Manifesting Your Dreams
- Be strategic in your relationships and vet the people you call friends.
- Use your words auspiciously and powerfully.
- Learn which communication skills have power in each World.
- Pay attention to your body's signals and commit to self-care.

Integrated Mental and Physical/Biological Worlds
Channel 12-22 *(Gemini-Pisces)*

Keywords: Communication, Openness, Translation, Elusiveness

You are sensitive to the energy around you and read people's energy. Your breathing is key to your unconscious perceptions. Pay attention.

You are spiritually connected to your physical body, giving you an energetic way of knowing that defies description. Thus, your sensitivity to energetic perceptions maximizes your physical consciousness. Pay attention to your breath and breathing because it reveals your stress level at any given moment. You are a highly social being who likes to engage with others, and you can, and often are, a person who influences others, especially with something you do. You have a talent for using powerful words and language that carry impact, and you can change someone's course of action based on your influence. This capacity to be influential arises from the kind of spiritual knowing you naturally bring into expression. You also like to take time alone to clarify where and when you want to be social. Pay attention to your breathing to monitor your stress levels and gauge where and when you want to be social based on your unique chemistry and emotional state. Use your words carefully, remembering your power of influence through language. Do the Microcosmic Orbit and chant or sing. Any use of your voice can release debris from your energy field. Take time to be with yourself.

Your Keys to Empowerment
- Pay attention to your breathing. Changes in your breathing pattern indicate stress; use your Mind to regulate your breathing for optimal HRV (Heart Rate Variability).
- Your words are powerful. Use them with discretion, always being kind and compassionate.
- Speak your truth courageously and wisely to prevent throat issues.
- Using the Microcosmic Orbit Meditation can keep your energy clear.

Action Points for Manifesting Your Dreams
- Be strategic in your relationships and vet the people you call friends.
- Use your words auspiciously and powerfully.
- Learn which communication skills have power in each World.
- Pay attention to your body's signals and commit to self-care.

Integrated Spiritual/Archetypal Portal and Physical/Biological Worlds
Gate 12 and Channel 12-22 *(Gemini-Pisces)*

Keywords: Communication, Openness, Translation, Elusiveness

You are sensitive to the energy around you and read people's energy. Your breathing is key to your unconscious perceptions. Pay attention.

You sense a solid connection to your physical perceptions that activates a relationship between the Physical and Spiritual/Archetypal Worlds. The Spiritual/Archetypal Worlds bring the energy of dreams, and you can understand instinctively toned language through voice frequencies.

Pay attention to your breath because it reveals your stress level at any given moment. You are finely tuned into your physical state and may even be sensitive enough to be aware of generally unconscious physical sensations. Be aware and mindful of what self-care your body needs.

When you sleep, you lay down horizontally to rest, and your energy field shifts, as does how energy impacts your body. Because of your spiritual connection to your physical body, you are very in tune with what is healthy for you or not. Use your voice to express your deep spiritual knowing rather than repressing it. Speaking up frees your energy, whereas "holding your tongue" may put you under stress. Be strategic. Do the Microcosmic Orbit, chant, or sing. Any use of your voice can release debris from your energy field. Take time to be with yourself.

Your Keys to Empowerment
- Pay attention to your breathing. Changes in your breathing pattern indicate stress; use your Mind to regulate your breathing for optimal HRV (Heart Rate Variability).
- Your words are powerful. Use them with discretion, always being kind and compassionate.
- Speak your truth courageously and wisely to prevent throat issues.
- Using the Microcosmic Orbit Meditation can keep your energy clear.

Action Points for Manifesting Your Dreams
- Be strategic in your relationships and vet the people you call friends.
- Use your words auspiciously and powerfully.
- Learn which communication skills have power in each World.
- Pay attention to your body's signals and commit to self-care.

Mental World
Channel 12-22 *(Gemini-Pisces)*

Keywords: Communication, Openness, Translation, Elusiveness

You are sensitive to the energy around you and read people's energy. Your breathing is key to your unconscious perceptions. Pay attention.

Pay attention to your breathing because it reveals your stress level at any given moment. You are a highly social being who likes to engage with others, and you can, and often are, a person who influences others, especially with something you do. You have a talent for using powerful words and language that carry impact, and you can change someone's course of action based on your influence. You also like to take time alone to clarify where and when you want to be social. Pay attention to your breathing to monitor your stress levels and gauge where and when you want to be social based on your unique chemistry and emotional state. Use your words carefully, remembering your power of influence through language. Do the Microcosmic Orbit, the Lamas Lotus, chant or sing. Any use of your voice can release debris from your energy field. Take time to be with yourself.

Your Keys to Empowerment
- Pay attention to your breathing. Changes in your breathing pattern indicate stress; use your Mind to regulate your breathing for optimal HRV (Heart Rate Variability).
- Your words are powerful. Use them with discretion, always being kind and compassionate.
- Speak your truth courageously and wisely to prevent throat issues.
- Using the Microcosmic Orbit Meditation can keep your energy clear.

Action Points for Manifesting Your Dreams
- Be strategic in your relationships and vet the people you call friends.
- Use your words auspiciously and powerfully.
- Learn which communication skills have power in each World.
- Pay attention to your body's signals and commit to self-care.

Physical/Biological World
Channel 12-22 *(Gemini-Pisces)*

Keywords: Communication, Openness, Translation, Elusiveness

You are sensitive to the energy around you and read people's energy. Your breathing is key to your unconscious perceptions. Pay attention.

You are spiritually connected to your physical body, giving you an energetic way of knowing that defies description. Thus, your sensitivity to energetic perceptions maximizes your physical consciousness. Pay attention to your breath and breathing because it reveals your stress level at any given moment. You are a highly social being who likes to engage with others, and you can, and often are, a person who influences others, especially with something you do. This capacity to be influential arises from the kind of spiritual knowing you naturally bring into expression. You have a talent for using powerful words and language that carry impact, and you can change someone's course of action based on your influence. You also like to take time alone to clarify where and when you want to be social. Pay attention to your breathing to monitor your stress levels and gauge where and when you want to be social based on your unique chemistry and emotional state. Use your words carefully, remembering your power of influence through language. Do the Microcosmic Orbit, chant, or sing. Any use of your voice can release debris from your energy field. Take time to be with yourself.

Your Keys to Empowerment
- Pay attention to your breathing. Changes in your breathing pattern indicate stress; use your Mind to regulate your breathing for optimal HRV (Heart Rate Variability).
  Your words are powerful. Use them with discretion, always being kind and
- compassionate.
- Speak your truth courageously and wisely to prevent throat issues.
- Using the Microcosmic Orbit Meditation can keep your energy clear.

Action Points for Manifesting Your Dreams
- Be strategic in your relationships and vet the people you call friends.
- Use your words auspiciously and powerfully.
- Learn which communication skills have power in each World.
- Pay attention to your body's signals and commit to self-care.

Channel 13-33

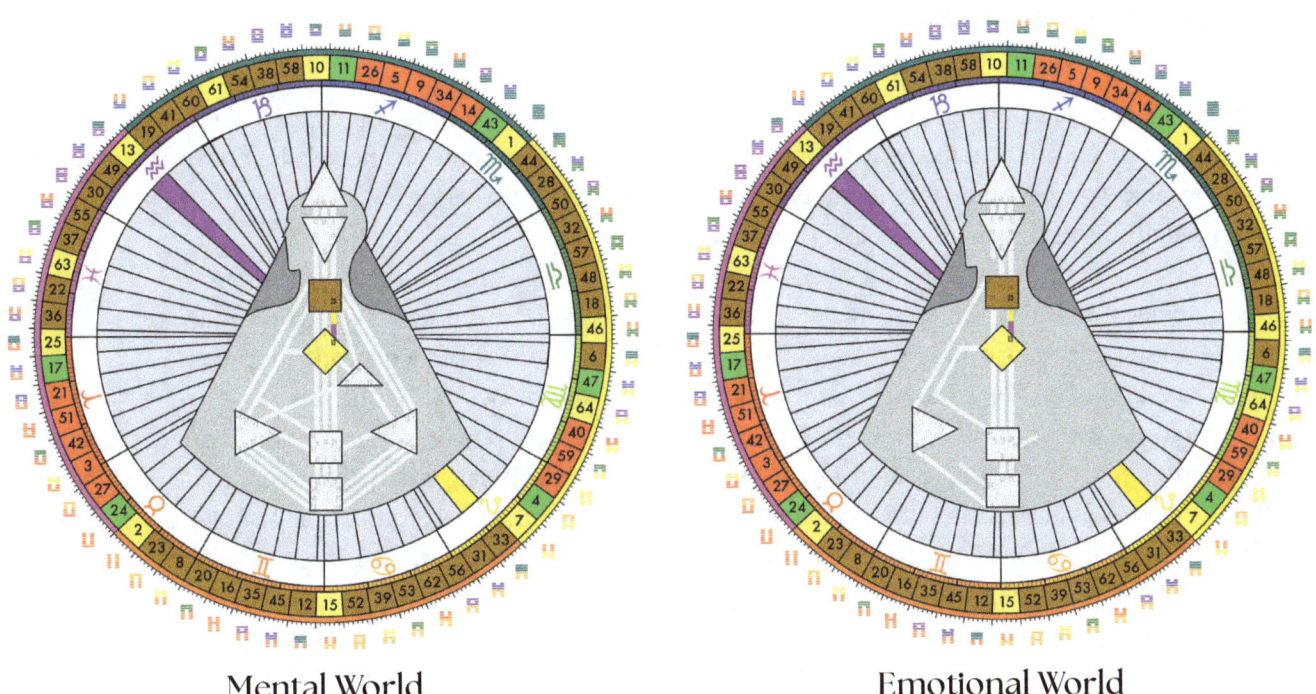

Mental World

Emotional World

Channel 13-33

Integrated Mental and Emotional/Angelic Worlds
Channel 13-33 *(Aquarius-Leo)*

Keywords: Remembrance, The Prodigal, Sharing

You are an excellent listener because your depth of awareness includes synchronicity and other dimensions of consciousness.

You have a deep awareness and remembrance of past events in your life, aligning with the cosmic dance around you. You may frequently experience synchronicity or past life memories, and your acceptance of the cosmos and its transcendence of third-dimensional reality seems natural. You are an excellent listener and may find others seeking to tell their story. Professionally, you might be a coach or a psychologist with a talent for recognizing partial information that leads you to unravel the whole story. You excel as both a listener and an interpreter of past knowledge. Hone your communication and listening skills by learning to ask open-ended questions and using Clean Communication.

You are likely working through the Constituting Path of Intelligence on the Kabbalistic Tree of Life. This path involves maintaining the rightful order of things and having a commanding manner. This energy connects makes you someone whose consciousness is involved in your life mission, and you likely have a sense of connectivity to the greater cosmos. Make sure you take time for yourself daily and develop excellent communication skills appropriate for each of the Four Worlds.

Your Keys to Empowerment
- Self-discipline allows you to maximize your sense of order and creativity.
- Explore meditation and self-growth tools.
- Use your power of visualization to project what you want to have happen.
- Set boundaries on your time and energy, so you take time to care for yourself.

Action Points for Manifesting Your Dreams
- Develop listening skills in all Four Worlds.
- Pay attention to synchronistic events and their messages for you.
- Work on your organizational skills and maintain order in your life.
- You are a good listener; learn how to manage your time and energy as a help agent.

Mental World
Channel 13-33 *(Aquarius-Leo)*

Keywords: Remembrance, The Prodigal, Sharing

You are an excellent listener because your depth of awareness includes synchronicity and other dimensions of consciousness.

You have a deep awareness and remembrance of past events in your life, aligning with the cosmic dance around you. You may experience synchronicity or past life memories frequently, and your acceptance of the cosmos and its transcendence of third-dimensional reality seems natural to you. You are an excellent listener and may find that others seek you out to tell their story. Professionally, you might be a coach or a psychologist with a talent for recognizing partial information that leads you to unravel the full story. You are gifted as both a listener and an interpreter of past knowledge. Hone your communication and listening skills by learning to ask open-ended questions and using Clean Communication. Work on maintaining the rightful order of things, so you feel in command of your life and home. Your consciousness is involved in your life mission and your connectivity to the greater cosmos. Make sure you take time for yourself daily and develop excellent communication skills in all Four Worlds.

Your Keys to Empowerment

- Self-discipline allows you to maximize your sense of order and creativity.
- Explore meditation and self-growth tools.
- Use your power of visualization to project what you want to have happen.
- Set boundaries on your time and energy, so you take time to care for yourself.

Action Points for Manifesting Your Dreams

- Develop listening skills in all Four Worlds.
- Pay attention to synchronistic events and their messages for you.
- Work on your organizational skills and maintain order in your life.
- You are a good listener; learn how to manage your time and energy as a help agent.

Emotional/Angelic World
Channel 13-33 *(Aquarius-Leo)*

Keywords: Remembrance, The Prodigal, Sharing

You are an excellent listener because your depth of awareness includes synchronicity and other dimensions of consciousness.

You are working on your Constituting Intelligence, one of the life lessons depicted on the Tree of Life. This path has to do with maintaining the rightful order of things and having a commanding manner. Thus, you are likely to feel uneasy if you are in a chaotic or disorderly situation. Your consciousness drives and motivates you, and you likely have a sense of connectivity to the greater cosmos. Make sure you take time for yourself daily and develop excellent communication skills in all Four Worlds. Your deep awareness and remembrance of past events in your life tune you into the cosmic dance around you. You may experience synchronicity or past life memories frequently, and your acceptance of the cosmos and its transcendence of third-dimensional reality seems natural to you. You are an excellent listener and may find that others seek you out to tell their story. Professionally, you might be a coach or a psychologist with a talent for recognizing partial information that leads you to unravel the full story. You are gifted as both a listener and an interpreter of past knowledge. Hone your communication and listening skills by learning to ask open-ended questions and using Clean Communication.

Your Keys to Empowerment
- Self-discipline allows you to maximize your sense of order and creativity.
- Explore meditation and self-growth tools.
- Use your power of visualization to project what you want to have happen.
- Set boundaries on your time and energy so you take time to care for yourself.

Action Points for Manifesting Your Dreams
- Develop listening skills in all Four Worlds.
- Pay attention to synchronistic events and their messages for you.
- Work on your organizational skills and maintain order in your life.
- You are a good listener; learn how to manage your time and energy as a help agent.

Channel 16-48

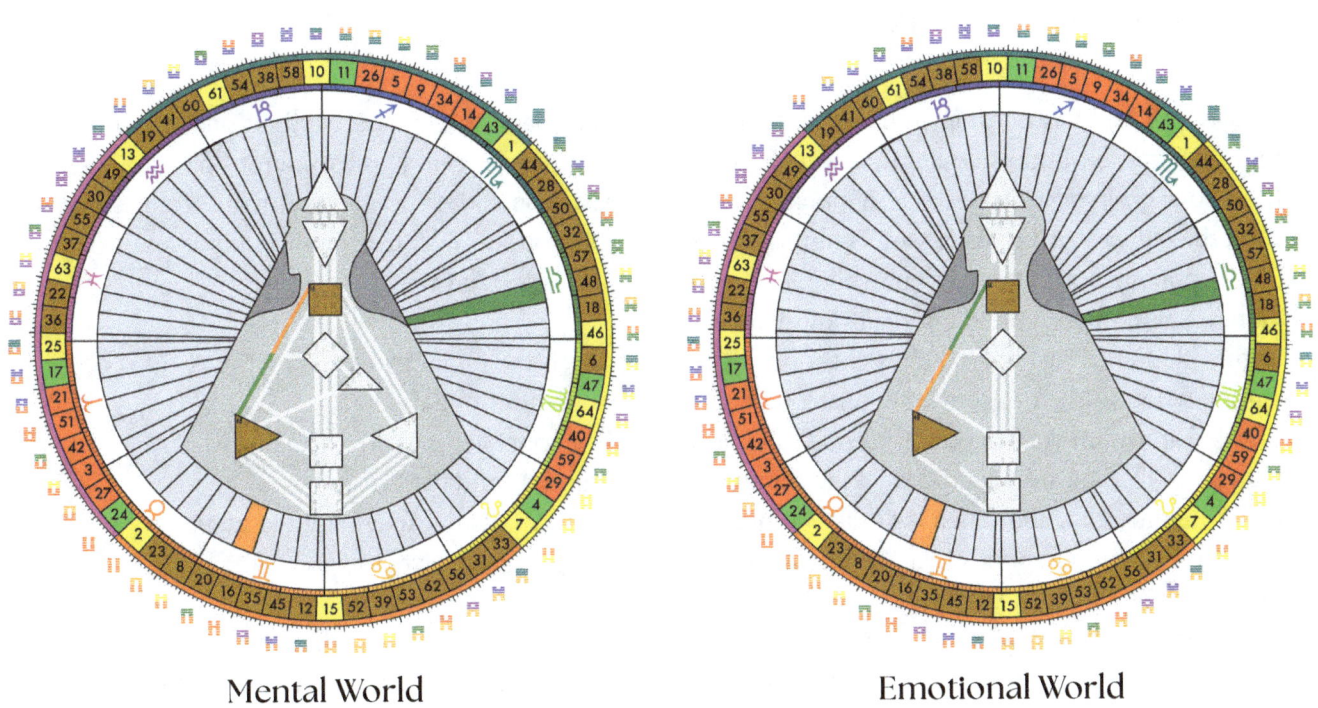

Mental World

Emotional World

Channel 16-48

Integrated Mental and Emotional/Angelic Worlds
Channel 16-48 *(Gemini-Libra)*

Keywords: Wisdom, Wavelength, Dimensionality, Depth

Your depth and wisdom go beyond ordinary awareness, challenging you to stay true to yourself and what you know.

Your depth and wisdom tap into deep memories that give you an understanding beyond the ordinary. Your grasp of what needs to happen to make something work or be successful often seems to come spontaneously and out of nowhere. You sense vibrational frequencies and internally know how to align with them. Trust that your insights come from a connection to the collective unconscious, and it drives you toward your depth of purpose and honing your skills. You are talented in all the things you feel committed to, and when you take something on, you do it entirely, honestly, and with integrity of higher values to which you feel committed. Never compromise your integrity; it is core to your very being and makes you who you are. Stand tall and trust God. When you feel challenged, take all the time you need to feel what aligns with your inner self. Wait before you act. Ask: "Does my action align with my goals?" "Are my deep core values being honored?" "What do I know about my depth and skills now?" Be mindful that not everyone has your level of ability to perceive vibrational alignment as you do, and your sensitivity and skill may set you apart from other people you relate to. Be firm in what you know is true, and be kind yet strong in holding your ground.

Your Keys to Empowerment
- Your depth and wisdom are exceptional.
- Use your talents to do what you love.
- Stand tall and trust God.
- You are sensitive to energy and have a depth of understanding. Use it.

Action Points for Manifesting Your Dreams
- Do what you love and love what you do.
- Your integrity is crucial to you. Do not compromise when you know you are internally aligned.
- You are highly sensitive. Honor your core values.
- What do you know about your depth and skills now?

Mental World
Channel 16-48 *(Gemini-Libra)*

Keywords: Wisdom, Wavelength, Dimensionality, Depth

Your depth and wisdom go beyond ordinary awareness, challenging you to stay true to yourself and what you know.

Your depth and wisdom tap into deep memories that give you an understanding beyond the ordinary. Your grasp of what needs to happen to make something work or be successful often seems to come spontaneously and out of nowhere. You sense vibrational frequencies and internally know how to align with them. Trust that your insights come from a connection to the collective unconscious, and it drives you toward your depth of purpose and honing your skills. You are talented in all the things you feel committed to, and when you take something on, you do it entirely, honestly, and with integrity of higher values to which you feel committed. Never compromise your integrity; it is core to your very being and makes you who you are. Stand tall and trust God. When you feel challenged, take all the time you need to feel what aligns with your inner self. Wait before you act. Ask: "Does my action align with my goals?" "Are my deep core values being honored?" "What do I know about my depth and skills now?"

Your Keys to Empowerment
- Trust your insights and wisdom.
- Use your talents to do what you love.
- Stand tall and trust God.
- You are sensitive to energy and have a depth of understanding. Use it.

Action Points for Manifesting Your Dreams
- Do what you love and love what you do.
- Your integrity is crucial to you. Do not compromise when you know you are internally aligned.
- Use your insights and depth to achieve your goals. Think "outside the box."
- What do you know about your depth and skills now?

Emotional/Angelic World
Channel 16-48 *(Gemini-Libra)*

Keywords: Wisdom, Wavelength, Dimensionality, Depth

Your depth and wisdom go beyond ordinary awareness, challenging you to stay true to yourself and what you know.

Your depth and wisdom tap into deep memories that give you an understanding beyond the ordinary. Your grasp of what needs to happen to make something work or be successful often seems to come spontaneously and out of nowhere. You sense vibrational frequencies and internally know how to align with them. Trust that your insights come from a connection to the collective unconscious, and it drives you toward your depth of purpose and honing your skills. You are talented in all the things you feel committed to, and when you take something on, you do it entirely, honestly, and with integrity of higher values to which you feel committed. Never compromise your integrity; it is core to your very being and makes you who you are. Stand tall and trust God. When you feel challenged, take all the time you need to feel what aligns with your inner self. Wait before you act. Ask: "Does my action align with my goals?" "Are my deep core values being honored?" "What do I know about my depth and skills now?" Be mindful that not everyone has your level.

Your Keys to Empowerment
- Trust your insights and wisdom.
- Use your talents to do what you love.
- Stand tall and trust God.
- You are sensitive to energy and have a depth of understanding. Use it.

Action Points for Manifesting Your Dreams
- Do what you love and love what you do.
- Your integrity is crucial to you. Do not compromise when you know you are internally aligned.
- Honor your core values.
- What do you know about your depth and skills now?

Channel 17-62

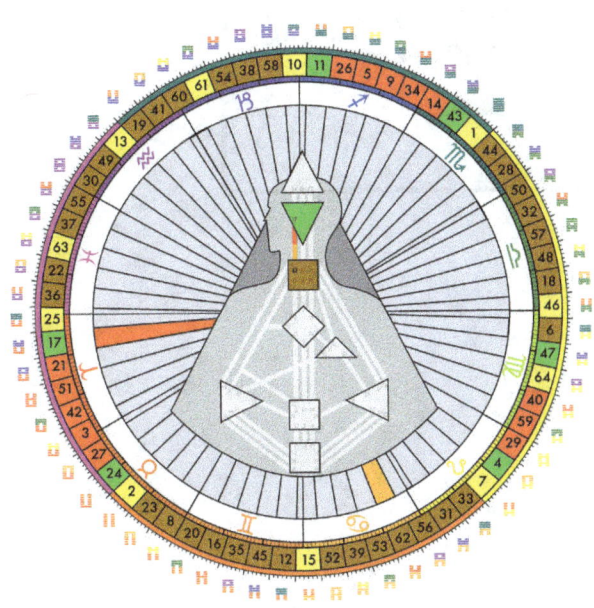

Mental World

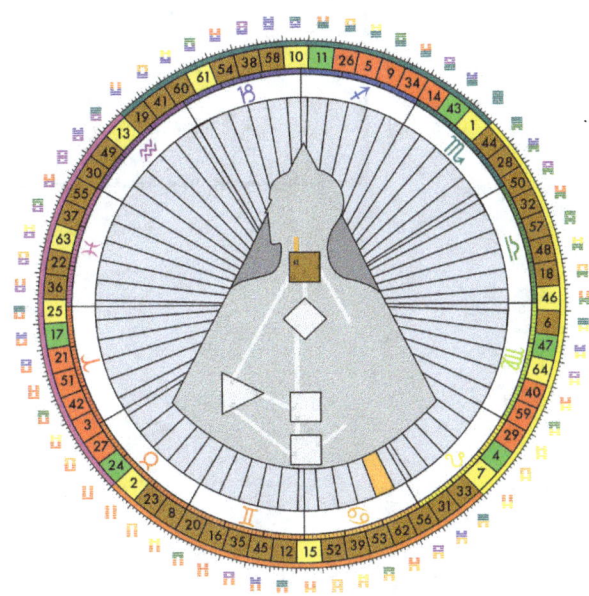

Spiritual World

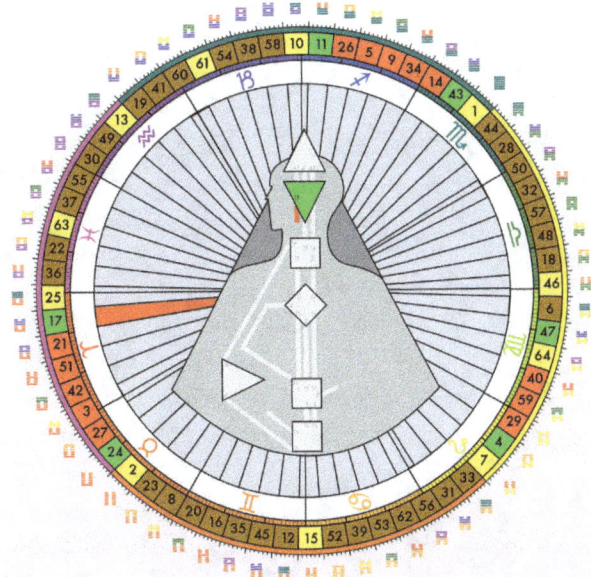

Emotional World

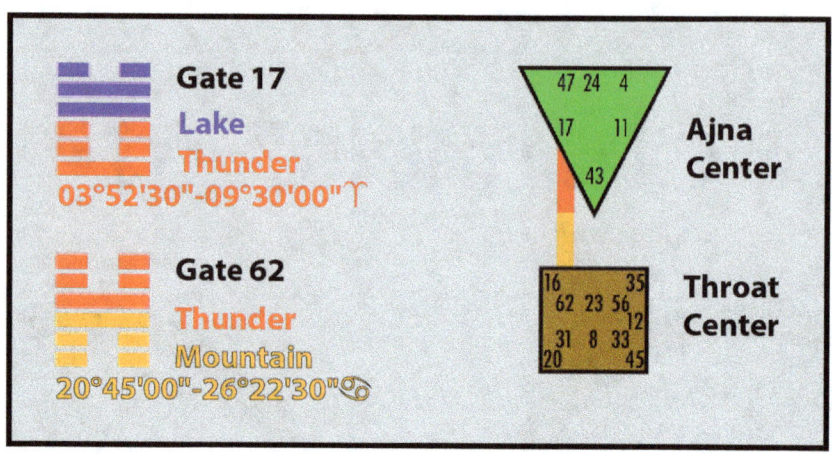

Channel 17-62

Integrated Mental, Emotional/Angelic, and Portal to the Spiritual/Archetypal World
Channel 17-62 *(Aries-Cancer)*

Keywords: Acceptance, Deference, Details, Transcendence, Love

You maintain high standards because you are highly sensitive on many levels of awareness. Be an example of clarity and faith.

Your spiritual connection runs deeply through all your communications with other people and animals. You maintain integrity by honoring your strong principles despite situational or personal preferences. You gain insights from being in situations and experiencing the energy of those around you. Sometimes, you pick up on what others think and feel, and you might speak for them. Remain true to your values and principles and listen to the energetic climate in which you find yourself. Be an example of consciousness by showing restraint and awareness to be an example of clarity and faith despite circumstances.

When you resonate with someone, you radiate love and compassion as a help agent, and when recognized for this quality, you are likely to feel empowered toward your life mission as a help agent. Speak when you know that your words ring true at your highest level of integrity. If you live by this rule, your energy will radiate love and compassion beyond any thought or words.

Because you are sensitive to energy and how it flows, you are likely to be sensitive to the feng shui of your environment. Be mindful of your need for order and honor it. In addition, you are a good animal communicator and a good dog trainer because you can tap into nonverbal communication. Take time daily to meditate in your own space, with or without a pet, and keep a journal, allowing your superconscious to write from beyond thinking. Allow words to flow from your higher mind. You might be surprised that you know more than you think you do.

Your Keys to Empowerment
- Trust your insights and wisdom.
- Use your talents to do what you love.
- Stand tall and trust God.
- You are sensitive to energy and have a depth of understanding.

Action Points for Manifesting Your Dreams
- Do what you love and love what you do.
- Your integrity is crucial to you. Do not compromise when you know you are internally aligned.
- Honor your core values.
- Speak your truth.

Integrated Mental, Emotional/Angelic Worlds
Channel 17-62 *(Aries-Cancer)*

Keywords: Acceptance, Deference, Details, Transcendence, Love

You maintain high standards because you are highly sensitive on many levels of awareness. Be an example of clarity and faith.

You connect deeply through all your communications with other people and animals. You maintain integrity by honoring your strong principles despite situational or personal preferences. You gain insights from being in situations and experiencing the energy of those around you. Sometimes, you pick up on what others think and feel, and you might speak for them. Remain true to your values and principles and listen to the energetic climate in which you find yourself. Be an example of consciousness by showing restraint and awareness to be an example of clarity and faith despite circumstances.

When you resonate with someone, you radiate love and compassion as a help agent, and when recognized for this quality, you are likely to feel empowered toward your life mission as a help agent. Speak when you know that your words ring true at your highest level of integrity. If you live by this rule, your energy will radiate love and compassion beyond any thought or words.

Because you are sensitive to energy and how it flows, you are likely to be sensitive to the Feng Shui of your environment. Be mindful of your need for order and honor it. In addition, you are a good animal communicator and a good dog trainer because you can tap into nonverbal communication. Take time daily to meditate in your own space, with or without a pet, and keep a journal, allowing your superconscious to write from beyond thinking. Allow words to flow from your higher mind. You might be surprised that you know more than you think you do.

Your Keys to Empowerment
- Trust your insights and wisdom.
- Use your talents to do what you love.
- Stand tall and trust God.
- You are sensitive to energy and have a depth of understanding.

Action Points for Manifesting Your Dreams
- Do what you love and love what you do.
- Your integrity is crucial to you. Do not compromise when you know you are internally aligned.
- You are sensitive to the Feng Shui of your environment. Pay attention and arrange your environment to align with your sensitivities.
- Speak your truth.

Integrated Mental and Portal to the Spiritual/Archetypal Worlds
Channel 17-62 *(Aries-Cancer)*

Keywords: Acceptance, Deference, Details, Transcendence, Love

You maintain high standards because you are highly sensitive on many levels of awareness. Be an example of clarity and faith.

You honor strong principles despite situational or personal preferences because you value your integrity. The connection you feel spiritually runs deeply through all your communications. You gain insights from being in situations and experiencing the energy of those around you. Sometimes, you pick up on what others think and feel, and you might speak for them. Remain true to your values and principles and listen to the energetic climate in which you find yourself. Be an example of consciousness by showing restraint and awareness to be an example of clarity and faith despite circumstances.

You are a good animal communicator and a good dog trainer. When you resonate with someone, you radiate love and compassion as a help agent, and when recognized for this quality, you are likely to feel empowered toward your life mission as a help agent. Speak when you know that your words ring true at your highest level of integrity. If you live by this rule, your energy will radiate love and compassion beyond any thought or words. Take time daily to meditate in your own space, with or without a pet, and keep a journal, allowing your superconscious to write from a room beyond thinking. Allow words to flow from your higher mind. You might be surprised that you know more than you think you do.

Your Keys to Empowerment
- You know more than you think you know. Trust yourself.
- You pick up on other people's thoughts, be aware, and choose your responses mindfully.
- Stand tall and trust God.
- Your sensitivity to energy gives you a depth of understanding. Trust it.

Action Points for Manifesting Your Dreams
- Be an example of consciousness by being loving and communicative.
- Stay true to your word.
- Meditate daily (allow your pets to meditate with you).
- Keep a journal and allow your thoughts to flow without censorship.

Mental World
Channel 17-62 *(Aries-Cancer)*

Keywords: Acceptance, Deference, Details, Transcendence, Love

You maintain high standards because you are highly sensitive on many levels of awareness. Be an example of clarity and faith.

You honor your strong principles despite situational or personal preferences because you value your integrity. You gain insights from being in situations and experiencing the energy of those around you. Sometimes, you pick up on what others think and feel, and you might speak for them. Remain true to your values and principles and listen to the energetic climate in which you find yourself. Be an example of consciousness by showing restraint and awareness to be an example of clarity and faith despite circumstances. You are a good animal communicator and a good dog trainer. When you resonate with someone, you radiate love and compassion as a help agent, and when recognized for this quality, you are likely to feel empowered toward your life mission as a help agent. Speak when you know that your words ring true at your highest level of integrity. If you live by this rule, your energy will radiate love and compassion beyond any thought or words.

Your Keys to Empowerment
- You know more than you think you know. Trust yourself.
- You pick up on the feelings of others; be aware.
- Stand tall and trust God.
- Your sensitivity to energy gives you a depth of understanding. Trust it.

Action Points for Manifesting Your Dreams
- Be an example of consciousness by being loving and communicative.
- Speak when you know your words ring true and have integrity.
- Meditate daily (allow your pets to meditate with you).
- Keep a journal and allow your thoughts to flow without censorship.

Emotional/Angelic World
Channel 17-62 *(Aries-Cancer)*

Keywords: Acceptance, Deference, Details, Transcendence, Love

You maintain high standards because you are highly sensitive on many levels of awareness. Be an example of clarity and faith.

You honor strong principles despite situational or personal preferences because you value your integrity. The connection you feel spiritually runs deeply through all your communications. You gain insights from being in situations and experiencing the energy of those around you. Sometimes, you pick up on what others think and feel, and you might speak for them. Remain true to your values and principles and listen to the energetic climate in which you find yourself. Be an example of consciousness by showing restraint and awareness to be an example of clarity and faith despite circumstances.

You are a good animal communicator and a good dog trainer. When you resonate with someone, you radiate love and compassion as a help agent, and when recognized for this quality, you are likely to feel empowered toward your life mission as a help agent. Speak when you know that your words ring true at your highest level of integrity. If you live by this rule, your energy will radiate love and compassion beyond any thought or words. Take time daily to meditate in your own space, with or without a pet, and keep a journal, allowing your superconscious to write from a room beyond thinking. Allow words to flow from your higher mind. You might be surprised that you know more than you think you do.

Your Keys to Empowerment
- When you have a strong sense of someone, trust your perceptions.
- You pick up on other people's thoughts, be aware, and choose your responses mindfully.
- Stand tall and trust God.
- You perceive energy and understand it without words. Trust it.

Action Points for Manifesting Your Dreams
- Be an example of consciousness by being loving and communicative.
- Stay true to your word.
- Meditate daily using Transcendental Meditation (allow your pets to meditate with you).
- Keep a journal and allow your thoughts to flow without censorship.

Channel 18-58

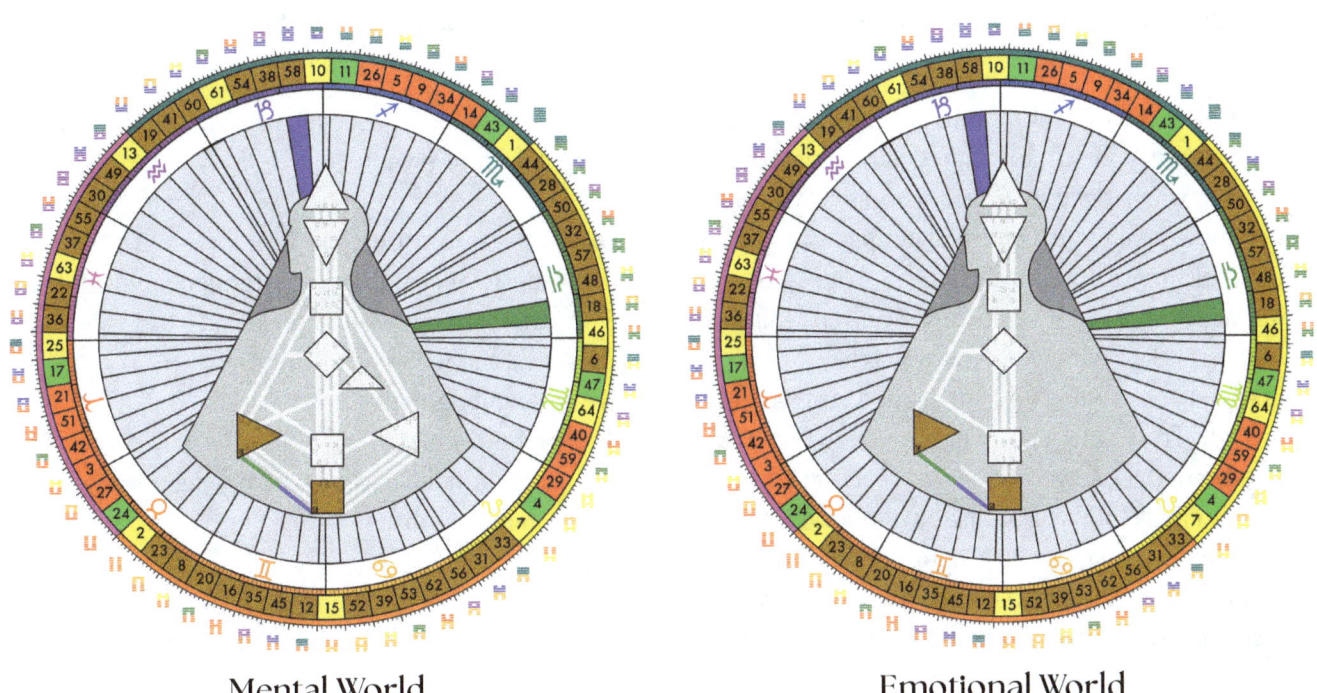

Mental World Emotional World

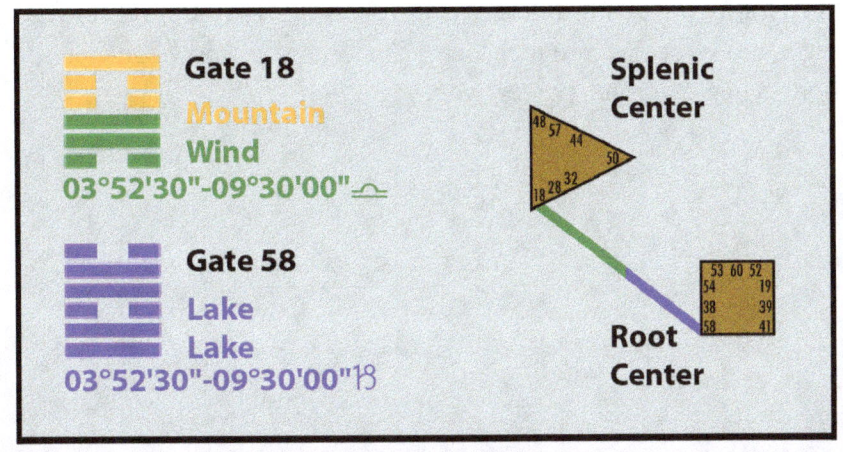

Channel 18-58

Integrated Mental and Emotional/Angelic Worlds
Channel 18-58 *(Libra-Capricorn)*

Keywords: Vibrations, Judgment, Energy, Perceptiveness, Sensitivity

You are extremely sensitive to vibrational frequencies and know when something "rings true" or not. Trust your perceptiveness and stand up for what you know.

Your sensitivity to vibrational frequencies is acute. You attune yourself to aligned energetic patterns and know what energy frequencies are likely to play out successfully and which will not play out because of their misaligned frequencies. Your judgment about where you are and how you feel will likely perfectly align with what you want to have happen, and you know when you are aligned and when you are not. Trust your judgment about your sensitivity to vibrational energy. When you feel uneasy or like something is "off," you are likely right on target, and you need to take action to put yourself in a more aligned or comfortable situation. Compromising what you know is aligned with its capacity to manifest compromises your integrity. Thus, to feel inwardly aligned with your highest self and the divine, when you know at a level of depth that something is right, stand up for it confidently and firmly. You are a child of light and very wise. You may feel alone among those less sensitive and perceptive. Remain grounded in your self-knowledge and maintain faith in your divinity.

Your Keys to Empowerment
- Your sensitivity to vibrational frequencies is acute.
- You know when you are aligned and balanced and when you are not.
- Trust your judgment about what feels right to you or not.
- Remain grounded in your self-knowledge and maintain faith in your divinity.

Action Points for Manifesting Your Dreams
- Stand up for your perceptions and trust them.
- Your judgment is usually on target. Believe in yourself.
- Use your perceptiveness and sensitivity to use good judgment.
- Honor your knowingness.

Mental World
Channel 18-58 *(Libra-Capricorn)*

Keywords: Vibrations, Judgment, Energy, Perceptiveness, Sensitivity

You are extremely sensitive to vibrational frequencies and know when something "rings true" or not. Trust your perceptiveness and stand up for what you know.

Your sensitivity to vibrational frequencies is acute. You attune yourself to aligned energetic patterns and know what energy frequencies are likely to play out successfully and which will not play out because of their misaligned frequencies. Your judgment about where you are and how you feel will likely perfectly align with what you want to have happen, and you know when you are aligned and when you are not. Trust your judgment about your sensitivity to vibrational energy. When you feel uneasy or like something is "off," you are likely right on target, and you need to take action to put yourself in a more aligned or comfortable situation. Compromising what you know is aligned with its capacity to manifest compromises your integrity. Thus, to feel inwardly aligned with your highest self and the divine, when you know at a level of depth that something is right, stand up for it confidently and firmly. You are a child of light and very wise.

Your Keys to Empowerment
- Your sensitivity to vibrational frequencies is acute.
- You know when you are aligned and balanced and when you are not.
- Trust your judgment about what feels right to you or not.
- Stand up for what you deeply know.

Action Points for Manifesting Your Dreams
- Stand up for your perceptions and trust them.
- Your judgment is usually on target. Believe in yourself.
- Use your perceptiveness and sensitivity to use good judgment.
- Honor your knowingness.

Emotional/Angelic World
Channel 18-58 *(Libra-Capricorn)*

Keywords: Vibrations, Judgment, Energy, Perceptiveness, Sensitivity

You are extremely sensitive to vibrational frequencies and know when something "rings true" or not. Trust your perceptiveness and stand up for what you know.

You are sensitive to vibrational frequencies throughout your body and perceptively. You attune yourself to aligned energetic patterns and know what energy frequencies are likely to play out successfully and which will not play out because of their misaligned frequencies. Your judgment about where you are and how you feel is usually perfectly aligned with what you want to have happen, and you know when you are aligned and when you are not. Trust your judgment regarding your high sensitivity to vibrational energy. When you feel uneasy or like something is "off," you are usually right on target, and you need to take action to put yourself in a more aligned or comfortable situation. Compromising what you know is aligned with its capacity to manifest compromises your integrity. Thus, to feel inwardly aligned with your highest self and the divine, when you know at a level of depth that something is right, stand up for it confidently and firmly. You are a child of light and very wise. You may feel alone among those less sensitive and perceptive. Remain grounded in your self-knowledge and your faith in your divinity.

Your Keys to Empowerment
- Your sensitivity to vibrational frequencies is acute.
- You know when you are aligned and balanced and when you are not.
- Trust your judgment about what feels right to you or not.
- Remain grounded in your self-knowledge and maintain faith in your divinity.

Action Points for Manifesting Your Dreams
- Stand up for your perceptions and trust them.
- Your judgment is usually on target. Believe in yourself.
- Use your perceptiveness and sensitivity to use good judgment.
- Honor your knowingness.

Channel 19-49

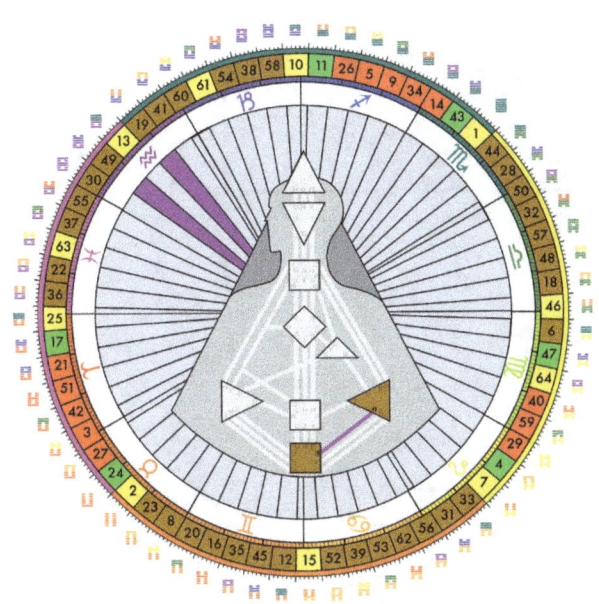

Mental World

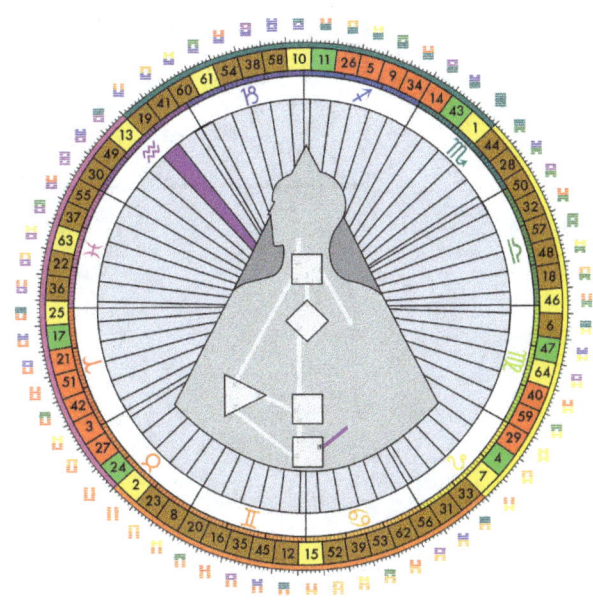

Spiritual World

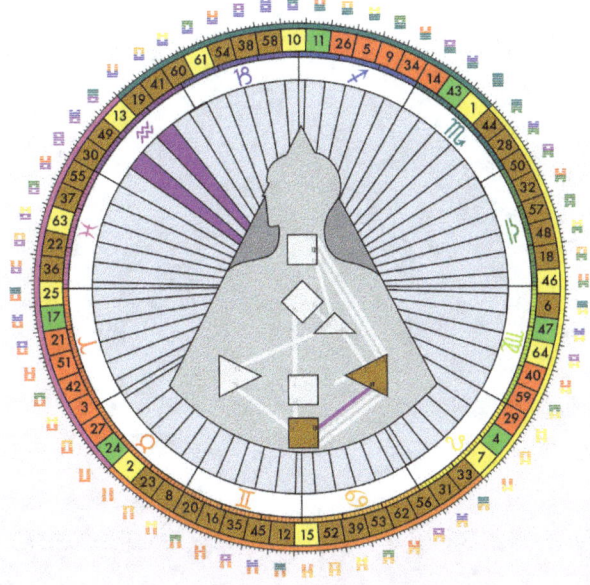

Physical World

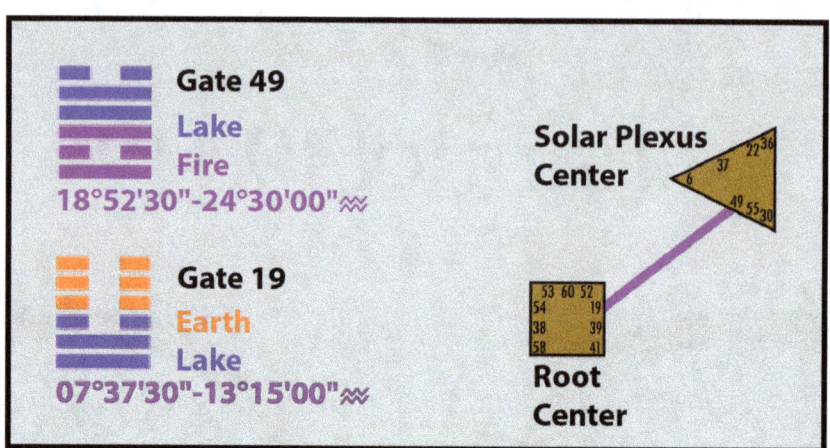

Channel 19-49

Integrated Mental, Emotional/Angelic, Physical/Biological World and Portal to the Spiritual/Archetypal Worlds
Channel 19-49 and Gate 19 *(Aquarius-Aquarius)*

Keywords: Acuteness, Synthesis, Responsiveness, Nuance

You are emotionally sensitive to nuances of communication, and you feel compassion for others.

You are acutely sensitive to emotional energy that impacts your health and feelings. You tune into your chemistry and spiritually attune to subtle feelings within your body. Because you perceive multidimensional information, you react quickly to situational nuances that emotionally impact you. Use your breathing and consciousness to realign and rebalance.

Because of your sensitivity, you will likely feel great compassion for those who cannot speak for themselves. If you find you are taking on the feelings of others and those emotions intrude on your clarity about your own emotions, you may have to discern more acutely to protect yourself and your health. Emotional waves are everyday experiences you can master by breathing through the wave and balancing its energies. You can also release energy from within your energetic aura by exhaling and releasing it into the earth. Because you are spiritually attuned and highly sensitive, alternative and holistic medical options are the best treatments for you. Grounding keeps you in touch with what your physiological reactions communicate to you unconsciously. Your capacity for sensitivity and compassion is great. Just be mindful not to deplete yourself by caring more for others than yourself.

Your Keys to Empowerment
- Pay attention to your body and its nuances and respond accordingly.
- Because you are highly sensitive, you tune in to the needs of those around you.
- Transform emotional reactivity by breathing, balancing energy, and releasing emotions.
- Remain grounded in your self-knowledge and maintain faith in your divinity.

Action Points for Manifesting Your Dreams
- When you feel emotional reactivity, breathe and rebalance.
- Take care of your needs before you take care of other's needs.
- Your spiritual sensitivity makes you suitable for holistic and alternative healing modalities.
- Recognize your sensitivity and your multidimensional consciousness.

Integrated Mental, Physical/Biological World and Portal to the Spiritual/Archetypal Worlds
Channel 19-49 and Gate 19 *(Aquarius-Aquarius)*

Keywords: Acuteness, Synthesis, Responsiveness, Nuance

You are emotionally sensitive to nuances of communication, and you feel compassion for others.

You sense the universe's multidimensional nature, tune in to subtle feelings within your body, and energy and things that impact your health and emotions. Grounding keeps you in touch with what your physiological reactions communicate to you unconsciously. Based on this multidimensional information, you react quickly to situational nuances that impact you emotionally. If you are reactive, use your breathing and consciousness to realign and rebalance. Because of your sensitivity, you will likely feel great compassion for those who cannot speak for themselves. If you find you are taking on the feelings of others and those emotions intrude on your clarity about your own emotions, you may have to discern more acutely to protect yourself and your health. Master your reactions by breathing through the wave and balancing its energies. You can also release energy from within your energetic aura by exhaling and releasing it into the earth. Your capacity for sensitivity and compassion is great. You have a talent for healing yourself and others. Reiki, Homeopathy, and Access Consciousness Bars are a few tools that might be useful for you. Just be mindful not to deplete yourself by caring more for others than yourself.

Your Keys to Empowerment
- Pay attention to your body and its nuances and respond accordingly.
- Because you are highly sensitive, you tune in to the needs of those around you. Be diligent in asking if you are picking up energy from your environment and others in it.
- Transform emotional reactivity by breathing, balancing energy, and releasing emotions.
- Remain grounded in your self-knowledge and maintain faith in your divinity.

Action Points for Manifesting Your Dreams
- When you feel emotional reactivity, breathe and rebalance.
- Take care of your needs before you take care of other's needs.
- Your spiritual openness makes tools like Heart Math, Self-Hypnosis, Access Consciousness Bars, and Essential Oils beneficial for you.
- Recognize your sensitivity and your multidimensional consciousness.

Integrated Physical/Biological World and Portal to the Spiritual/Archetypal Worlds
Channel 19-49 and Gate 19 *(Aquarius-Aquarius)*

Keywords: Acuteness, Synthesis, Responsiveness, Nuance

You are emotionally sensitive to nuances of communication, and you feel compassion for others.

You sense the universe's multidimensional nature, tune in to subtle feelings within your body, and energy and things that impact your health and emotions. Grounding keeps you in touch with what your physiological reactions communicate to you unconsciously. Based on this multidimensional information, you react quickly to situational nuances that impact you emotionally. If you are reactive, use your breathing and consciousness to realign and rebalance. Because of your sensitivity, you will likely feel great compassion for those who cannot speak for themselves. If you find you are taking on the feelings of others and those emotions intrude on your clarity about your own emotions, you may have to discern more acutely to protect yourself and your health. Master your reactions by breathing through the wave and balancing its energies. You can also release energy from within your energetic aura by exhaling and releasing it into the earth. Your capacity for sensitivity and compassion is great. You have a talent for healing yourself and others. Reiki, Homeopathy, and Access Consciousness Bars are a few tools that might be useful for you. Just be mindful not to deplete yourself by caring more for others than yourself.

Your Keys to Empowerment
- Pay attention to your body and its nuances and respond accordingly.
- Because you are highly sensitive, you tune in to the needs of those around you. Be diligent in asking if you are picking up energy from your environment and others in it.
- Transform emotional reactivity by breathing, balancing energy, and releasing emotions.
- Remain grounded in your self-knowledge and maintain faith in your divinity.

Action Points for Manifesting Your Dreams
- When you feel emotional reactivity, breathe and rebalance.
- Take care of your needs before you take care of other's needs.
- Your spiritual openness makes tools like Heart Math, Self-Hypnosis, Access Consciousness Bars, and Essential Oils beneficial for you.
- Recognize your sensitivity and your multidimensional consciousness.

Integrated Mental World and Portal to the Spiritual/Archetypal World
Channel 19-49 and Gate 19 *(Aquarius-Aquarius)*

Keywords: Acuteness, Synthesis, Responsiveness, Nuance

You are emotionally sensitive to nuances of communication, and you feel compassion for others.

You are acutely sensitive to emotional energy and things that impact your health and feelings. You react quickly to situational nuances that affect you emotionally. If you are reactive, you can use your breathing and consciousness to realign and rebalance. Because of your sensitivity, you will likely feel great compassion for those who cannot speak for themselves. If you find you are taking on the feelings of others and those emotions intrude on your clarity about your own emotions, you may have to discern more acutely to protect yourself and your health. Emotional waves are everyday experiences you can master by breathing through the wave and balancing its energies. You can also release energy from within your energetic aura by exhaling and releasing it into the earth. Your capacity for sensitivity and compassion is great. Just be mindful not to deplete yourself by caring more for others than yourself. Because you have a strong spiritual connection, consider using alternative tools for balancing your emotions, such as heart math (HRV training), essential oils, and self-hypnosis.

Your Keys to Empowerment
- Pay attention to your body and its nuances and respond accordingly.
- Because you are highly sensitive, you tune in to the needs of those around you.
- Transform emotional reactivity by breathing, balancing energy, and releasing emotions.
- Remain grounded in your self-knowledge and maintain faith in your divinity.

Action Points for Manifesting Your Dreams
- When you feel emotional reactivity, breathe and rebalance.
- Take care of your needs before you take care of other's needs.
- Your spiritual openness makes tools like Heart Math, Self-Hypnosis, Access
- Consciousness Bars, and Essential Oils beneficial for you.
- Recognize your sensitivity and your multidimensional consciousness.

Integrated Mental and Physical/Biological Worlds
Channel 19-49 and Gate 19 *(Aquarius-Aquarius)*

Keywords: Acuteness, Synthesis, Responsiveness, Nuance

You are emotionally sensitive to nuances of communication, and you feel compassion for others.

You are acutely sensitive to emotional energy that impacts your health and feelings. You tune into your chemistry and spiritually attune to subtle feelings within your body. Because you perceive multidimensional information, you react quickly to situational nuances that emotionally impact you. . Use your breathing and consciousness to realign and rebalance if you feel reactive. Because of your sensitivity, you will likely feel great compassion for those who cannot speak for themselves. If you find you are taking on the feelings of others and those emotions intrude on your clarity about your own emotions, you may have to discern more acutely to protect yourself and your health. Emotional waves are everyday experiences you can master by breathing through the wave and balancing its energies. You can also release energy from within your energetic aura by exhaling and releasing it into the earth. Grounding keeps you in touch with what your physiological reactions communicate to you unconsciously. Your capacity for sensitivity and compassion is great. Just be mindful not to deplete yourself by caring more for others than yourself.

Your Keys to Empowerment
- Pay attention to your body and its nuances and respond accordingly.
- Because you are highly sensitive, you tune in to the needs of those around you.
- Transform emotional reactivity by breathing, balancing energy, and releasing emotions.
- Remain grounded in your self-knowledge and maintain faith in your divinity.

Action Points for Manifesting Your Dreams
- When you feel emotional reactivity, breathe and rebalance.
- Take care of your needs before you take care of other's needs.
- Self-care is essential for you. You are highly sensitive to your body's needs, so make taking care of yourself a priority.
- Recognize your sensitivity and your multidimensional consciousness.

Mental World
Channel 19-49 *(Aquarius-Aquarius)*

Keywords: Acuteness, Synthesis, Responsiveness, Nuance

You are emotionally sensitive to nuances of communication, and you feel compassion for others.

You are acutely sensitive to emotional energy and things that impact your health and feelings. You react quickly to situational nuances that affect you emotionally. If you are reactive, you can use your breathing and consciousness to realign and rebalance. Because of your sensitivity, you will likely feel great compassion for those who cannot speak for themselves. If you find you are taking on the feelings of others and those emotions intrude on your clarity about your own emotions, you may have to discern more acutely to protect yourself and your health. Emotional waves are everyday experiences you can master by breathing through the wave and balancing its energies. You can also release energy from within your energetic aura by exhaling and releasing it into the earth. Your capacity for sensitivity and compassion is great. Just be mindful not to deplete yourself by caring more for others than yourself.

Your Keys to Empowerment
- Pay attention to your body and its nuances and respond accordingly.
- Because you are highly sensitive, you tune in to the needs of those around you.
- Transform emotional reactivity by breathing, balancing energy, and releasing emotions.
- Remain grounded in your self-knowledge and maintain faith in your divinity.

Action Points for Manifesting Your Dreams
- When you feel emotional reactivity, breathe and rebalance.
- Take care of your needs before you take care of other's needs.
- Self-care is essential for you. You are highly sensitive to your body's needs, so make taking care of yourself a priority.
- Recognize your sensitivity and your multidimensional consciousness.

Physical/Biological Worlds
Channel 19-49 *(Aquarius-Aquarius)*

Keywords: Acuteness, Synthesis, Responsiveness, Nuance

You are emotionally sensitive to nuances of communication, and you feel compassion for others.

You sense the universe's multidimensional nature, tune in to subtle feelings within your body, and are acutely sensitive to emotional energy and things that impact your health and emotions. Your grounding keeps you in touch with what your physiological reactions communicate to you unconsciously. Based on this multidimensional information, you react quickly to situational nuances that impact you emotionally. If you are reactive, you can use your breathing and consciousness to realign and rebalance. Because of your sensitivity, you will likely feel great compassion for those who cannot speak for themselves. If you find you are taking on the feelings of others and those emotions intrude on your clarity about your own emotions, you may have to discern more acutely to protect yourself and your health. Emotional waves are everyday experiences you can master by breathing through the wave and balancing its energies. You can also release energy from within your energetic aura by exhaling and releasing it into the earth. Your capacity for sensitivity and compassion is great. Just be mindful not to deplete yourself by caring more for others than yourself.

Your Keys to Empowerment
- Pay attention to your body and its nuances and respond accordingly.
- Because you are highly sensitive, you tune in to the needs of those around you.
- Transform emotional reactivity by breathing, balancing energy, and releasing emotions.
- Remain grounded in your self-knowledge and maintain faith in your divinity.

Action Points for Manifesting Your Dreams
- When you feel emotional reactivity, breathe and rebalance.
- Take care of your needs before you take care of other's needs.
- Self-care is essential for you. You are highly sensitive to your body's needs, so make taking care of yourself a priority.
- Recognize your sensitivity and your multidimensional consciousness.

Channel 20-57

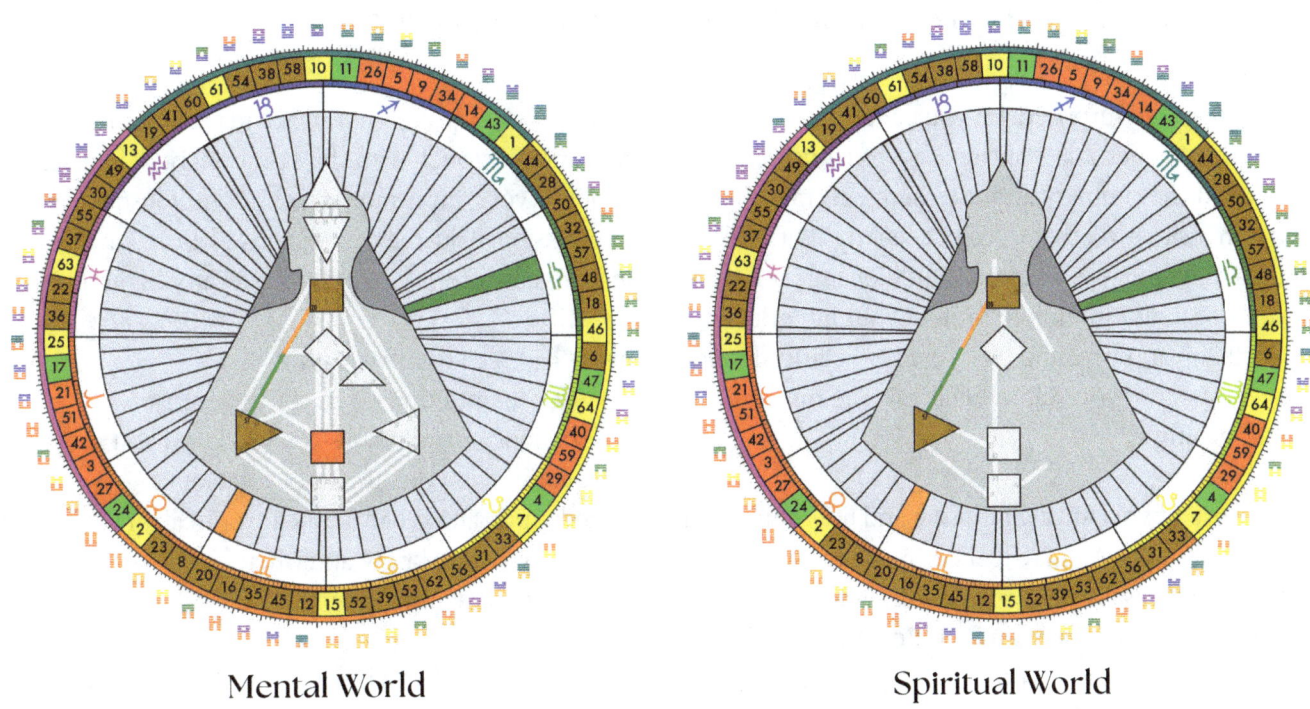

Mental World　　　　　　　　　　　Spiritual World

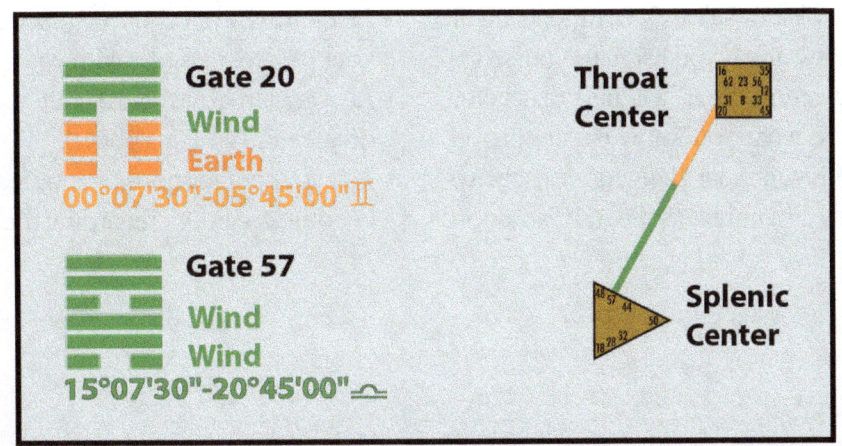

Channel 20-57

137

Integrated Mental and Spiritual/Archetypal Worlds
Channel 20-57 *(Gemini-Libra)*

Keywords: Knowingness, Brainwave, Acuity, Clarity, Intuitive Knowing

You are strongly intuitive and know when things are right for you and when they are not. Pay attention to your inner voice and wait for clarity before acting.

You may be surprised by your acute insights and intuitive penetrating awareness. You know things beyond the ordinary and use them naturally. If you are in a situation that does not feel right, it is likely unhealthy for you, and you should change your status. Use your intuition to protect your integrity. You are highly intuitive and can trust your clarity. Honor that aspect of yourself to fulfill your life mission and stay healthy.

Because of your strong intuition and how acute and accurate it is, you may feel compelled to act when you sense misalignments. Always wait for the appropriate time and energy to act. Be patient and hold tight until you know with a K that the time is right to speak or to work. Knowing with a K means knowing what you know so deeply that no one can tell you that what you know is not valid. Over time, you can test your perceptions, and if you listen to yourself at the level of this awareness, you will find that when you know with a K, what you know is true proves to be so. With this Channel defined, you always do best if you have a mammal as a pet. In addition, meditation in your own space daily is critical to remaining in touch with this component of yourself, which is very important to your consciousness and life mission. You may be surprised by your acute insights and intuitive penetrating awareness at times.

Your Keys to Empowerment
- Trust your intuition when you have clarity.
- Be patient and only act when you know you are acting from the depths of your soul.
- Meditation and dream work are critical for you.
- Know what you know, and when you know it, stand firm for it.

Action Points for Manifesting Your Dreams
- Learn to discern what comes from the depth of your knowing and what is superficial.
- Meditate daily in your own space, allowing your pets to meditate with you.
- Keep a journal to record your dreams and your insights.
- Test your perceptions over time so you become confident regarding their truth.

Mental World
Channel 20-57 *(Gemini-Libra)*

Keywords: Knowingness, Brainwave, Acuity, Clarity, Intuitive Knowing

You are strongly intuitive and know when things are right for you and when they are not. Pay attention to your inner voice and wait for clarity before acting.

You may be surprised by your acute insights and intuitive penetrating awareness at times. You know things beyond the ordinary and use them naturally. If you are in a situation that does not feel right, it is likely unhealthy for you, and you should change your situation. Because of your strong intuition and how acute it is, you may feel pressed to act but are wise to wait for the appropriate time and energy. Be patient and hold tight until you know with a K that the time is right to speak or to work. Knowing with a K means knowing what you know so deeply that no one can tell you that what you know is not valid. Over time, you can test your perceptions, and if you listen to yourself at the level of this awareness, you will find that when you know with a K, what you know is true proves to be so. With this Channel defined, you always do best if you have a mammal as a pet. In addition, meditation in your own space daily is critical to remaining in touch with this component of yourself, which is very important to your consciousness and life mission. Give priority to your intuition over your mind. Let your mind serve your spirit, and use your mental acumen appropriately and strategically.

Your Keys to Empowerment
- Trust your intuition.
- Be patient and only act when you know you are acting from the depths of your soul.
- Meditation and dream work are critical for you.
- Let your mind be in service to your spirit.

Action Points for Manifesting Your Dreams
- Learn to discern what comes from the depth of your knowing and what is superficial.
- Meditate daily in your own space, allowing your pets to meditate with you.
- Keep a journal to record daily observations.
- Use your mental acumen appropriately and strategically.

Spiritual/Archetypal World
Channel 20-57 *(Gemini-Libra)*

Keywords: Knowingness, Brainwave, Acuity, Clarity, Intuitive Knowing

You are strongly intuitive and know when things are right for you and when they are not. Pay attention to your inner voice and wait for clarity before acting.

You may be surprised by your acute insights and intuitive penetrating awareness at times. You know things beyond the ordinary and naturally use your intuition to protect your integrity. You are highly intuitive and must honor that aspect of yourself to fulfill your life mission and stay healthy. When you are in a situation that does not feel right, it is not fit for you to be in, and you should change your status. Because of your strong intuition and it's acute, you may feel pressed to act and have to wait for the appropriate time and energy to act. Be patient and hold tight until you know with a K that the time is right to speak or to work. Learning with a K means knowing what you know so deeply that no one can tell you that what you know is not valid. Over time, you can test your perceptions, and if you listen to yourself at the level of this awareness, you will find that when you know with a K, what you know is true proves to be so. With this Channel defined, you always do best if you have a mammal as a pet. In addition, meditation in your own space daily is critical to remaining in touch with this component of yourself, which is very important to your consciousness and life mission. Let your mind serve your spirit and use your mental acumen appropriately and strategically.

Your Keys to Empowerment
- Trust your intuition.
- Be patient and only act when you know you are acting from the depths of your soul.
- Meditation and dream work are critical for you.
- Let your mind be of service to your spirit.

Action Points for Manifesting Your Dreams
- Learn to discern what comes from the depth of your inner knowing and what is superficial.
- Meditate daily in your own space, allowing your pets to meditate with you.
- Keep a journal to record your dreams and your insights.
- Use your mental acumen appropriately and strategically.

Channel 20-34-57

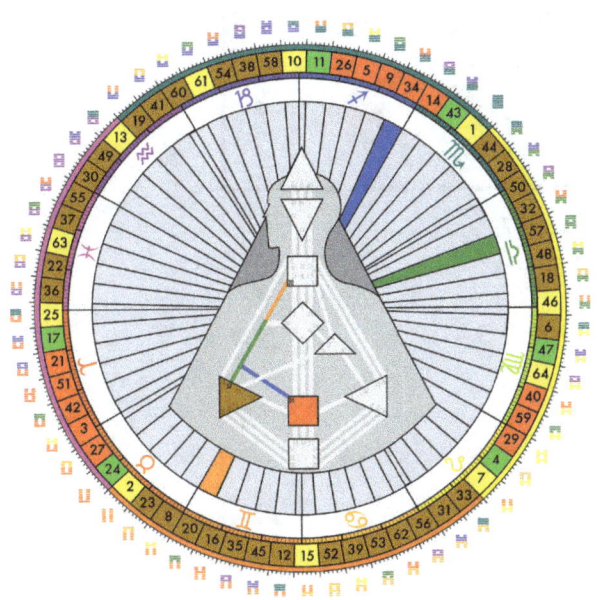

Mental World

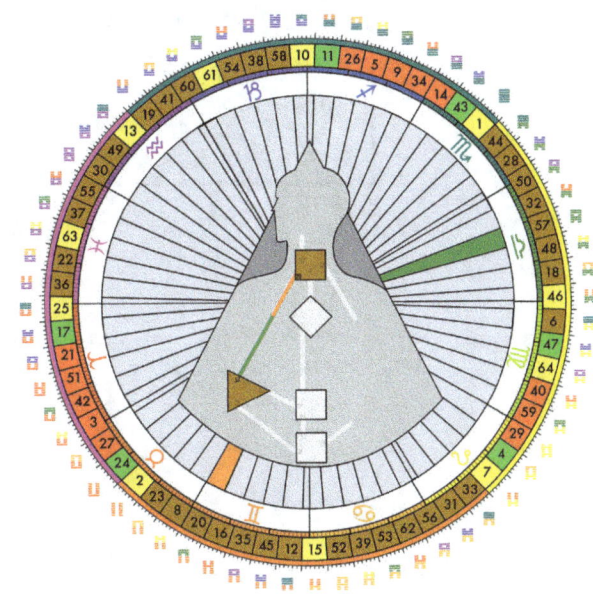

Spiritual World

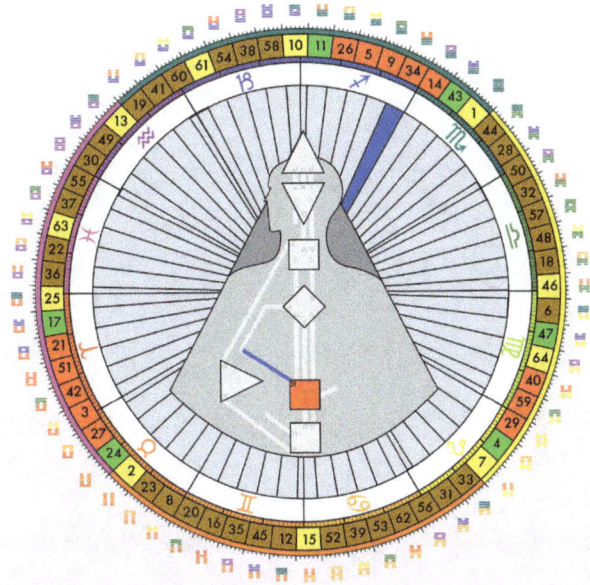

Emotional World

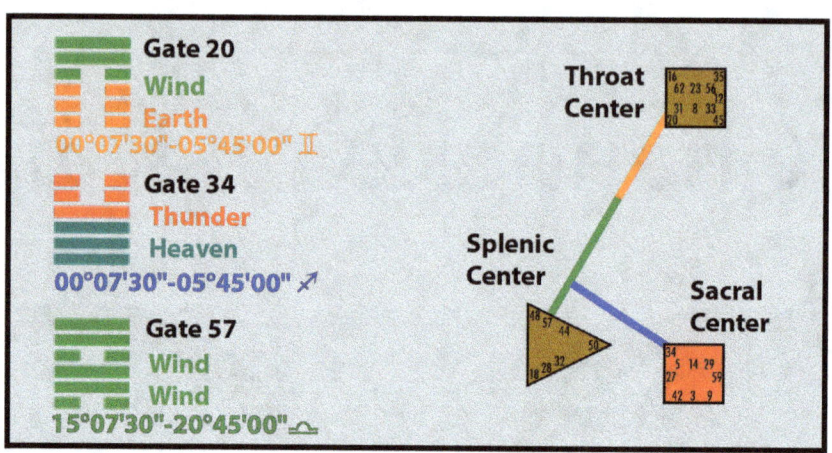

Channel 20-34-57

Integrated Mental and Spiritual/Archetypal Worlds and Emotional/Angelic Portal
Channel 20-34-57 *(Gemini-Sagittarius-Libra)*

Keywords: Knowingness, Brainwave, Acuity, Clarity, Intuitive Knowing

You are highly sensitive and driven to manifest your potential, and you attract people to you when you emotionally align with your values. You have strong intuition and know when things are right for you and when they are not. Focus on your inner voice and wait for clarity before acting despite feeling impatient.

You have Charisma and excellent timing, and you may be surprised by your acute insights and intuitive penetrating awareness. You know things beyond the ordinary and use them naturally. You are driven from within the depth of your being to manifest your highest potential and to act when you feel the instinct to do so. Because you are such a strongly motivated person whose core values connect to higher principles and consciousness, you may feel pushed from within at times when you are exhausted and are not confident about your considered action. The pressure to act in the present comes from your spiritually driven awareness of what will serve the collective's highest good. This activation is perceptive and unconscious.

If you are in a situation that does not feel right, it is likely unhealthy for you, and you should change your status. Use your intuition to protect your integrity. Use your power strategically and carefully. You are highly intuitive, and you can trust your clarity. Honor that aspect of yourself to fulfill your life mission and stay healthy. Always wait until your inner voice of truth speaks to you. You internally hear this voice when you take time alone and are uninfluenced by anyone around you.

Because of your strong intuition and how acute and accurate it is, you may feel compelled to act when you sense misalignments. Always wait for the appropriate time and energy to act. Be patient and hold tight until you know with a K that the time is right to speak or to work. Knowing with a K means knowing what you know so deeply that no one can tell you that what you know is not valid. Over time, you can test your perceptions, and if you listen to yourself at the level of this awareness, you will find that when you know with a K, what you know is true proves to be so. You always do best if you have a mammal as a pet. In addition, Meditation in your own space daily is critical to remaining in touch with this component of yourself, which is very important to your consciousness and life mission.

Always envision how what you are considering doing is likely to play out and reevaluate constantly. Following this strategy helps you avoid missteps from precipitous action. Thus, take time daily for Meditation and do so in your own space, with your pets, if you have any. Your pets will keep you spiritually aligned, which is crucial in your decision-making as a priority. Always visualize what you want to have happen and play our various scenarios until you get inner confirmation of the right action. Be patient and go SLOW.

Use the Four Worlds Clarity Worksheet to review factors you consider about any major decisions to ensure you are balanced and aligned in all worlds before acting. In addition, meditate daily in your own space, allowing your pets to be with you so you listen for the voice of wisdom that guides your truth.

Your Keys to Empowerment
- Before acting, be certain that you wait until your inner voice of truth speaks to you.
- You connect energetically to the Four Worlds: Mental, Spiritual, Emotional, and Physical, and you do best when you align in all worlds.
- You attract people to you when you radiate your energy outward.
- Know what you know, and when you know it, stand firm for it.
- Always consider how your intuitive knowing aligns with what you value. Use your strength of powerful knowing wisely.

Action Points for Manifesting Your Dreams
- Always wait until you feel that internal Knowing guides your actions.
- Meditate daily in your own space, allowing your pets to meditate with you.
- Keep a journal to record your dreams and your insights.
- Visualize what you want to have happen and play out various scenarios until you get inner confirmation of the right action.
- When you know what you know and no one can tell you otherwise, wait for an opportunity to speak or act. Be patient and strategic.

Channel 20-34

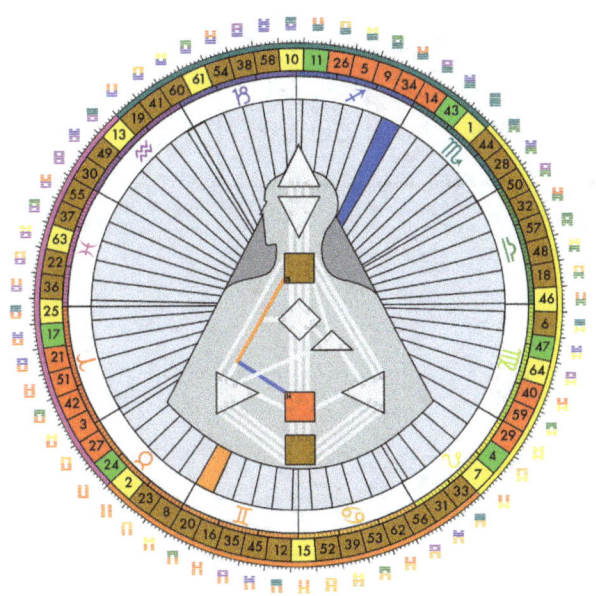

Mental World

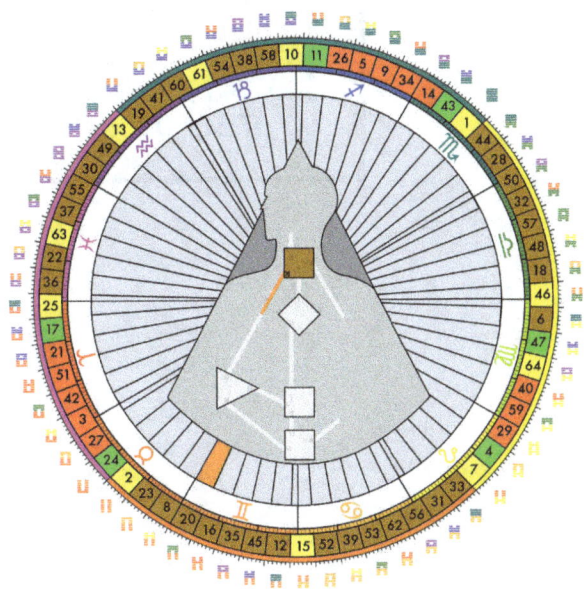

Spiritual World

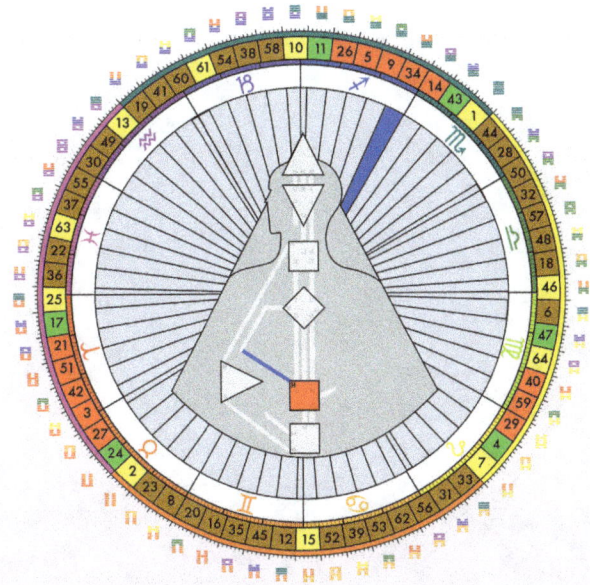

Emotional World

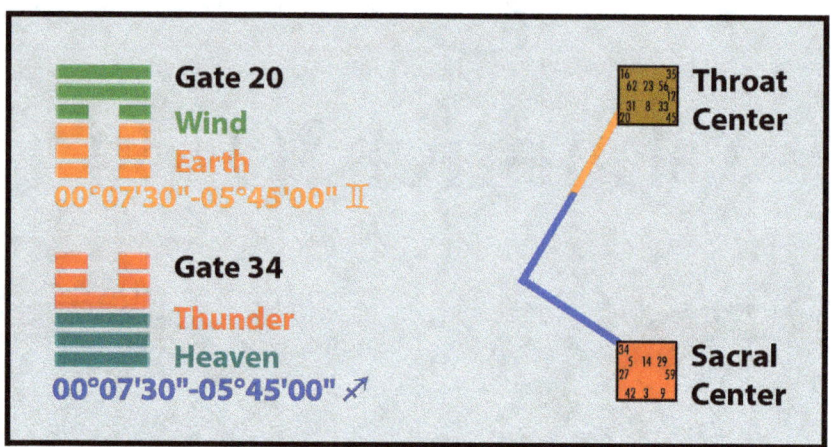

Channel 20-34

Integrated Mental World, Spiritual/Archetypal and Emotional/Angelic World Portals
Channel 20-34 *(Gemini-Sagittarius)*

Keywords: Power, Charisma, Thoughts Manifest

You are highly sensitive and driven to manifest your potential. When you are emotionally aligned with your values, you attract people to you. Wait for clarity before acting.

You are connected energetically and want to integrate the Mental, Spiritual/Archetypal, and Emotional/Angelic worlds. You are driven from within the depth of your being to manifest your highest potential and to act when you feel the instinct to do so. Because you are such a strongly motivated person whose core values are connected to higher principles and consciousness, you may feel pushed from within at times when you are exhausted and are not confident about your considered action. The pressure to act in the present comes from your spiritually driven awareness of what will serve the collective's highest good. This activation is perceptive and unconscious. Thus, when in doubt at any level of your being, WAIT. Always envision how what you are considering doing is likely to play out and reevaluate constantly. Following this strategy helps you avoid missteps from precipitous action.

You are someone with Charisma and excellent timing. Be mindful to use your power strategically and carefully to not deplete or misuse your energy. Always wait until your inner voice of truth speaks to you. You internally hear this voice when you take time alone and are uninfluenced by anyone around you. Thus, take time daily for meditation and do so in your own space, with your pets, if you have any.

Your pets will keep you spiritually aligned, which is crucial in your decision-making as a priority. Always visualize what you want to have happen and play our various scenarios until you get inner confirmation of the right action. Be patient and go SLOW.

Your Keys to Empowerment
- Before acting, be certain that you wait until your inner voice of truth speaks to you.
- You connect energetically to the Four Worlds: Mental, Spiritual, Emotional and Physical, and you do best when you are aligned in all worlds.
- You attract people to you when you radiate your energy outward.
- Only take on roles that bring you fulfillment.

Action Points for Manifesting Your Dreams
- Always wait until you feel that internal Knowing guides your actions.
- Meditate daily in your own space, allowing your pets to meditate with you.
- Keep a journal to record your dreams and your insights.
- Visualize what you want to have happen and play out various scenarios until you get inner confirmation of the right action.

Integrated Mental World and Spiritual/Archetypal Portal
Channel 20-34 *(Gemini-Sagittarius)*

Keywords: Power, Charisma, Thoughts Manifest

You are highly sensitive and driven to manifest your potential. When you are emotionally aligned with your values, you attract people to you. Wait for clarity before acting.

You are connected energetically and want to integrate the Mental, Spiritual, Emotional, and Physical worlds. Your drive comes from within the depth of your being to manifest your highest potential and to act when you feel the instinct to do so. The pressure to work in the present comes from your spiritually driven awareness of what will serve the collective's highest good. This activation is perceptive and unconscious. Thus, when in doubt at any level of your being, WAIT. You can always envision how what you are considering doing is likely to play out, and you do well to reevaluate constantly. Following this strategy helps you avoid missteps from precipitous action. You have intense energy and excellent timing. Be mindful to use your power strategically and carefully so as not to deplete or misuse your energy. Always wait until your inner voice of truth speaks to you. You internally hear this voice when you take time alone and are uninfluenced by anyone around you. Thus, take time daily for meditation and do so in your own space, with your pets, if you have any. Your pets will keep you aligned spiritually, which is crucial in your decision-making as a priority. Always visualize what you want to have happen and play our various scenarios until you get inner confirmation of the right action. Be patient and go SLOW.

Your Keys to Empowerment
- Before acting, take a few days to feel confident about your proposed action.
- You connect energetically to the Four Worlds: Mental, Spiritual, Emotional, and
- Physical, and you do best when you align in all worlds.
- You attract people to you when you radiate your energy outward.
  Meditation helps you clarify your deepest values.

Action Points for Manifesting Your Dreams
- Always wait until you feel that internal Knowing guides your actions.
- Meditate daily in your own space, allowing your pets to meditate with you.
- Keep a journal to record your dreams and your insights.
- Visualize what you want to have happen and play out various scenarios until you get inner confirmation of the right action.

Integrated Mental World and Emotional/Angelic World Portal
Channel 20-34 *(Gemini-Sagittarius)*

Keywords: Power, Charisma, Thoughts Manifest

You are highly sensitive and driven to manifest your potential. When you are emotionally aligned with your values, you attract people to you. Wait for clarity before acting.

You recognize yourself as a multidimensional being living in the Mental, Spiritual, Emotional, and Physical Worlds. Your drive comes from within the depth of your being to manifest your highest potential and to act when you feel the instinct to do so. Because you are such a strongly motivated person whose core values connect to higher principles and consciousness, you may feel pushed from within at times when you are exhausted and are not confident about your considered action. The pressure to act in the present comes from the spiritually driven awareness of what will serve the collective's highest good. This activation is perceptive and unconscious. Thus, when in doubt at any level of your being, WAIT. On the Emotional/Angelic level, you are always able to envision how what you are considering doing is likely to play out, and you do well to reevaluate constantly. Following this strategy helps you avoid missteps from precipitous action. You have intense energy and excellent timing. Be mindful to use your power strategically and carefully so as not to deplete or misuse your energy. Always wait until your inner voice of truth speaks to you. This voice is the one you hear internally when you take time alone and are uninfluenced by anyone around you. Thus, take time daily for meditation and do so in your own space, with your pets, if you have any. Your pets will keep you aligned spiritually, which is crucial in your decision-making as a priority. Always visualize what you want to have happen and play our various scenarios until you get inner confirmation of the right action. Be patient and go SLOW.

Your Keys to Empowerment
- Before acting, be confident that you wait until your inner voice of truth speaks to you.
- You connect energetically to the Four Worlds: Mental, Spiritual, Emotional, and Physical, and you do best when you align in all worlds.
- You attract people to you when you radiate your energy outward.
- Avoid missteps by waiting for inner confirmation about considered actions.

Action Points for Manifesting Your Dreams
- When you feel emotional, wait for balance before considering any actions.
- Meditate daily in your own space, allowing your pets to meditate with you.
- Keep a journal to record your dreams and your insights.
- Visualize what you want to have happen and play out various scenarios until you get inner confirmation of the right action.

Integrated Spiritual/Archetypal and Emotional/Angelic World Portals
Channel 20-34 *(Gemini-Sagittarius)*

Keywords: Power, Charisma, Thoughts Manifest

You are highly sensitive and driven to manifest your potential. When you are emotionally aligned with your values, you attract people to you. Wait for clarity before acting.

Your awareness often arises from the depth of your being, driving you to manifest your highest potential and to act when you feel the instinct to do so. You connect your feelings and deeply rooted values to your spiritual core and what serves others and yourself. You are wise to delay any action until you are certain that your envisioned action is correct for you. Because you have a strong energy that attracts others to you, you are vulnerable in listening to their needs above your own. Be mindful to use your inner power strategically not to deplete or misuse your energy. Always wait until your inner voice of truth speaks to you. This voice is the one you hear internally when you take time alone and are uninfluenced by anyone around you. Thus, take time daily for meditation and do so in your own space, with your pets, if you have any. Your pets will keep you aligned spiritually, which is crucial in your decision-making as a priority. Always visualize what you want to have happen and play our various scenarios until you get inner confirmation of the right action. Be patient and go SLOW.

Your Keys to Empowerment
- Before acting, be confident that you wait until your inner voice of truth speaks to you.
- You connect energetically to the Four Worlds. Take time to process your needs and wants.
- You attract people to you when you radiate your energy outward.
- Avoid missteps by waiting for inner confirmation about considered actions.

Action Points for Manifesting Your Dreams
- When you feel emotional, wait for balance before considering any actions.
- Meditate daily in your own space, allowing your pets to meditate with you.
- Keep a journal to record your dreams and your insights.
- Visualize what you want to have happen and play out various scenarios until you get inner confirmation of the right action.

Mental World
Channel 20-34 *(Gemini-Sagittarius)*

Keywords: Power, Charisma, Thoughts Manifest

You are highly sensitive and driven to manifest your potential. When you are emotionally aligned with your values, you attract people to you. Wait for clarity before acting.

You are driven from within the depth of your being to manifest your highest potential and to act when you feel the instinct to do so. Because you are such a strongly motivated person whose core values connect to higher principles and consciousness, you may feel pushed from within at times when you are exhausted and are not confident about your considered action. When in doubt at any level of your being, WAIT. Always envision how what you are considering doing is likely to play out and reevaluate constantly. Following this strategy helps you avoid missteps from precipitous action. You are someone with Charisma and excellent timing. Be mindful to use your power strategically and carefully not to deplete or misuse your energy. Always wait until your inner voice of truth speaks to you. You internally hear this voice when you take time alone and are uninfluenced by anyone around you. Thus, take time daily for meditation and do so in your own space, with your pets, if you have any. Your pets will keep you spiritually aligned, which is crucial in your decision-making as a priority. Always visualize what you want to have happen and play our various scenarios until you get inner confirmation of the right action. Be patient and go SLOW.

Your Keys to Empowerment
- Before acting, wait until your inner voice of truth speaks to you.
- You connect energetically to the Four Worlds: Mental, Spiritual, Emotional, and Physical, and you do best when you know you align in all worlds.
- You attract people to you when you radiate your energy outward.
- Avoid missteps by waiting for inner confirmation about considered actions.

Action Points for Manifesting Your Dreams
- Always wait until you feel that internal Knowing guides your actions.
- Meditate daily in your own space, allowing your pets to meditate with you.
- Keep a journal to record your dreams and your insights.
- Visualize what you want to have happen and play out various scenarios until you get inner confirmation of the right action.

Channel 21-45

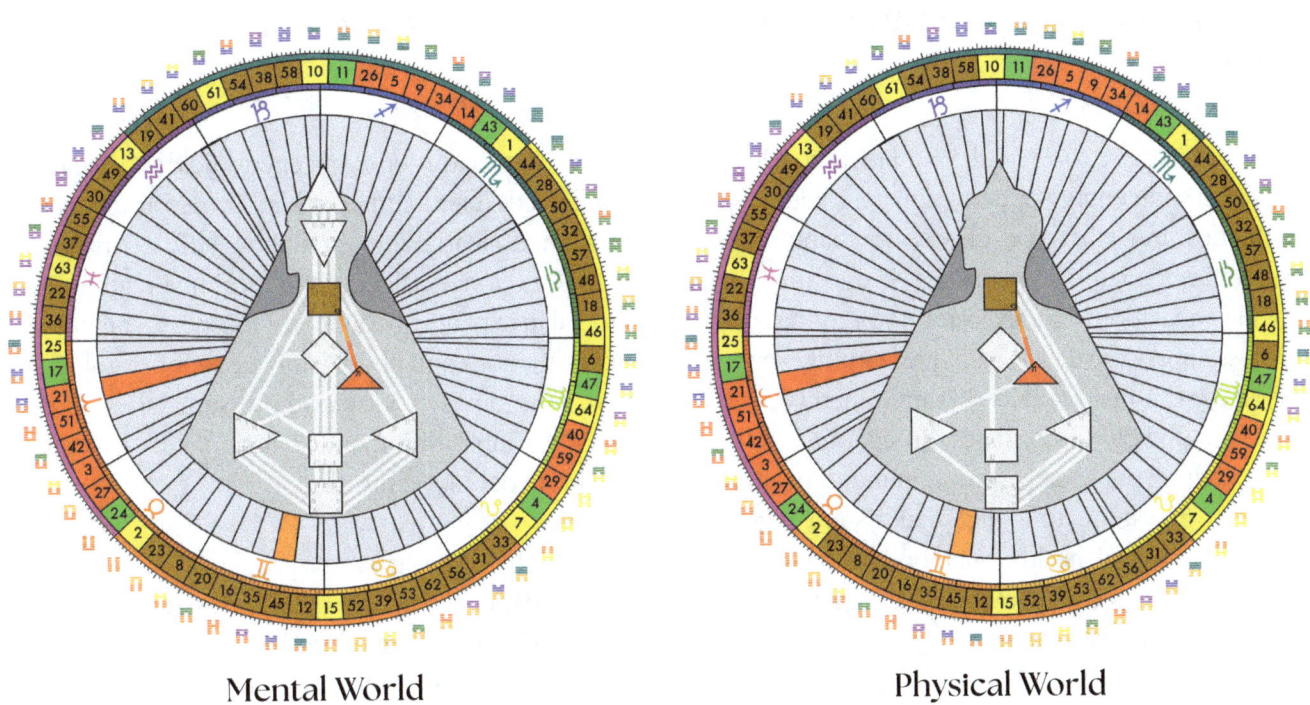

Mental World　　　　　　　　Physical World

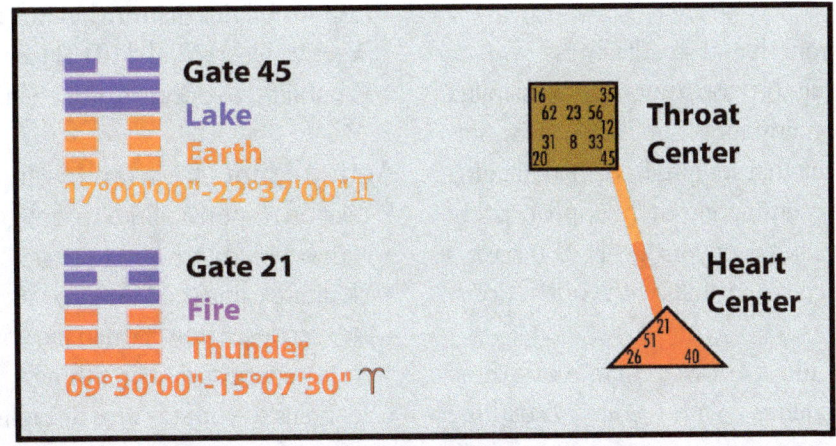

Channel 21-45

Integrated Mental and Physical/Biological Worlds
Channel 21-45 (Aries-Gemini)

Keywords: Dominion over Resources, Oxygen, Breathing, Abundance

You like to orchestrate where you are and what you are doing and recognize when you can be of service. Watch your breathing as a way to monitor stress and commit only to what is right for you.

You are in close touch with your life force itself, and you carry an energy of dominion over your responsibilities and what you choose to manifest. How you manage stress in your body is essential. Watch your inhalation and exhalation to monitor your stress level. You have a unique, intuitive connection to your heart and its rhythm. When you inhale, oxygenated blood circulates throughout your body, impacting your creative drive, immune health, and digestive system. Your digestive system relates to your emotional health. Your body awareness and sensitivity make integrating health practices into your life essential.

When you set your intention on what you want to orchestrate in your life, you can achieve it.

Because of your strength and steadfastness, you are vulnerable to taking on too much responsibility and managing too many tasks simultaneously. Stay mindful that you are naturally gifted in managing resources and in disseminating them appropriately. Be clear on your values and your goals. You have a responsibility to align your values with your actions.

Be cautious and move slower than you think you should. Meditate with your breathing daily. The Microcosmic Orbit is an excellent meditation because you learn your breathing circulates consciousness through your energy field and releases what needs releasing. Heart Math would also benefit you since Heart Rate Variability (HRV) correlates with emotional balance and health. Breathing is crucial in expanding your consciousness. Thus, note how situations and people impact your breathing. If you want to raise your blood pressure, take a more extended inhalation than exhalation and vice versa to lower your blood pressure.

Your Keys to Empowerment
- You are tuned in to your body and especially to your heartbeat. Pay attention.
- When you intend to achieve something, you can make it happen.
- Be cautious about taking on more responsibilities than are healthy for you.
- Practice Heart Math HRV (Heart Rate Variability) to optimize your health.

Action Points for Manifesting Your Dreams
- Take on responsibilities that align with your life path and values.
- Meditate using the Microcosmic Orbit to learn how to manage your body's energy using breathing.
- Set goals so you stay on a disciplined path.
- Learn how to delegate responsibilities.

Mental World
Channel 21-45 *(Aries-Gemini)*

Keywords: Dominion over Resources, Oxygen, Breathing, Abundance

You like to orchestrate where you are and what you are doing and recognize when you can be of service. Watch your breathing as a way to monitor stress and commit only to what is right for you.

You are in close touch with your life force itself, and you carry an energy of dominion over your responsibilities and what you choose to manifest. You are tuned in to your heart rhythm and your body's circulatory system. You use oxygen intake to balance energy in stressful daily life situations. Your heart circulates oxygenated blood to the rest of your body, impacting your creative drive, immune health, and digestive system. In addition, your digestive system relates to your emotional health. To manage stress in your body is essential. Watch your inhalation and exhalation to monitor your stress level.

Because you can set your intention on what you want to orchestrate in your life and achieve it, you are vulnerable to taking on too much responsibility and managing too many tasks simultaneously. Stay mindful that you are naturally gifted in managing resources and in disseminating them appropriately. Be clear on your values and your goals.

You have a responsibility to align your values with your actions. Be cautious and move slower than you think you should. Meditate with your breathing daily. The Microcosmic Orbit circulates your breathing through your energy field and releases what needs to be released. Since breathing is crucial to expanding your consciousness, note how situations and people impact your breathing. If you want to raise your blood pressure, take a more extended inhalation than exhalation and vice versa to lower your blood pressure.

Your Keys to Empowerment
- You are tuned in to your body and especially to your heartbeat. Pay attention.
- When you intend to achieve something, you can make it happen.
- Be cautious about taking on more responsibilities than are healthy for you.
- Practice Heart Math HRV (Heart Rate Variability) to optimize your health.

Action Points for Manifesting Your Dreams
- Take on responsibilities that align with your life path and values.
- Meditate using the Microcosmic Orbit to learn how to manage your body's energy using breathing.
- Set goals so you stay clear and follow a disciplined path.
- Learn how to delegate responsibilities.

Physical/Biological World
Channel 21-45 *(Aries-Gemini)*

Keywords: Dominion over Resources, Oxygen, Breathing, Abundance

You like to orchestrate where you are and what you are doing and recognize when you can be of service. Watch your breathing as a way to monitor stress and commit only to what is right for you.

Your high sensitivity to your heart and its rhythm energizes you through oxygen intake. Oxygenated blood circulates from your heart to the rest of your body, impacting your creative drive, immune health, and digestive system. It also affects your digestive system as it relates to your emotional health. You are at your healthiest when you integrate health practices into your life. When you set your intention on what you want to orchestrate in your life, you achieve it. You are not at your best when you take on too much responsibility and manage too many tasks simultaneously.

How you manage stress in your body is essential. Watch your inhalation and exhalation to monitor your stress level. If you want to raise your blood pressure, take a more extended inhalation than exhalation and. vice versa to lower your blood pressure. Stay mindful that you are naturally gifted in managing resources and in disseminating them appropriately. Be cautious and move slower than you think you should. Manage the resources of your Self-Care. Meditate with your breathing daily using the Microcosmic Orbit. Heart Math regulates Heart Rate Variability (HRV), regulating your breathing and releasing what needs releasing. Since breathing is crucial in expanding your consciousness, note how situations and people impact your breathing.

Your Keys to Empowerment
- You are tuned in to your body and especially to your heartbeat. Pay attention.
- Take dominion over your body by serving its needs.
- Be cautious about taking on responsibilities that are healthy for you.
- Practice Heart Math HRV (Heart Rate Variability) to optimize your health.

Action Points for Manifesting Your Dreams
- Take on responsibilities that align with your life path and values.
- Meditate using the Microcosmic Orbit to learn how to manage your body's energy using breathing.
- Follow self-care routines with discipline.
- Learn how to delegate responsibilities.

Channel 23-43

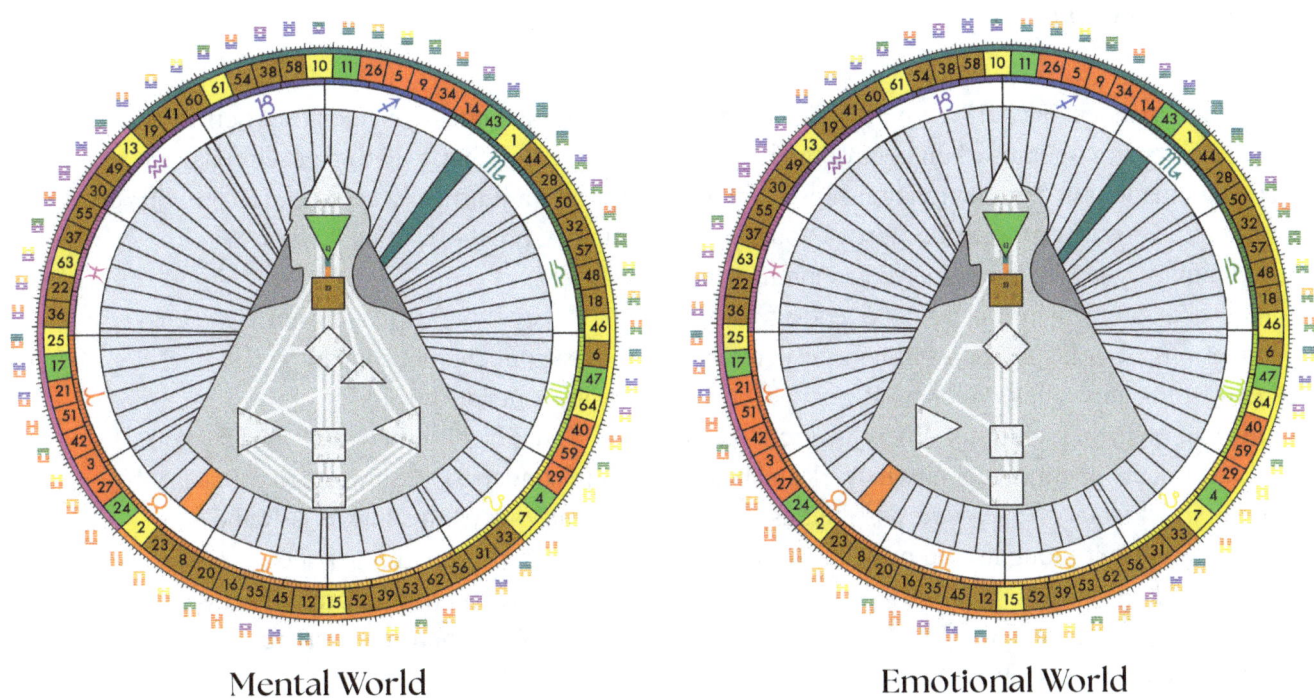

Mental World · Emotional World

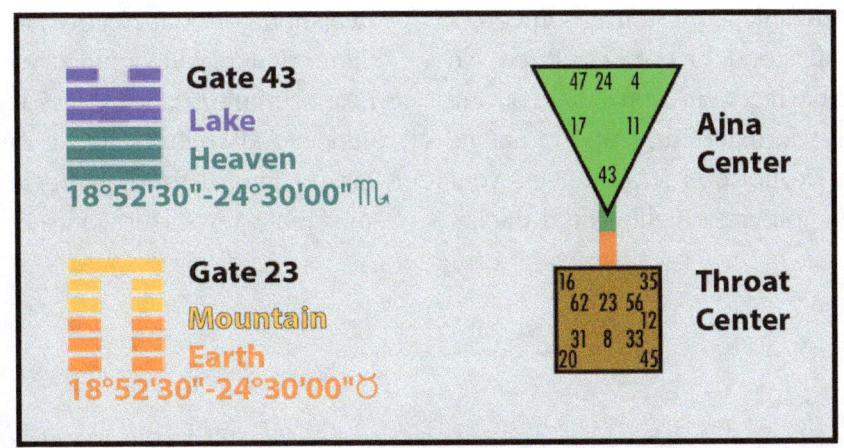

Channel 23-43

Integrated Mental and Emotional/Angelic Worlds
Channel 23-43 *(Taurus-Scorpio)*

Keywords: Uniqueness, Structuring, Intensity, Creative Thinking

You are a creative thinker who likes to consider all possibilities despite not always being understood.

If you are confident in your creative intelligence, you trust your creative genius when confronted by challenging situations or complex relationships. Thinking outside the box is your forte. Because of your depth of creativity, you may be perceived as intense and unique. Be confident in your perceptiveness to other dimensions. Your heightened sensitivity to creative energy stimulates your focus on whatever challenges you focus on to find solutions. When you focus on an issue, you set your intuitive genius to work and begin to pull in all kinds of energetic possibilities. These energies transmit thoughts you probably don't fully understand.

Your mental process opens you up to innovative possibilities and directions. You combine information creatively, resulting in unique perspectives that can benefit a broad audience. You may sometimes feel alone, not understood, or even criticized. No matter what outside reactions you face, you are brilliant at putting information together in unique and original ways. Do not ever second guess your thought processes. You are a highly gifted thinker who contributes your genius when confident and courageous. Stay true to yourself. Take time daily to write in a journal. Keeping notes on your creative thinking process is valuable for you.

Your Keys to Empowerment
- Trust your creative thinking and think "outside the box."
- You are a highly gifted thinker who often is misunderstood. Stay true to yourself.
- Speak your truth courageously and wisely to prevent throat issues.
- Keep notes on your creative process and apply it where appropriate.

Action Points for Manifesting Your Dreams
- Stay true to yourself.
- Keep notes on your creative process; do not discuss it until you formulate your perspective.
- Learn communication skills so you can be better understood when you have creative ideas.
- You put information together in innovative and unique ways. Trust yourself.

Mental World
Channel 23-43 *(Taurus-Scorpio)*

Keywords: Uniqueness, Structuring, Intensity, Creative Thinking

You are a creative thinker who likes to consider all possibilities despite not always being understood.

If you are confident in your creative intelligence, you trust your creative genius when confronted by challenging situations or complex relationships. Thinking outside the box is your forte. Use it confidently in your perceptiveness to other dimensional energies that transmit thoughts you probably don't fully understand. Your mental process opens you up to innovative possibilities and directions. You combine information creatively, resulting in unique perspectives that can benefit a broad audience. You may sometimes feel alone, not understood, or even criticized. No matter what outside reactions you face, you are brilliant at putting information together in unique and original ways. Do not ever second guess your thought processes. You are a highly gifted thinker who contributes your genius when confident and courageous. Stay true to yourself. Take time daily to write in a journal. Keeping notes on your creative thinking process is valuable for you.

Your Keys to Empowerment
- Trust your creative thinking and think "outside the box."
- You are a highly gifted thinker who often is misunderstood. Stay true to yourself.
- Speak your truth courageously and wisely to prevent throat issues.
- Keep notes on your creative process and apply it where appropriate.

Action Points for Manifesting Your Dreams
- Stay true to yourself.
- Write in your journal daily and wait to discuss your ideas until you fully formulate them.
- Learn communication skills so you can be better understood when you have creative ideas.
- You put information together in innovative and unique ways. Trust yourself.

Emotional/Angelic World
Channel 23-43 *(Taurus-Scorpio)*

Keywords: Uniqueness, Structuring, Intensity, Creative Thinking

You are a creative thinker who likes to consider all possibilities despite not always being understood.

If you are confident in your creative intelligence, you trust your creative genius when confronted by challenging situations or complex relationships. Thinking outside the box is your forte. Because of your depth of creativity, you may be perceived as intense and unique. Be confident in your perceptiveness to other dimensions. Your heightened sensitivity to creative energy stimulates your focus on whatever challenges you focus on to find solutions. When you focus on an issue, you set your intuitive genius to work and begin to pull in all kinds of energetic possibilities. These energies transmit thoughts you probably don't fully understand.

Your mental process opens you up to innovative possibilities and directions. You combine information creatively, resulting in unique perspectives that can benefit a broad audience. You may sometimes feel alone, not understood, or even criticized. No matter what outside reactions you face, you are brilliant at putting information together in unique and original ways. Do not ever second guess your thought processes. You are a highly gifted thinker who contributes your genius when confident and courageous. Stay true to yourself. Take time daily to write in a journal. Keeping notes on your creative thinking process is valuable for you.

Your Keys to Empowerment
- Trust your creative thinking and think "outside the box."
- You are a highly gifted thinker who often is misunderstood. Stay true to yourself.
- Speak your truth courageously and wisely to prevent throat issues.
- Keep notes on your creative process and wait to discuss your ideas until they are fully formulated.

Action Points for Manifesting Your Dreams
- Stay true to yourself.
- Keep notes on your creative process; do not discuss it until you formulate your perspective.
- Be courageous in talking about and implementing your ideas.
- You put information together in innovative and unique ways. Trust yourself.

Channel 24-61

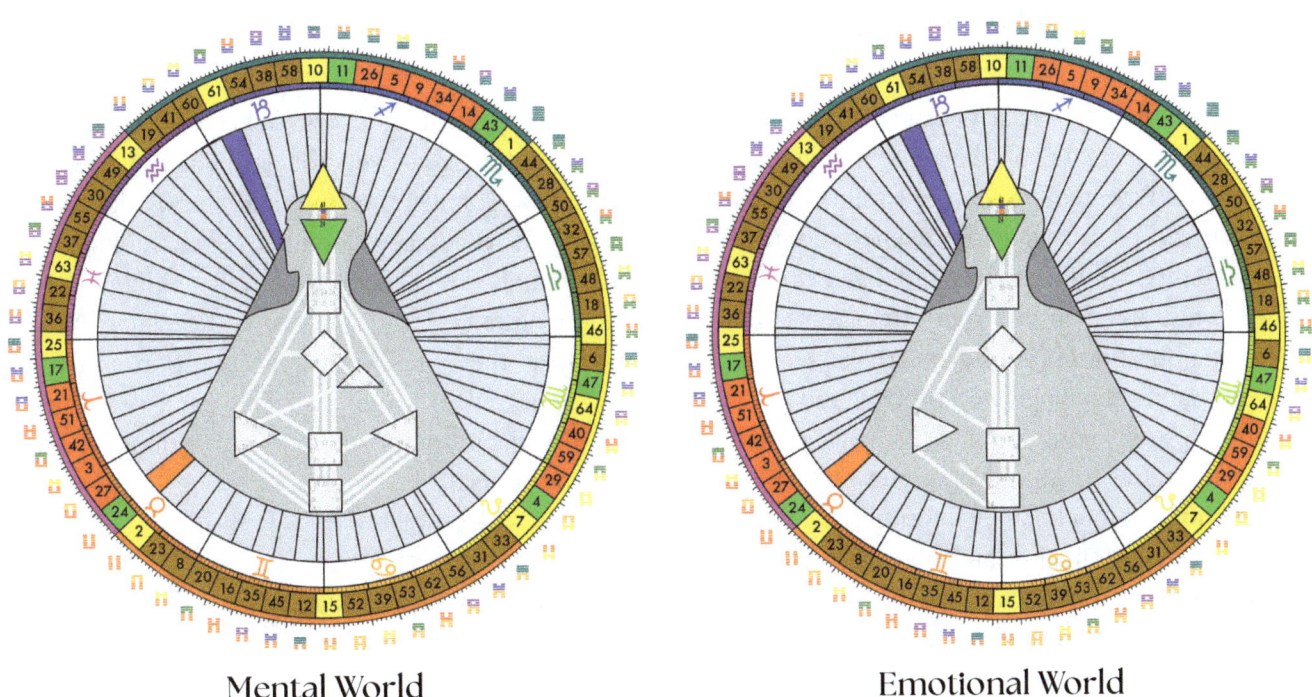

Mental World　　　　　　　　　　　Emotional World

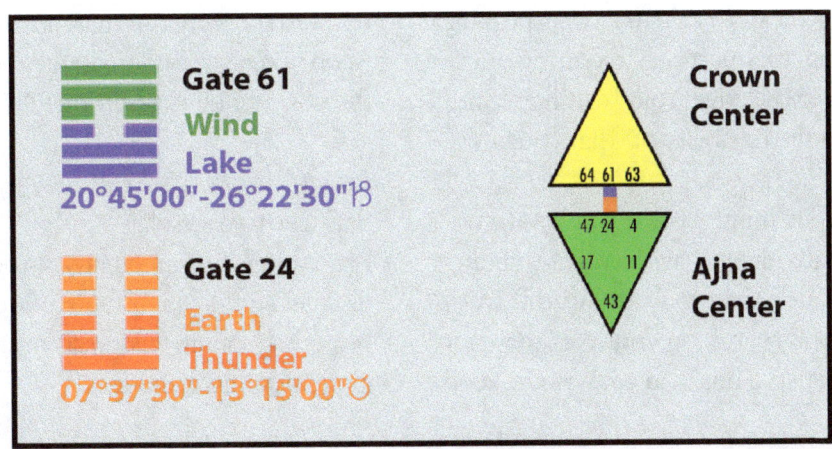

Channel 24-61

Integrated Mental and Emotional/Angelic Worlds
Channel 24-61 *(Taurus-Capricorn)*

Keywords: Inquisitiveness, Awareness, Probing, Dedication

You are a deep thinker who seeks answers to questions you want to understand, and you keep probing until the truth rings true for you.

Understanding universal questions motivates you strongly. You are a deep thinker who will likely ask questions repeatedly to find answers that eluded you in the past. Your inquisitiveness comes from your desire to understand the universe and its mysteries, and you are spurred forward in your probing questions because you are excited by clarity and understanding. Keep probing and following your questions until you find the answers that put your mysteries to rest. Always return to your roots and gather as much family information as possible. Epigenetic information and mysteries are part of your probing. Continue delving into what fascinates you, and you will be pleased with the wisdom you gain. Epigenetic information may date back 12 generations; delving into your consciousness's mysteries and structure is part of your quest to unravel the universe's spiraling mysteries. Trust your probing and keep returning to questions requiring more understanding and knowledge. Your search grounds you when you trust the reliability of what you know.

Because of how your mind works, you want your answers to resonate deeply with your thinking and awareness enough that you "know" the truth when you find it. This search on your part may not always be in your grasp. Thus, you are wise to keep a Journal handy at all times. Write down questions you are seeking answers for, and which world has the answer or whether multiple worlds do. Keep organized so you can document your thinking for your benefit–label sections of your writing: observations, awareness, questions, and feelings. Note which of the Four Worlds the question and the answer are likely to appear. This exercise is profound and can transform your way of thinking and trusting yourself.

Your Keys to Empowerment
- Trust your creative thinking and think "outside the box."
- You are a highly gifted thinker who often is misunderstood. Stay true to yourself.
- Speak your truth courageously and wisely to prevent throat issues.
- Keep notes on your creative process and wait to discuss your ideas until you fully formulate them.

Action Points for Manifesting Your Dreams
- Stay true to yourself.
- Keep notes on your creative process; do not discuss it until you formulate your perspective.
- Be courageous in talking about and implementing your ideas.

Mental World
Channel 24-61 *(Taurus-Capricorn)*

Keywords: Inquisitiveness, Awareness, Probing, Dedication

You are a deep thinker who seeks answers to questions you want to understand, and you keep probing until the truth rings true for you.

You are a deep Thinker and will likely ask questions repeatedly to find answers that eluded you in the past. Your inquisitiveness comes from your desire to understand the universe and its mysteries, and you are spurred forward in your probing questions because you are excited by clarity and understanding. Keep probing and following your questions until you find the answers that put your mysteries to rest. Always return to your roots and gather as much family information as possible. Continue delving into what fascinates you, and you will be pleased with the wisdom you gain. Delving into the mysteries of your consciousness and its structure is part of your quest to unravel the universe's spiraling mysteries. Trust your probing and keep returning to questions requiring more understanding and knowledge. Your search grounds you when you trust the reliability of what you know.

Keep a Journal handy at all times. Write down questions you are seeking answers for, and which world has the answer or whether multiple worlds do. Keep organized so you can document your thinking. For your benefit, label sections of your writing: observations, awareness, questions, and feelings. Note which of the Four Worlds the question and the answer are likely to appear. This exercise is profound and can transform your way of thinking and trusting yourself.

Your Keys to Empowerment
- You are deep and inquisitive. Trust your probing process.
- Many of your questions come from the depths of your soul. Pay attention.
- When your questions remain unanswered, you return to them repeatedly.
- Keep a journal for observations in all worlds.

Action Points for Manifesting Your Dreams
- Respect your mental process and honor your questions when they surface.
- Gather as much of your and your family's history as possible and ask questions about significant events.
- Keep a journal to record observations, awareness, feelings, and questions and place them in the Four Worlds: Mental, Spiritual, Physical, and Emotional.
- Consider each question you ask: What difference will the answer make?

Emotional/Angelic World
Channel 24-61 *(Taurus-Capricorn)*

Keywords: Inquisitiveness, Awareness, Probing, Dedication

You are a deep thinker who seeks answers to questions you want to understand, and you keep probing until the truth rings true for you.

Understanding universal questions motivates you strongly. You are a deep thinker who will likely ask questions repeatedly to find answers that eluded you in the past. Your inquisitiveness comes from your desire to understand the universe and its mysteries, and you are spurred forward in your probing questions because you are excited by clarity and understanding. Keep probing and following your questions until you find the answers that put your mysteries to rest. Always return to your roots and gather as much family information as possible. Epigenetic information and mysteries are part of your probing. Continue delving into what fascinates you, and you will be pleased with the wisdom you gain. Epigenetic information may date back 12 generations. Thus, your delving into the mysteries of your consciousness and its structure is part of your quest to unravel the universe's spiraling mysteries. Trust your probing and keep returning to questions requiring more understanding and knowledge. Your search grounds you when you trust the reliability of what you know.

Write down questions you are seeking answers for, and which world has the answer or whether multiple worlds do. Keep organized so you can document your thinking for your benefit–label sections of your writing: observations, awareness, questions, and feelings. Note which of the Four Worlds the question and the answer are likely to appear.

Meditate with your questions in mind and stay focused on the question while allowing yourself to be open to total receptivity as you receive intuitive answers to your questions. Be patient with yourself and this process. If you are disciplined and patient, this profound exercise can transform your way of thinking and trusting yourself.

Your Keys to Empowerment
- You are deep and inquisitive. Trust your probing process.
- Many of your questions come from the depths of your soul. Pay attention.
- When your questions remain unanswered, return to them repeatedly.
- Keep a journal for observations in all worlds.

Action Points for Manifesting Your Dreams
- Respect your mental process and honor your questions when they surface.
- Gather as much of your and your family's history as possible and ask questions about significant events.
- Keep a journal to record observations, awareness, feelings, and questions and place them in the Four Worlds: Mental, Spiritual, Physical, and Emotional.
- As you consider your question, ask: What do I know about _____ now?
- Remain curious and follow your inspirations.

Channel 25-51

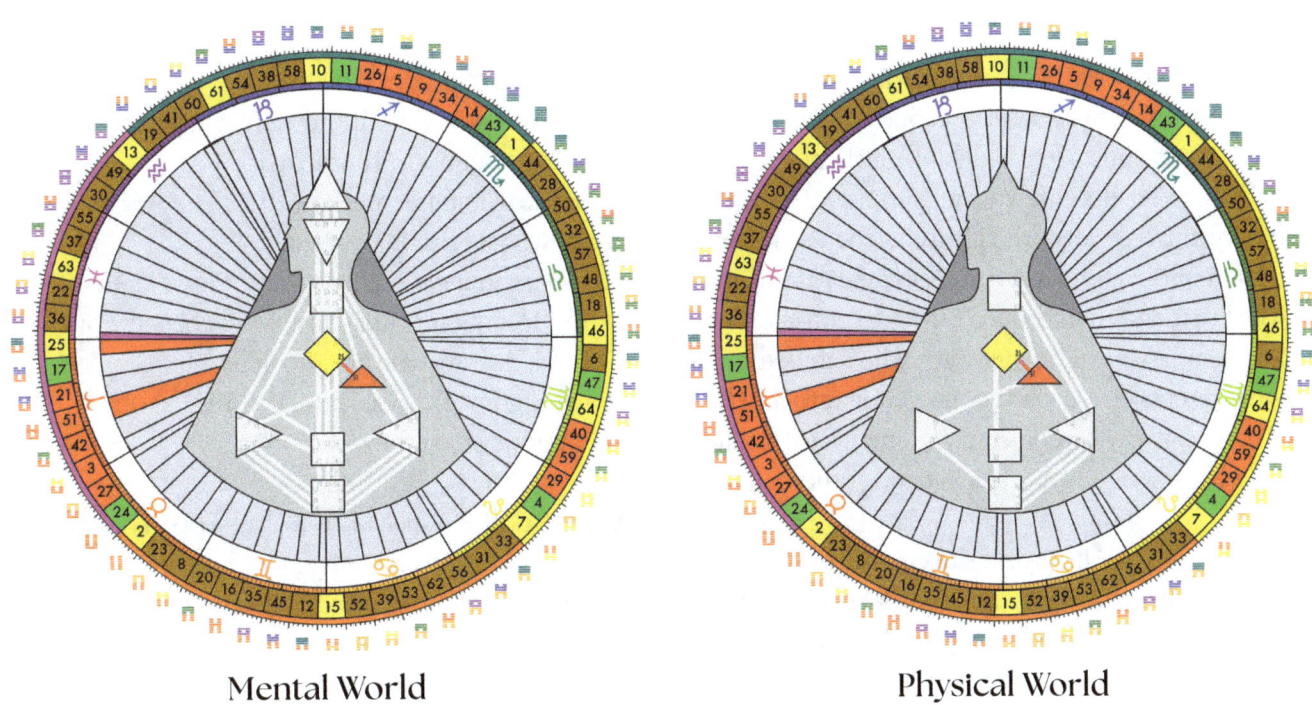

Mental World   Physical World

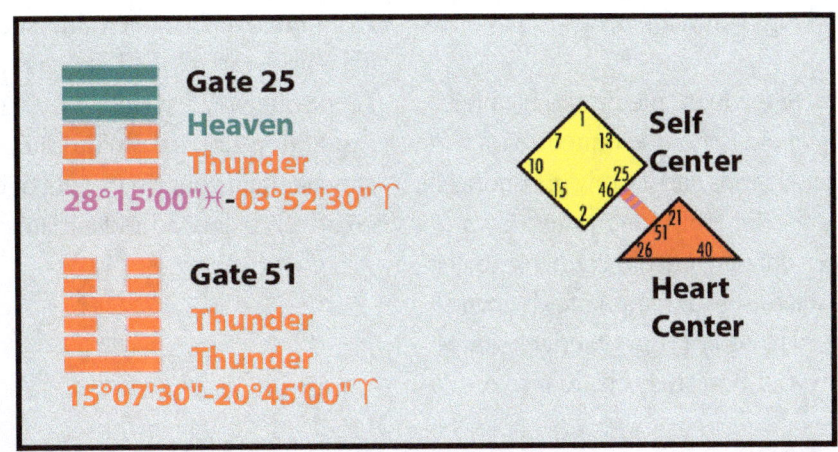

Channel 25-51

Integrated Mental and Physical/Biological Worlds
Channel 25-51 *(Pisces/Aries-Aries)*

Keywords: Initiation, Creative Intelligence, Competent

You are tuned in to your creative drive and like initiating things and being first.

When blood flows from your heart, it circulates oxygenated blood throughout your body. Thus, you carry the physical, hormonal, and biological energy of initiation in you. Because you are in tune with the flow of oxygenated blood, the life force energy that initiates life processes, you are likely in tune with wanting to be first and to introduce others to consciousness and health. You are an innovator who can determine what direction you want to move forward and how you want to use your creative energy to manifest your highest potential while initiating others.

Because you are highly sensitive to the flow of energy through your connection to your heart and blood flow through your body, you can also use awareness of your breathing to optimize your consciousness and direct your mind using your breath. Take all the time you need daily to be clear with your intentions and only engage in things you value deeply.

Meditate using the Sun/Moon meditation, which activates your energy field fully and connects you to higher-frequency dimensions and earthly grounding ones. In addition, daily Tai Chi Gung practice can maintain your flow of chi or energy in creatively balanced ways. MELT exercises for lymphatic drainage may be very beneficial to add to your practices since releasing stress from your body may challenge you.

Your Keys to Empowerment
- You are in tune with the flow of oxygen through your body. Tune in to it.
- You like to initiate things and be first. Respect that in yourself.
- Use a breathing meditation daily. Heart Math HRV (Heart Rate Variability) would benefit you.
- Take all the time you need to determine what aligns with your values before committing to action.

Action Points for Manifesting Your Dreams
- Trust your creative intelligence and stand up for it.
- When you take on a project, ensure it aligns with your values so you enjoy competently delivering what you promise.
- Make daily to-do lists and prioritize what sparks your interests most.
- Commit to daily movements such as Tai Chi Gung or MELT exercise to keep your lymph system moving.
- In addition, doing daily Tai Chi Gung practice can maintain your flow of chi or energy in creatively balanced and initiatory ways.

Mental World
Channel 25-51 *(Pisces/Aries-Aries)*

Keywords: Initiation, Creative Intelligence, Competent

You are tuned in to your creative drive and like initiating things and being first.

When blood flows from your heart, it circulates oxygenated blood throughout your body. Thus, you carry the physical, hormonal, and biological energy of initiation in you. Because you are in tune with the flow of oxygenated blood, the life force energy that initiates life processes, you are likely in tune with wanting to be first and to introduce others to consciousness and health. You are an innovator who can determine what direction you want to move forward and how you want to use your creative energy to manifest your highest potential while initiating others.

Because you are highly sensitive to the flow of energy through your connection to your heart itself and to the flow of blood through your body, you are also able to use awareness of your breathing to optimize your consciousness and direct your mind using your breath. Take all the time you need daily to be clear with your intentions and only engage in things you value deeply. Meditate using the Sun/Moon meditation that activates your energy field fully and connects you to higher frequency dimensions and earthly grounding ones.

Your Keys to Empowerment
- You are in tune with the flow of oxygen through your body. Tune in to it.
- You like to initiate things and be first. Respect that in yourself.
- Use a breathing meditation daily. Heart Math HRV (Heart Rate Variability) would benefit you.
- Take all the time you need to determine what aligns with your values before committing to action.

Action Points for Manifesting Your Dreams
- Trust your creative intelligence and stand up for it.
- When you take on a project, ensure it aligns with your values so you enjoy competently delivering what you promise.
- Journal daily, focusing on what creative thoughts might be worthy of noting.
- Commit to daily movements such as Tai Chi Gung or MELT exercise to keep your lymph system moving.

Physical/Biological World
Channel 25-51 *(Pisces/Aries-Aries)*

Keywords: Initiation, Creative Intelligence, Competent

You are tuned in to your creative drive and like initiating things and being first.

When blood flows from your heart, it circulates oxygenated blood throughout your body. Thus, you carry the physical, hormonal, and biological energy of initiation in you. Because you are in tune with the flow of oxygenated blood, the life force energy that initiates life processes, you are likely in tune with wanting to be first and to introduce others to consciousness and health. You are an innovator who can determine what direction you want to move forward and how you want to use your creative energy to manifest your highest potential while initiating others.

Because you are highly sensitive to the flow of energy through your connection to your heart and to the flow of blood through your body, you can also use awareness of your breathing to optimize your consciousness and direct your mind using your breath. Take all the time you need daily to be clear with your intentions and only engage in things you value deeply.

Meditate using the Sun/Moon meditation that activates your energy field fully and connects you to higher frequency dimensions and earthly grounding ones.

In addition, doing daily Tai Chi Gung practice can maintain your flow of chi or energy in creatively balanced ways. MELT exercises for lymphatic drainage may be very beneficial to add to your practices since releasing stress from your body may challenge you.

Your Keys to Empowerment
- You are in tune with the flow of oxygen through your body. Tune in to it.
- You like to initiate things and be first. Respect that in yourself.
- Use a breathing meditation daily. Heart Math HRV (Heart Rate Variability) would benefit you.
- Take all the time you need to determine what aligns with your values before committing to action.

Action Points for Manifesting Your Dreams
- Trust your creative intelligence and stand up for it.
- When you take on a project, ensure it aligns with your values so you enjoy competently delivering what you promise.
- Take time daily to Journal, paying special attention to perceptions from your body awareness.
- Commit to daily movements such as Tai Chi Gung or MELT exercise to keep your lymph system moving.

Channel 26-44

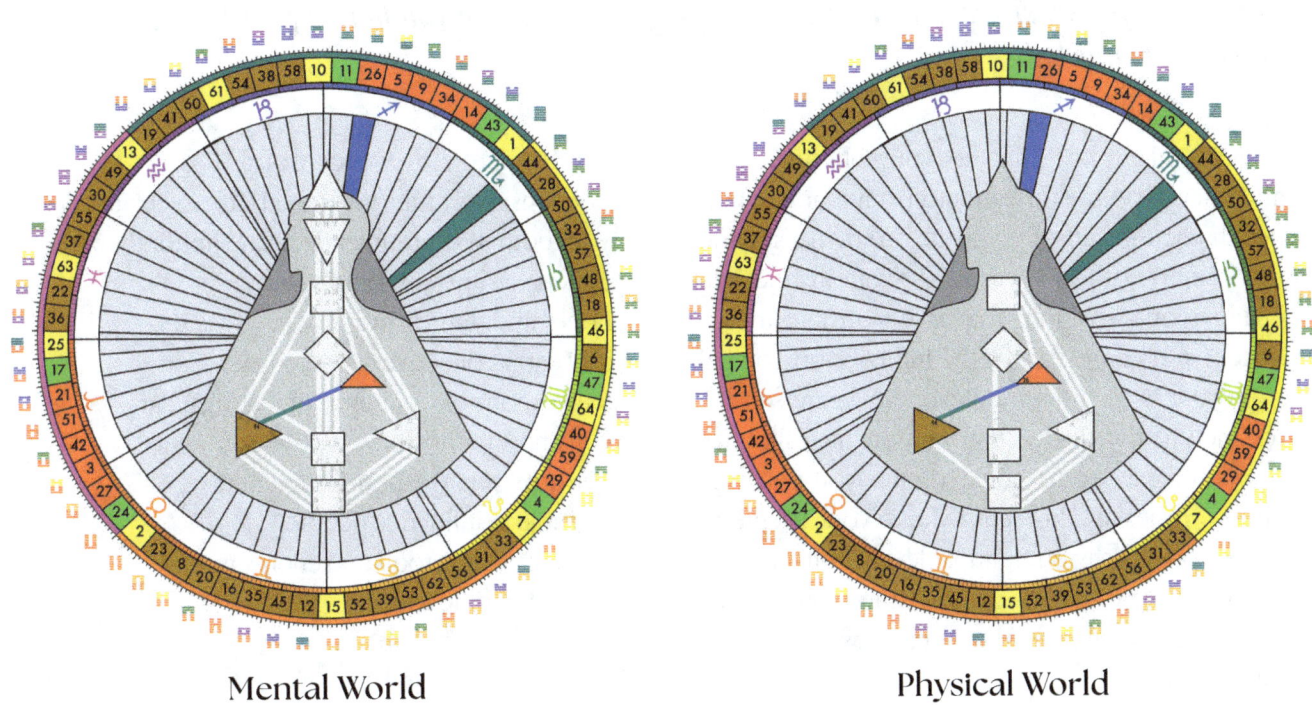

Mental World   Physical World

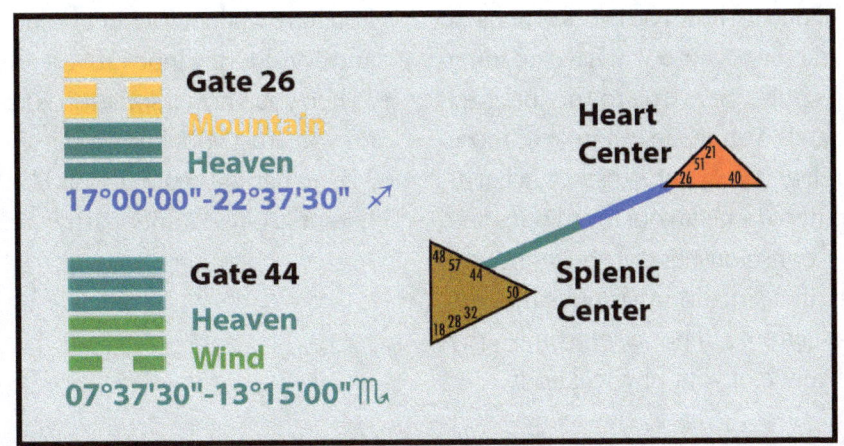

Channel 26-44

Integrated Mental and Physical/Biological Worlds
Channel 26-44 *(Sagittarius-Scorpio)*

Keywords: Transmission and Surrender, Sensory Integration, Immune Sensitivity, and perceptiveness

You are highly sensitive to what is healthy for you, and when you honor your perceptions, you are at your best.

You are highly sensitive to your physical health and energy body, and you intuitively know what is healthy or unhealthy for you. If you are in a situation and you do not feel at ease, trust your instincts and change your situation. You have a strong immune system and can use it for the information you gain from your five senses and beyond. You are sensitive to smell to the degree that you might walk into a room, and if it doesn't "smell" right to you, you might choose to leave. This sensitivity is your friend and keeps you healthy on multiple levels. You carry collective energy for those with whom you connect. Thus, you can help them by serving as a role model for self-care.

Align your values so what you manifest to benefit the collective is congruent with how you live and behave. You are a good marketer because you have an inner sense of the group's pulse. Stay true to the integrity of your word and deeds. You are an example to those with whom you relate. Use your sense of what is healthy or not healthy to benefit your loved ones and shift and uplift the consciousness of those around you. When you are in a situation that does not feel "right," leave the situation. Do not compromise the integrity and intelligence of your physical body.

Your Keys to Empowerment
- You sensitively tune into your body. Listen to your body's communications and honor them.
- When you know what is healthy, honor and stand firm about it.
- You carry collective consciousness and feel responsible for communicating what you know to those you care about.
- You are strong, responsive to energy, and able to influence people.
- Natural healing tools and energy work are compatible with your sensitivity.

Action Points for Manifesting Your Dreams
- You have the power to influence people and do it with word and deed integrity.
- You have a talent for integrating information and considering innovative solutions.
- When you know a situation is unhealthy for you, trust your knowledge. Act on it.
- Master natural healing tools like Reiki, Essential Oils, Homeopathy, etc.

Mental World
Channel 26-44 *(Sagittarius-Scorpio)*

Keywords: Transmission and Surrender, Sensory Integration, Immune Sensitivity, and perceptiveness

You are highly sensitive to what is healthy for you, and when you honor your perceptions, you are at your best.

You are highly sensitive to your physical health and energy body, and you intuitively know what is healthy or unhealthy for you. If you are in a situation and you do not feel at ease, trust your instinct and change your situation. You have a robust immune system and can use it for the information you gain from your five senses and beyond. You carry collective energy for those with whom you connect. Thus, you can help them by serving as a role model for self-care. Align your values so what you manifest to benefit the collective is congruent with how you live and behave. You are a good marketer because you have an inner sense of the group's pulse. Stay true to the integrity of your word and deeds. You are an example to those with whom you relate. Use your sense of what is healthy or not healthy to benefit your loved ones and shift and uplift the consciousness of those around you. When you are in a situation that does not feel "right," leave the situation. Do not compromise the integrity and intelligence of your physical body.

Your Keys to Empowerment
- You sensitively tune into your body. Listen to your body's communications and honor them.
- When you know what is healthy, honor and stand firm about it.
- You are strong, responsive to energy, and able to influence people.
- Natural healing tools and energy work are compatible with your sensitivity.

Action Points for Manifesting Your Dreams
- You can influence people and do it with word and deed integrity.
- You have a talent for integrating information and considering innovative solutions.
- When you know a situation is unhealthy for you, trust your knowledge. Act on it.
- Essential Oils and other natural modalities are healing for you. Check them out.

Physical/Biological World
Channel 26-44 *(Sagittarius-Scorpio)*

Keywords: Transmission and Surrender, Sensory Integration, Immune Sensitivity, and perceptiveness

You are highly sensitive to what is healthy for you, and when you honor your perceptions, you are at your best.

You are highly sensitive to your physical health and energy body, and you intuitively know what is healthy or unhealthy for you. If you are in a situation and you do not feel at ease, trust your instincts, and change your situation. You have a strong immune system and can use it for the information you gain from your five senses and beyond. You are sensitive to smell to the degree that you might walk into a room, and if it doesn't "smell" right to you, you might choose to leave. This sensitivity is your friend and keeps you healthy on multiple levels. You carry collective energy for those with whom you connect. Thus, you can help them by serving as a role model for self-care. Align your values so what you manifest to benefit the collective is congruent with how you live and behave. You are a good marketer because you have an inner sense of the group's pulse. Stay true to the integrity of your word and deeds. You are an example to those with whom you relate. Use your sense of what is healthy or not healthy to benefit your loved ones and shift and uplift the consciousness of those around you. When you are in a situation that does not feel "right," leave the situation. Do not compromise the integrity and intelligence of your physical body.

Your Keys to Empowerment
- You sensitively tune into your body. Listen to your body's communications and honor them
- When you know what is healthy, honor and stand firm about it.
- You carry collective consciousness and feel responsible for communicating what you know to those you care about.
- Natural healing tools and energy work are compatible with your sensitivity.

Action Points for Manifesting Your Dreams
- You can influence people and do it with word and deed integrity.
- You have a talent for integrating information and considering innovative solutions.
- When you know a situation is unhealthy for you, trust your knowledge. Act on it.
- Master natural healing tools like Reiki, Essential Oils, Homeopathy, etc.

Channel 27-50

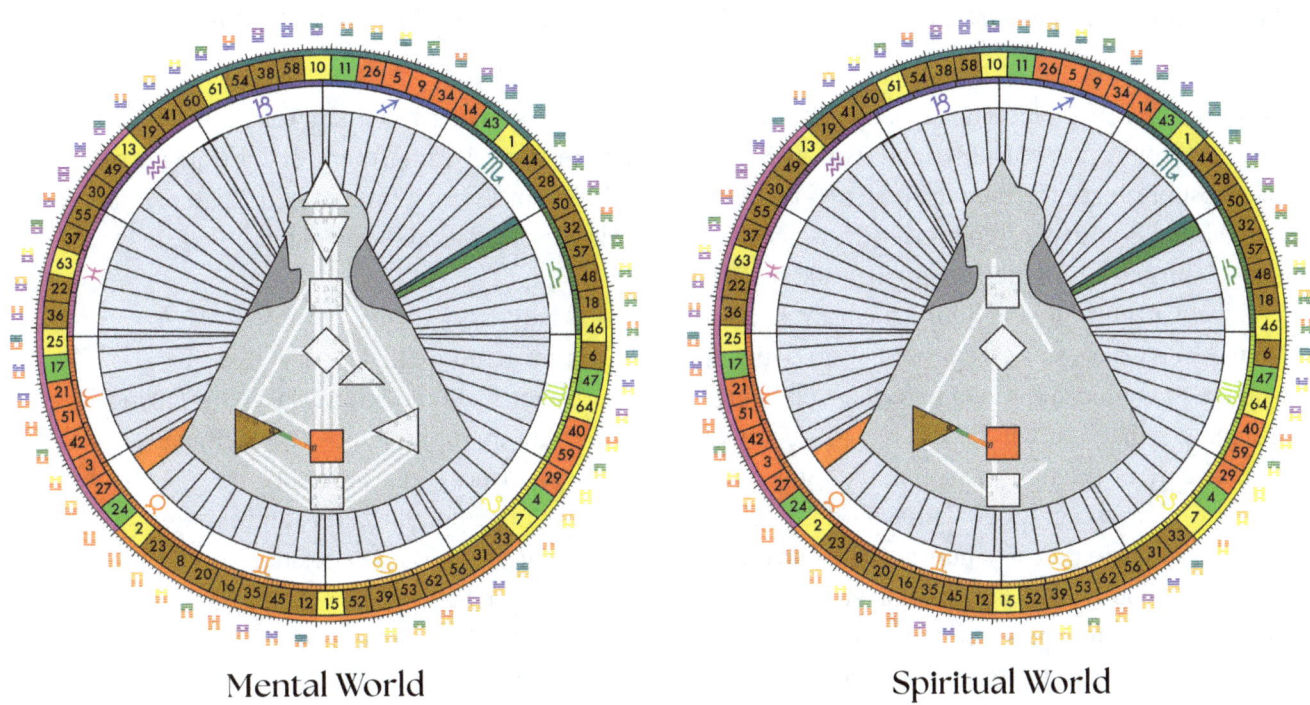

Mental World　　　　　　　　　　　Spiritual World

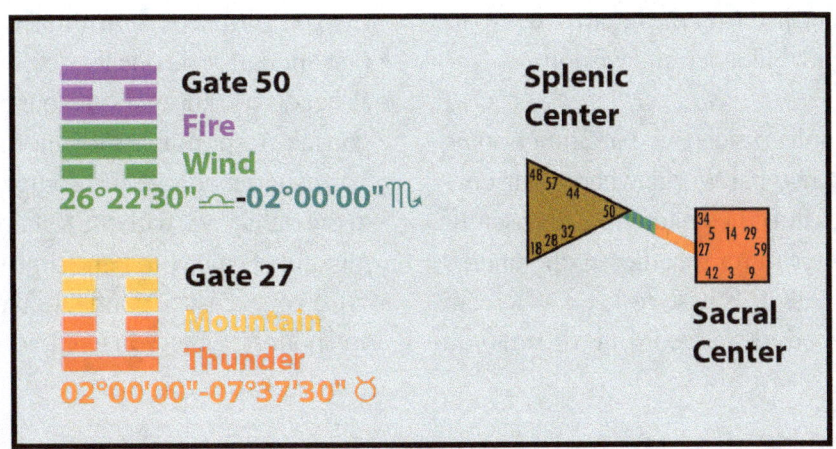

Channel 27-50

Integrated Mental and Spiritual/Archetypal Worlds
Channel 27-50 *(Taurus-Libra/Scorpio)*

Keywords: Responsibility, Preservation, Guardianship

You are naturally caring and compassionate; you often feel you have a mission and do not know what it is. Be introspective and caretaking of yourself before you care for others.

Your strong sense of compassion and caring permeates your consciousness, and you will likely take responsibility for the well-being of those you care about. You may often awaken with a sense of angst. The angst is the feeling upon awakening that you were given a mission during the night and can't quite place what you are supposed to do. Trust that you are empathic and tuned in to the well-being of others and that you will be where you need to be to take care of the right person at the right time. If you stay alert and in touch with your deep self and compassionate nature as a nurturer, you can be confident that you are fulfilling your divine mission and purpose. You must make certain that you use self-discipline in your self-care routines because they are essential in keeping you healthy and giving you the reserves of energy to help others when called to do so. Meditate daily and listen for the intuitive whispers that provide you with guidance and wisdom.

When you are in a deep sleep, you are functioning in the Spiritual/Archetypal World, where your consciousness expands into the collective unconscious that links all living creatures together in one unified field of consciousness. It is wise to keep a "Dream Journal" near your bedside to record any dreams you can access when you first awaken. Work with your dreams by rewriting them or by doing a dialogue with them to bring unconscious material into consciousness for growth and clarity.

Your Keys to Empowerment
- You are in tune with the collective consciousness and often awaken the feeling that you are supposed to do something, and you're not sure what to do.
- Trust your empathic nature and express your caring when appropriate.
- Disciplined Self-Care is essential for your well-being and health.
- Meditate upon awakening to clear your energy from the night and to tune in to yourself.

Action Points for Manifesting Your Dreams
- Get enough good quality sleep.
- What do you know about your boundaries when you take responsibility for another's care?
- You experience love and compassion when in the right place with the right people. Be mindful of who you spend time with.
- Trust your sense of connection with others and honor it when you feel spiritually guided.

Mental World
Channel 27-50 *(Taurus-Libra/Scorpio)*

Keywords: Responsibility, Preservation, Guardianship

You are naturally caring and compassionate; you often feel you have a mission and do not know what it is. Be introspective and caretaking of yourself before you care for others.

Your strong sense of compassion and caring permeates your consciousness, and you will likely take responsibility for the well-being of those you care about. You may often awaken with a sense of angst. The angst is the feeling upon awakening that you were given a mission during the night, and you can't quite place what you are supposed to do. Trust that you are empathic and tuned in to the well-being of others and that you will be where you need to be to take care of someone at the right time. If you stay alert and in touch with your deep self and compassionate nature as a nurturer, you can be confident that you are fulfilling your divine mission and purpose. You must use self-discipline in your self-care routines because they are essential in keeping you healthy and giving you the energy to help others when called to do so. Meditate daily and listen for the intuitive whispers that provide you with guidance and wisdom.

Your Keys to Empowerment
- You are in tune with the collective consciousness and often awaken the
- You awaken feeling that you are supposed to do something, and you're not sure what to do.
- Trust your empathic nature and express your caring when appropriate.
- Disciplined Self-Care is essential for your well-being and health.
- Meditate upon awakening to clear your energy from the night and to tune in to yourself.
- Keep a "Dream Journal" near your bedside with a pen. Recall dreams upon awakening.

Action Points for Manifesting Your Dreams
- Get enough good quality sleep.
- What do you know about your boundaries when you take responsibility for another's care?
- You experience love and compassion when in the right place with the right people. Be mindful of who you spend time with
- Meditate daily and listen for the intuitive whispers that provide you with guidance and wisdom.

Spiritual/Archetypal World
Channel 27-50 *(Taurus-Libra/Scorpio)*

Keywords: Responsibility, Preservation, Guardianship

You are naturally caring and compassionate; you often feel you have a mission and do not know what it is. Be introspective and caretaking of yourself before you care for others.

When you are in a deep sleep, you are functioning in the Spiritual/Archetypal World, where your consciousness expands into the collective unconscious that links all living creatures together as one unified field of consciousness. You are driven by your strong sense of compassion and caring that permeates your consciousness. You will likely take responsibility for the well-being of those you care about. Moreover, you may often awaken with a sense of angst. The angst is the feeling upon awakening that you were given a mission during the night and can't quite place what you are supposed to do. Trust that you are empathic and tuned in to the well-being of others and that you will be where you need to be to take care of someone at the right time. If you stay alert and in touch with your deep self and compassionate nature as a nurturer, you can be confident that you are fulfilling your divine mission and purpose. It is wise to keep a journal near your bedside to record any dreams you can access first thing when you awaken. Work with your dreams by rewriting them or by doing a dialogue with them to bring unconscious material into consciousness for growth and clarity.

Your Keys to Empowerment
- You are in tune with the collective consciousness and often awaken with "angst," feeling that you are supposed to do something and are unsure what to do.
- Disciplined Self-Care is essential for your well-being and health.
- Meditate upon awakening to clear your energy from the night and to tune in to yourself.
- Keep a "Dream Journal" near your bedside with a pen. Recall dreams upon awakening.
- You are a healer. Learn healing modalities you feel connected to.

Action Points for Manifesting Your Dreams
- Get enough good quality sleep.
- Trust your empathic nature and express your caring when appropriate.
  You experience love and compassion when in the right place with the right people.
- Be mindful of who you spend time with.
- Meditate daily and listen for the intuitive whispers that provide you with guidance and wisdom.

Channel 28-38

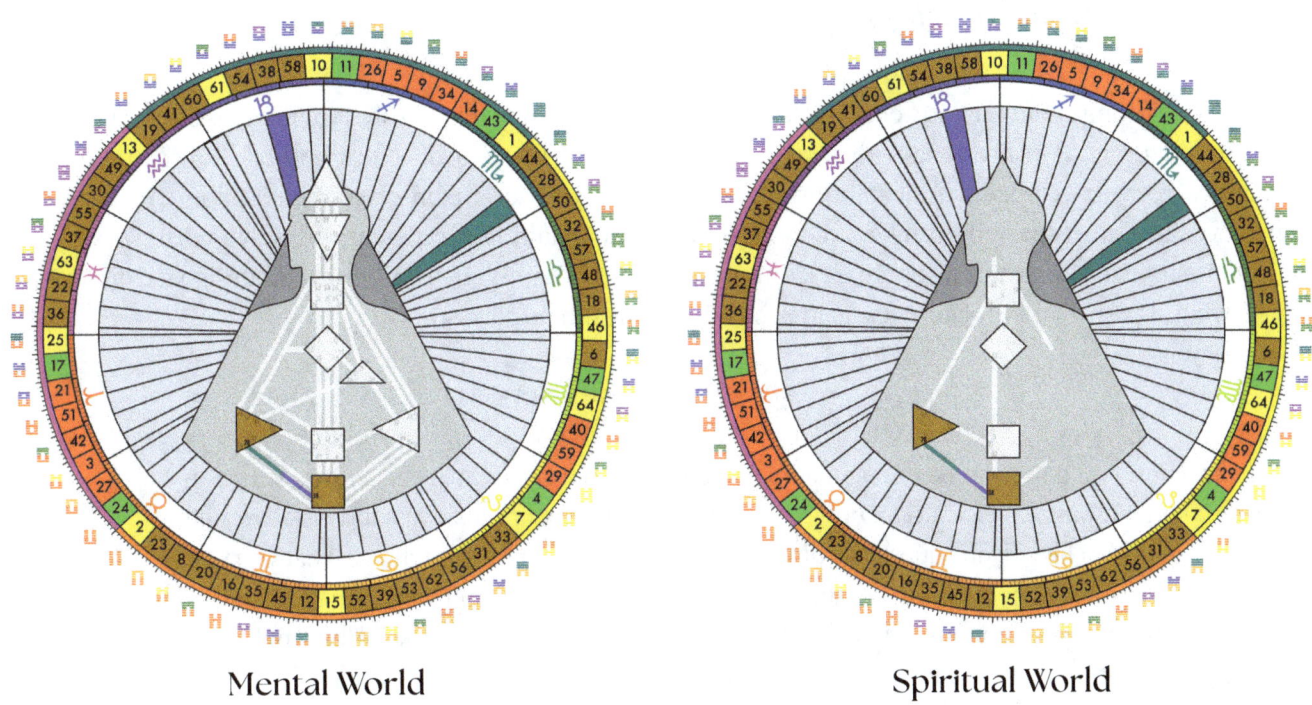

Mental World   Spiritual World

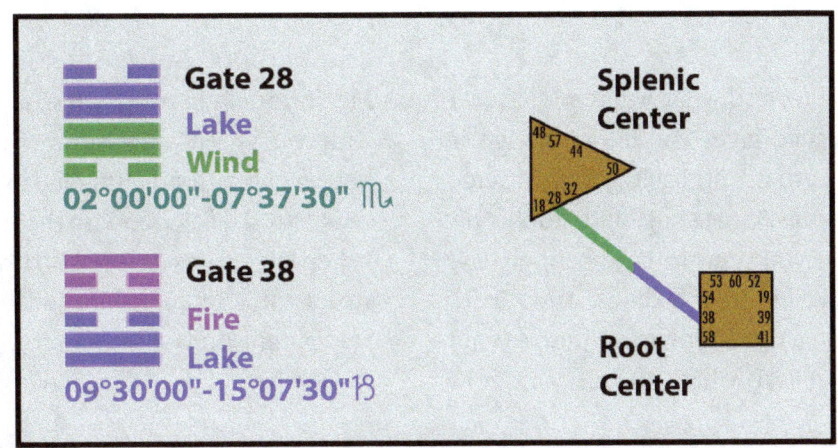

Channel 28-38

Integrated Mental and Spiritual/Archetypal World
Channel 28-38 *(Scorpio-Capricorn)*

Keywords: Preservation, Struggle, Selection, Intuitive Direction

Your intuition drives you toward mastery when confronting life challenges. Trust your inner sense of what is healthy for you.

Life always confronts you with challenges to your health and survival. How you deal with the challenges is critical to your well-being. Your stubbornness and perseverance are a strength. You have a good sense of your survival needs and instinctively commit to following a path that will likely result in a healthy outcome.

However, you have a sixth sense that alerts you to danger. Thus, you may, at times, feel anxiety. When anxiety surfaces, ask: "What do I know about this anxiety now?" This clean question directs you toward your inner process; take all the time you need to delve into your unconscious and ask: "What is the past situation that reminds you of what is triggering my anxiety now?" Once you identify a source of your anxiety, ask again: "What do I know about this anxiety now?"

Your insight is vital toward what will work for you, and your perseverance gives you an advantage in considering options that will result in your desired outcome. Stay optimistic, trusting, and stubbornly committed to what you want to have happen. Use your sensitivity and intuitive abilities. Tune in to what you need to do to transform frustration to your advantage by tuning in to what you know and how you can creatively solve whatever issues are before you. Trust your deep self and take all the time you need to set a plan of action. Tune in to what you know and how to creatively solve whatever issues are before you. Time to meditate is vital for your health on all levels.

Your Keys to Empowerment

- Your perseverance and stubbornness are your strength in challenging situations.
- Use your sensitivity and intuitive abilities to find a way to achieve what you want to have happen in all situations.
- When anxious, ask: "What am I reminded of from my past?"
- You sensitively tune in to what is healthy; do not compromise when you know what is right for you.

Action Points for Manifesting Your Dreams

- Meditate daily in your own space with your pets if you have any.
- Keep a journal for dreams and experiences that cause stress–dialogue with the stress to gain clarity.
- When anxious, ask: "What do I know about this anxiety now?" Keep asking until you gain clarity.
- Stay optimistic, you overcome challenges and learn from your experiences.

Mental World
Channel 28-38 *(Scorpio-Capricorn)*

Keywords: Preservation, Struggle, Selection, Intuitive Direction

Your intuition drives you toward mastery when confronting life challenges. Trust your inner sense of what is healthy for you.

Life always confronts you with challenges to your health and survival. How you deal with the challenges is critical to your well-being. Your stubbornness and perseverance are a strength. You have a good sense of your survival needs and instinctively commit to following a path that will likely result in a healthy outcome. Your insight is strong toward what will work for you, and your perseverance gives you an advantage in considering options that will result in your desired outcome. Stay optimistic, trusting, and stubbornly committed to what you want to have happen. Use your sensitivity and intuitive abilities. Tune in to what you need to do to transform frustration to your advantage by tuning in to what you know and how you can creatively solve whatever issues are before you. Trust in your deep self and take all the time you need to set a plan of action that will transform frustration and set you on a path of ease and fulfillment.

Your Keys to Empowerment
- Your perseverance and stubbornness are your strength in challenging situations.
- Use your sensitivity and intuitive abilities to find a way to achieve what you want to have happen in all situations.
- When anxious, ask: "What am I reminded of from my past?"
- Trust your deep self and take time to set your path forward.

Action Points for Manifesting Your Dreams
- Meditate daily in your own space with your pets if you have any.
- Keep a journal for dreams and experiences that cause stress–dialogue with the stress to gain clarity.
- When anxious, ask: "How can I transform this frustration into my advantage?"
- Stay optimistic, you overcome challenges and learn from your experiences.

Spiritual/Archetypal World
Channel 28-38 *(Scorpio-Capricorn)*

Keywords: Preservation, Struggle, Selection, Intuitive Direction

Your intuition drives you toward mastery when confronting life challenges. Trust your inner sense of what is healthy for you.

At an intuitive level, you know that life often confronts you with challenges to your health and survival. How you deal with the challenges is critical to your well-being. Your stubbornness and perseverance are a strength. You have a good sense of your survival needs and instinctively commit to following a path that will likely result in a healthy outcome. Your insight is strong toward what will work for you, and your perseverance gives you an advantage in considering options that will result in your desired outcome. Stay optimistic, trusting, and stubbornly committed to what you want to have happen.

Go within and depend on your spiritual guides to guide you on how to proceed when uncertain. Rely on your sensitivity and intuitive abilities to tune in to what you must do to transform frustration to your advantage. Tune in to what you know and how to creatively solve whatever issues are before you. Trust in your deep self and take all the time you need to set a plan of action that will transform frustration and set you on a path of ease and fulfillment.

Your Keys to Empowerment
- Your perseverance and stubbornness are your strength in challenging situations.
- Use your sensitivity and intuitive abilities to find a way to achieve what you want to have happen in all situations.
- When anxious, ask: "What am I reminded of from my past?"
- Rely on your sensitivity and intuitive abilities to guide you toward your goals.

Action Points for Manifesting Your Dreams
- Meditate daily in your own space with your pets if you have any.
- Keep a journal for dreams and experiences that cause stress–dialogue with the stress to gain clarity.
- When struggling, ask: "What is so important for me to learn that God would put this challenge before me?"
- Stay optimistic, you overcome challenges and learn from your experiences.

Channel 29-46

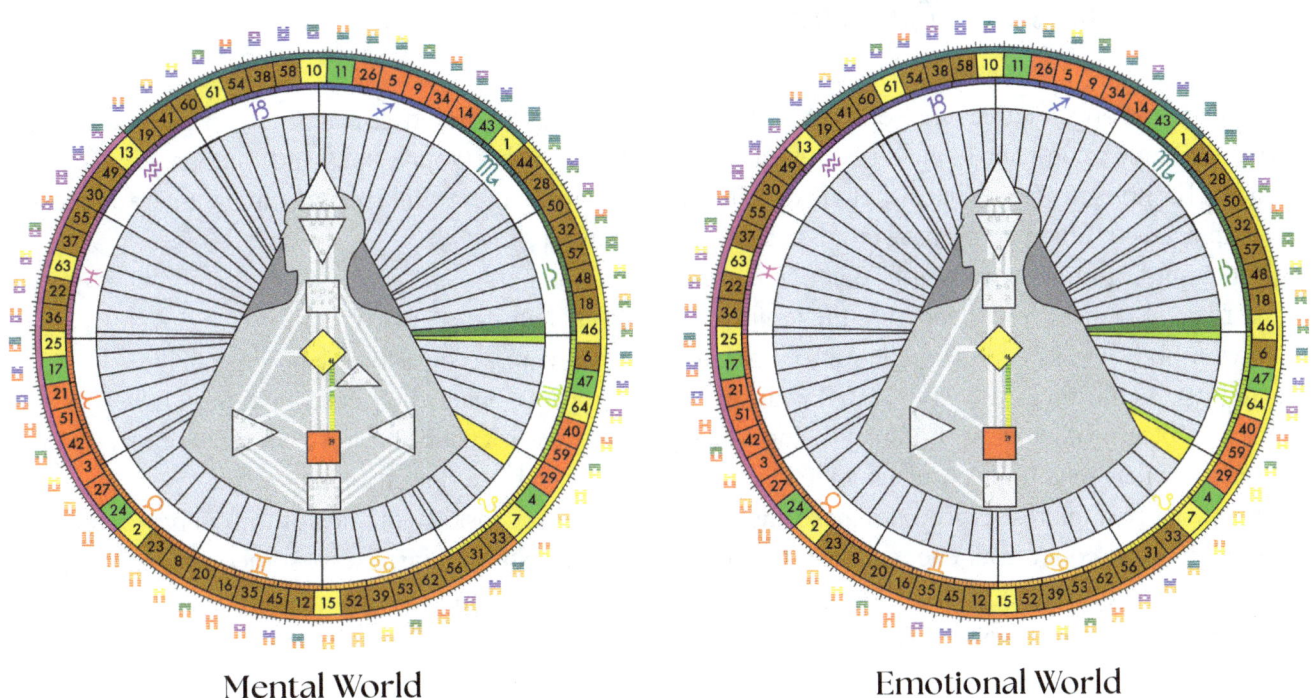

Mental World　　　　　　　　　　　　Emotional World

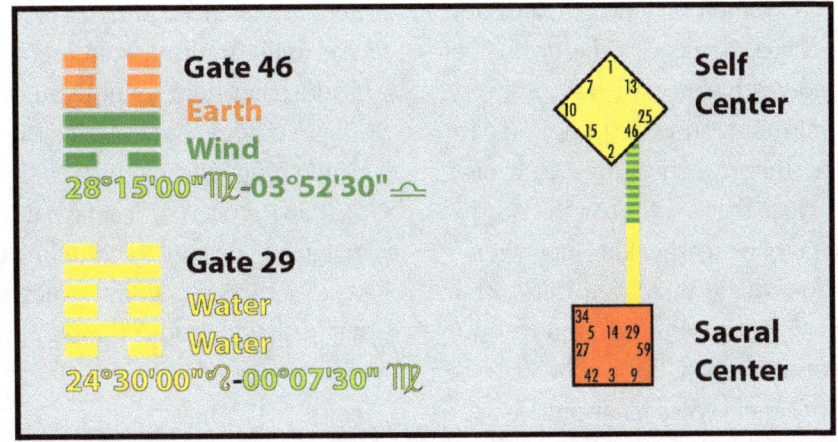

Channel 29-46

Integrated Mental and Emotional/Angelic Worlds
Channel 29-46 *(Leo/Virgo-Virgo/Libra)*

Keywords: Love of Body, Discovery, Body Feeling, Instinct

Although you have a strong sense of what is healthy for you, you sometimes compromise yourself for others. Be self-protective.

You have a strong intuitive sense of what is ideal for your body and value it and its health greatly. At times, you feel conflicted about what tasks to take on to be a help agent to others and what you need to do to protect and maintain your health. When you commit to actions that do not recognize the limitations on your body and its energy, you compromise your integrity and the integrity of your body. Because you want to please others and you enjoy being a help agent, you may tend to put yourself aside when it is not in your best interest. Before you make any commitments that require your energy outlay, take time to be clear on the impact your decision may have on your health and your body.

You can succeed beyond what others can accomplish by maintaining a balance that honors all involved participants. Remember, your health and body are vehicles for good deeds when you feel rested, available, and ready to serve. Take time to consider your commitments and take things on with mindful intelligence. Before committing to a task, ask yourself: "Am I clear that I want to take on this task now?" Be courageous in speaking up when a job is not suitable for you, as taking on things that put you under stress is not in your best interest nor the interest of the other person. Be as protective of yourself as you are of others you care about.

Writing daily gratitude statements in all Four Worlds helps anchor your values and offers a strategy for balancing them while maintaining self-care and relationships.

Your Keys to Empowerment
- Self-care is crucial for balance in your life.
- You love being a help agent, at times, at the expense of yourself. Only commit to others when you feel rested, available, and ready to serve.
- Always consider your health and energy reserves when committing to serve someone else.
- Do not compromise your integrity and that of your body.

Action Points for Manifesting Your Dreams
- Take time for yourself daily. Meditate, exercise, and relax.
- Write daily gratitude statements in all Four Worlds; they help anchor your values and offer a strategy for balancing them while maintaining self-care and relationships.
- You can succeed beyond what you imagine if you care for your health.
- Avoid activities or commitments that push your body's limits.

Mental World
Channel 29-46 *(Leo/Virgo-Virgo/Libra)*

Keywords: Love of Body, Discovery, Body Feeling, Instinct

Although you have a strong sense of what is healthy for you, you sometimes compromise yourself for others. Be self-protective.

You have a strong intuitive sense of what is ideal for your body and value it and its health greatly. When you commit to actions that do not recognize the limitations on your body and its energy, you compromise your integrity and the integrity of your body. Before you make any commitments that require your energy outlay, take time to be clear on the impact your decision may have on your health and your body.

You can succeed beyond what others can accomplish, but you must consider your health and how you are cared for while helping others. Remember, your health and body are vehicles for good deeds when you feel rested, available, and ready to commit. Take time to consider your commitments and take things on with mindful intelligence. Before committing to a task, ask yourself: "Am I clear that I want to take on this task now?" Be courageous in speaking up when a job is not suitable for you, as taking on things that put you under stress is not in your best interest nor the interest of the other person. Be as protective of yourself as you are of others you care about.

Your Keys to Empowerment
- Self-care is crucial for balance in your life.
- You love being a help agent, at times, at the expense of yourself. Only commit to others when you feel rested, available, and ready to serve.
- Always ask: "Am I clear that I want to take on this task now?"
- Do not compromise your integrity and that of your body.

Action Points for Manifesting Your Dreams
- Take time for yourself daily. Meditate, exercise, and relax.
- Write daily gratitude statements in all Four Worlds; they help anchor your values and offer a strategy for balancing them while maintaining self-care and relationships.
- You can succeed beyond what you imagine if you care for your health.
- Avoid activities or commitments that push your body's limits.

Emotional/Angelic World
Channel 29-46 *(Leo/Virgo-Virgo/Libra)*

Keywords: Love of Body, Discovery, Body Feeling, Instinct

Although you have a strong sense of what is healthy for you, you sometimes compromise yourself for others. Be self-protective.

At times, you feel conflicted about what tasks to take on to be a help agent to others and what you need to do to protect yourself and maintain your health. Because you want to please others and enjoy being a help agent, you often put yourself aside when it is not in your best interest. You have a strong instinctive sense of what is right for your body and value it and its health greatly. When you commit to actions that do not recognize the limitations on your body and its energy, you compromise your integrity and the integrity of your body. Before you make any commitments that require your energy outlay, take time to be clear on the impact your decision may have on your health and your body. Ask, before committing to take on a task, if you are acting from a "want for approval" or if you are acting in service.

You can succeed beyond what others can accomplish, but you must consider your health and how you are cared for while helping others. Remember, your health and body are vehicles for good deeds when you feel rested, available, and ready to commit. Take time to consider your commitments and take things on with mindful intelligence. Before committing to a task, ask yourself: "Am I clear that I want to take on this task now?" Be courageous in speaking up when a job is not suitable for you, as taking on things that put you under stress is not in your best interest nor the interest of the other person. Be as protective of yourself as you are of others you care about.

Your Keys to Empowerment
- Self-care is crucial for balance in your life.
- You love being a help agent, at times, at the expense of yourself. Only commit to others when you feel rested, available, and ready to serve.
- Always ask: "Am I clear that I want to take on this task now?"
- Do not compromise your integrity and that of your body.

Action Points for Manifesting Your Dreams
- Take time for yourself daily. Meditate, exercise, and relax.
- Discern when you might choose to act from a "want for approval" rather than from a neutral place.
- You can succeed beyond what you imagine if you care for your health.
- Avoid activities or commitments that push your body's limits.

Channel 30-41

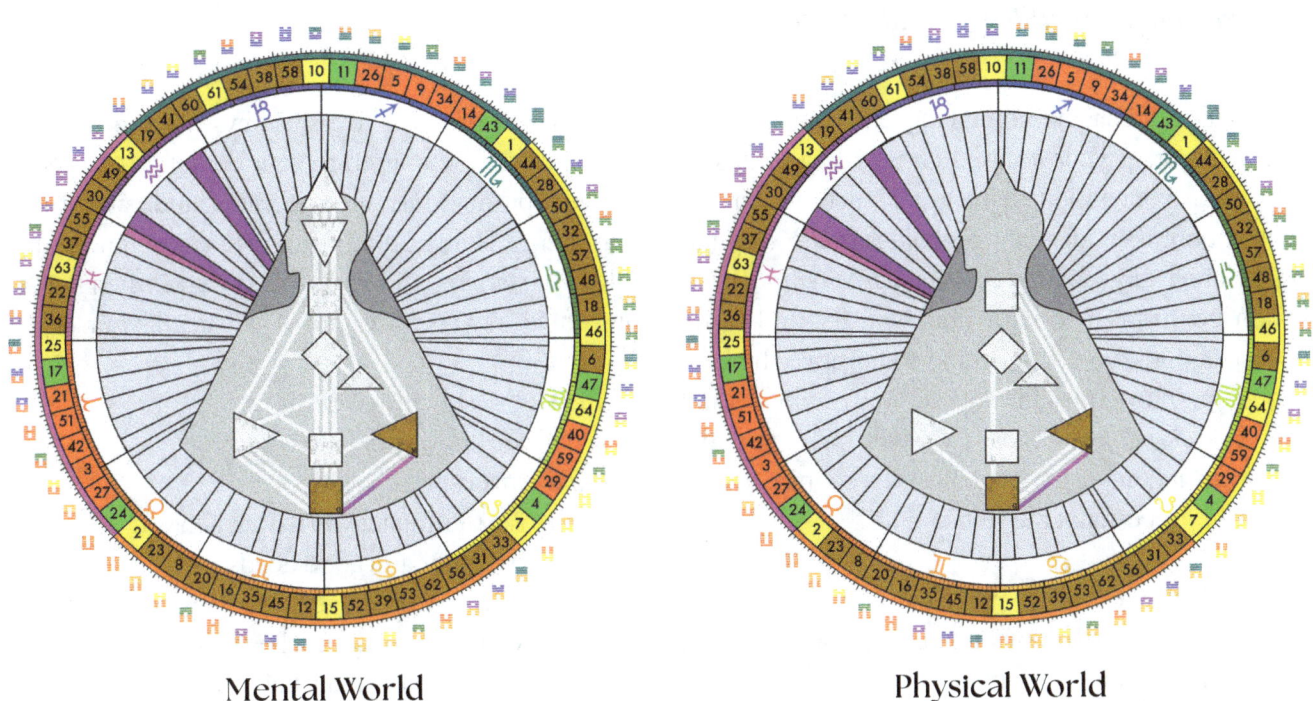

Mental World   Physical World

Gate 30
Fire
Fire
24°30'00"♒ - 00°07'30"♓

Gate 41
Mountain
Lake
02°00'00" - 07°37'30"♒

Solar Plexus Center

Root Center

Channel 30-41

Integrated Mental and Physical/Biological Worlds
Channel 30-41 *(Aquarius/Pisces-Aquarius)*

Keywords: Imagining, Recognition, Clarity, Stirrings

Your innovative creativity is a gift that needs nurturing and encouragement, especially when you face challenges and obstacles.

When you imagine something and can envision it manifesting your focused energy contributes to bringing your vision to reality. Sometimes, at the inception of an idea, all possibilities excite you, and you are exuberant inside yourself. When opposition confronts you with doubts, fears, and other obstructions, do not succumb to negative thinking but continue to imagine your desired outcomes and hang true to your vision. Consider many possible ways to accomplish your goals and recognize the joy in your process, not the result.

Your challenge is to use your innovative creativity to think outside the box of limitation and push through toward new ways of thinking and being that excite you. Your capacity to move through the frustration and come out of any situation, having used your creative intelligence, i.e., innovative thinking, is a true gift you deeply value. Make sure you acknowledge your integrity in sticking with a situation that challenges you to be your best self.

In the Physical World, you experience an inner dilemma. You must determine whether to push forward to accomplish your goals or to let go of your goals when they are stressful physically and emotionally. Stay committed to your path if it is correct for you spiritually. You are integrating and transforming energy. Thus, be mindful of your energy and your physical stamina, and keep this in mind when making choices so you take care of all parts of yourself.

Your Keys to Empowerment
- When you know your path is correct, stand firm despite challenges.
- Recognize the impact you have when you radiate brilliance and good deeds.
- Use your creative intelligence to reach your goals.
- Daily meditation and journaling help you assess how you can remain balanced.

Action Points for Manifesting Your Dreams
- Write out your Goals in the Four Worlds and visit them daily with notes on progress toward achieving them.
- Stay committed to your path if it aligns spiritually.
- Commit to disciplined Self-Care to optimize your health and to protect it.
- Only commit to an action plan when you have clarity.

Mental World
Channel 30-41 *(Aquarius/Pisces-Aquarius)*

Keywords: Imagining, Recognition, Clarity, Stirrings

Your innovative creativity is a gift that needs nurturing and encouragement, especially when you face challenges and obstacles.

When you imagine something and can envision it manifesting, your focused energy contributes to bringing your vision to reality. Sometimes, at the inception of an idea, all possibilities excite you, and you are exuberant inside yourself. When opposition confronts you with doubts, fears, and other obstructions, do not succumb to negative thinking but continue to imagine your desired outcomes and hang true to your vision. Consider many possible ways to accomplish your goals and recognize the joy in your process, not the result.

Your challenge is to use your innovative creativity to think outside the box of limitation and push through toward new ways of thinking and being that excite you. Your capacity to move through the frustration and come out of any situation feeling like your creative intelligence, i.e., innovative thinking, is a true gift you deeply value. Make sure you acknowledge your integrity in sticking with a situation that challenges you to be your best self. Even when you feel clarity around your goals, ensure you have the physical stamina to pursue your projects. Time is your friend. Be patient, go slow.

Your Keys to Empowerment
- When you know your path is correct, stand firm despite challenges.
- Recognize the impact you have when you radiate brilliance and good deeds.
- Time is your friend. Be patient, go slow.
- Daily meditation and journaling help you assess how you can remain balanced.

Action Points for Manifesting Your Dreams
- Write out your goals in the Four Worlds and visit them daily with notes on progress toward achieving them.
- When frustrated and challenged, use your creative intelligence to transform the situation.
- Commit to disciplined Self-Care to optimize your health and to protect it.
- Only commit to an action plan when you have clarity.

Physical/Biological Worlds
Channel 30-41 *(Aquarius/Pisces-Aquarius)*

Keywords: Imagining, Recognition, Clarity, Stirrings

Your innovative creativity is a gift that needs nurturing and encouragement, especially when you face challenges and obstacles.

The Physical World may present you with an inner dilemma. You must determine whether to push forward to accomplish your goals or to let go of your goals when they are stressful physically and emotionally. Be mindful of your energy and your physical stamina (Physical World) and keep this in mind when making choices so you take care of all parts of yourself.

When you imagine something, and you envision it manifesting your focused energy plays a part in bringing your vision to reality. Sometimes, at the inception of an idea, all possibilities excite you, and you are exuberant inside yourself. When opposition confronts you with doubts, fears, and other obstructions, do not succumb to negative thinking but continue to imagine your desired outcomes and hang true to your vision. Consider many possible ways to accomplish your goals and recognize the joy in your process, not the result. Your challenge is to use your innovative creativity to think outside the box of limitation and push through toward new ways of thinking and being that excite you. You can move through frustration and come out of any situation feeling like your creative intelligence, i.e., innovative thinking, is a true gift you deeply value. Make sure you acknowledge your integrity in sticking with a situation that challenges you to be your best self.

Your Keys to Empowerment
- When you know your path is correct, stand firm despite challenges.
- Recognize the impact you have when you radiate brilliance and good deeds.
- Think creatively when you feel challenged and frustrated. Time is your friend.
- Daily meditation and journaling help you assess how you can remain balanced.

Action Points for Manifesting Your Dreams
- Write out your goals in the Four Worlds and visit them daily with notes on progress toward achieving them.
- When frustrated and challenged, use your creative intelligence to transform the situation.
- Commit to disciplined Self-Care to optimize your health and to protect it.
- Only commit to an action plan when you have clarity.

Channel 32-54

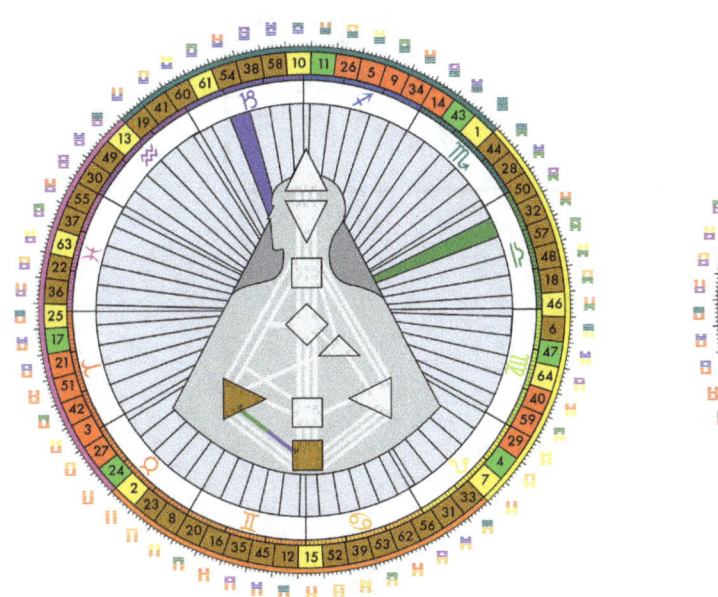

Mental World

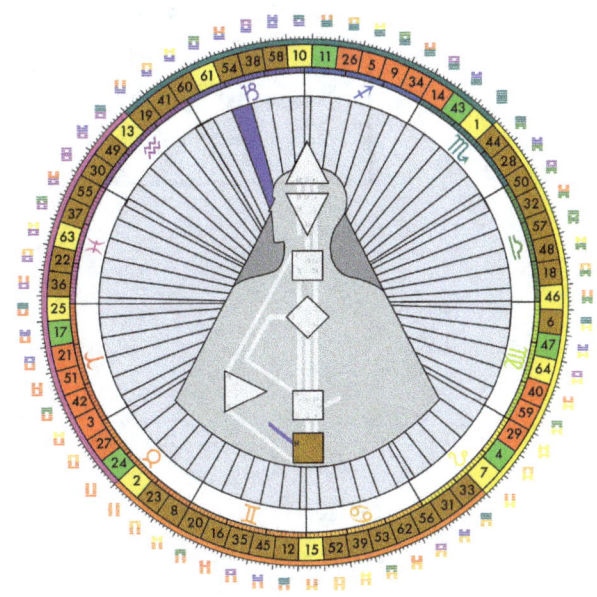

Emotional World

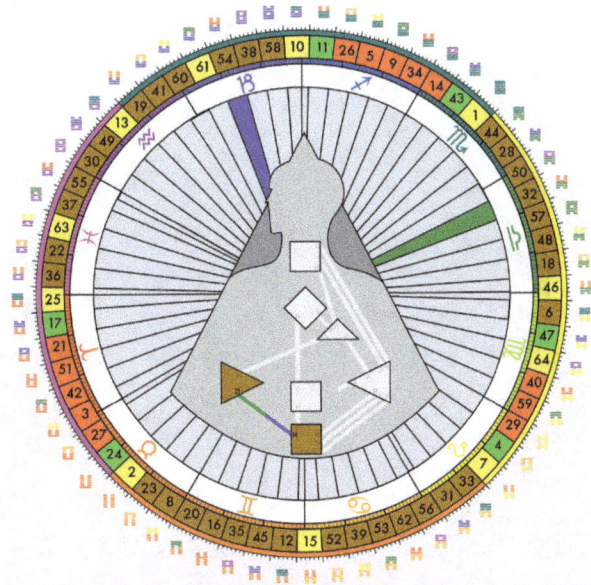

Physical World

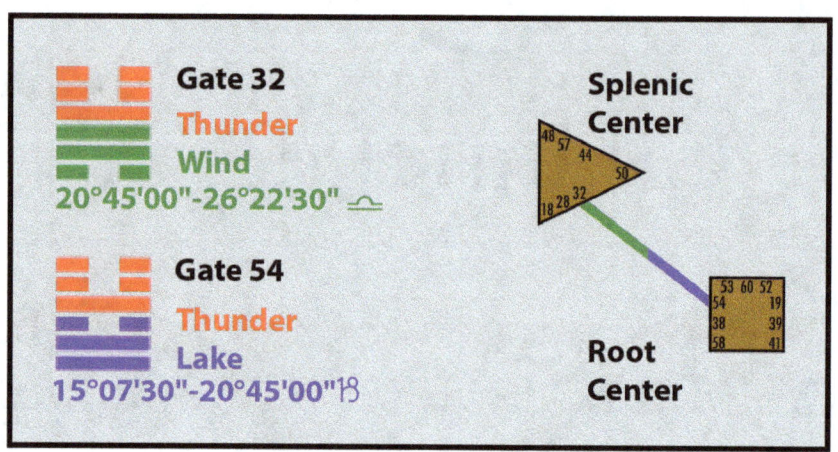

Channel 32-54

Integrated Mental and Physical/Biological Worlds and Gate 54 Portal to The Emotional/Angelic World
Channel 32-54 *(Libra-Capricorn)*

Keywords: Transformation, Sustenance, Duration, Goals

You are more motivated to achieve your goals when they align with your spiritual values.

You have a great deal of wisdom and inner knowing. At your core, you want to achieve your goals and transform your life to honor your life mission. Competence and achieving your goals underlie much of your motivation. Use this part of yourself wisely. Your values are strong and deeply spiritual, and your physical well-being depends on your balance. When they relate to your consciousness and growth, your goals will likely be more attainable and aligned with you than those that do not honor your life purpose and physical capacity to achieve them. Be mindful of this aspect of yourself so you can pay attention to how you frame your goals.

What you set as your goals and how you physically manage to achieve them affects your health and physical stamina. Your underlying unconscious motivations impact you because you internalize your goals, whether you write them down or not. You must recognize a power higher than your ego as the orchestrator of your success. To use this energy effectively, be strategic in your goal setting so you do not take on more than is healthy for you. To maximize your depth of purpose and the ability to manifest it, write down what you want to have happen and how it can happen. Also, consider writing down what you believe about your goals. The more internal processing you do, the more you will achieve.

Write your goals for all the worlds: Mental, Emotional, Spiritual, Physical, and Integrated. By recognizing that you live in multiple dimensions, you integrate all aspects of yourself and your values. This perspective is crucial in setting goals that manifest fully in your life. In addition, meditation and movement are essential for you. You can significantly benefit from breath work and movement that supports higher consciousness so you can mobilize energy to achieve your goals. The MELT technique for lymphatic drainage would be helpful for you, as would be regular Sauna treatment.

Your Keys to Empowerment
- Your connection to the depth of your soul drives your actions, consciously and unconsciously.
- You are a multidimensional being who recognizes that your choices impact your health and sense of fulfillment.
- Writing down your Goals in all Four Worlds and the Integrated World allows you to align your values and manage your resources in all Worlds.
- Do a moving exercise that connects you to cosmic energy.

Action Points for Manifesting Your Dreams
- Read what you wrote as your goals in all Four Worlds and the Integrated World daily.
- Always defer to a higher power who guides your path. Meditate daily to stay connected with your spiritual self.
- Use breathing to rebalance and realign when stressed.
- Daily movement and detoxing, such as MELT, Tai Chi Gung, walking, and Sauna treatments, are beneficial for you.

Integrated Mental World and Portal Through Gate 54 to Emotional/Angelic World
Channel 32-54 *(Libra-Capricorn)*

Keywords: Transformation, Sustenance, Duration, Goals

You are more motivated to achieve your goals when they align with your spiritual values.

When your goals relate to consciousness and growth, they will be more attainable and aligned when they honor your life purpose and physical capacity to achieve them. Be mindful of this aspect of yourself so you pay attention to how you frame your goals. You have a great deal of wisdom and inner knowing. At your core, you want to achieve your goals and transform your life to honor your life mission. Your values are strong, and your physical well-being depends on your balance to accomplish what you want. When you reach your goals, you are likely to feel great inner satisfaction and a sense of inner calm.

To maximize your depth of purpose and the ability to manifest it, write down what you want to have happen and how it can happen. Also, consider writing down what you believe about your goals. The more internal processing you do, the more you will achieve. Write your goals for all Four Worlds: Mental, Emotional, Spiritual, Physical, and Integrated. By recognizing that you live in multiple dimensions, you integrate all aspects of yourself and your values. This perspective is crucial in setting goals that manifest fully in your life. In addition, movement is essential for you. Tai Chi Gung can benefit you significantly because while doing it, you breathe and move energy in ways that will imprint your intentions emotionally.

Your Keys to Empowerment
- Your connection to the depth of your soul drives your actions, consciously and unconsciously.
- You are a multidimensional being who recognizes that your choices impact your health and sense of fulfillment.
- Writing down your goals in all Four Worlds and the Integrated World allows you to align your values and manage your resources in all Worlds.
- Do Tai Chi Gung or another moving exercise that connects you to cosmic energy and anchors your goals emotionally, making them more accessible to you.

Action Points for Manifesting Your Dreams
- Read what you wrote as your goals in all Four Worlds and the Integrated World daily.
- Always defer to a higher power who guides your path. Meditate daily to stay connected with your spiritual self.
- Use breathing to rebalance and realign when stressed.
- Daily movement and detoxing, such as Tai Chi Gung, walking, and Sauna treatments, are beneficial for you.

Integrated Mental and Physical/Biological Worlds
Channel 32-54 *(Libra-Capricorn)*

Keywords: Transformation, Sustenance, Duration, Goals

You are more motivated to achieve your goals when they align with your spiritual values.

You have great wisdom and inner knowing. At your core, you want to achieve your goals and transform your life to honor your life mission. Your values are strong, and your physical well-being depends on you having the right balance of accomplishment. To maximize your depth of purpose and the ability to manifest it, write down what you want to have happen and how it can happen. Also, consider writing down what you believe about your goals. The more internal processing you do, the more you will receive inner guidance and achieve.

What you set as your goals and how you physically manage to achieve them affects your health and physical stamina. Your underlying unconscious motivations impact you because you internalize your goals, whether you write them down or not. To use this energy effectively, be strategic in your goal setting so you do not take on more than is healthy for you. Pay attention to stress and have self-care practices that relieve stress.

Write your goals for all the worlds: Mental, Emotional, Spiritual, Physical, and Integrated. By recognizing that you live in multiple dimensions, you integrate all aspects of yourself and your values. This perspective is crucial in setting goals that manifest fully in your life. In addition, movement is essential for you.

Tai Chi Gung practice integrates movement and consciousness and can significantly benefit you. It teaches how to breathe and move energy so you can mobilize it to achieve your goals. Meditation, especially Transcendental Meditation, is an excellent way to discipline your mind so you connect to your higher, deep self. Honoring that aspect of yourself is crucial to feeling peaceful and fulfilled.

Your Keys to Empowerment
- Your connection to the depth of your soul drives your actions, consciously and unconsciously.
- Ensure you stay hydrated and mindful of your body chemistry and needs.
- Write down your goals in all Four Worlds and the Integrated World to align your values and manage your resources in all Worlds.
- When you feel challenged, assess where you are achieving your goals and revise your plans for your current situation.

Action Points for Manifesting Your Dreams
- Read what you wrote as your goals in all Four Worlds and the Integrated World daily.
- Modify your goals appropriately for your current situation.
- Pay attention to your body and how you feel. Make sure you put your body needs a priority.

Integrated Physical/Biological World and Gate 54 Portal to The Emotional/Angelic World
Channel 32-54 *(Libra-Capricorn)*

Keywords: Transformation, Sustenance, Duration, Goals

You are more motivated to achieve your goals when they align with your spiritual values.

What you set as your goals and how you physically manage to achieve them affects your health and physical stamina. Your underlying unconscious motivations impact you because you internalize your goals. In addition, if your goals relate to consciousness and growth, they will be more attainable and aligned when they honor your life purpose and physical capacity to achieve them. Be mindful of this aspect of yourself so you pay attention to how you frame your goals and use your energy effectively. Be strategic in your goal setting so you do not take on more than is healthy for you. Pay attention to stress and have self-care practices that relieve stress.

You have great wisdom and inner knowing. At your core, you want to achieve your goals and transform your life to honor your life mission. Your values are strong, and your physical well-being depends on having the right energy balance in all Four Worlds to accomplish your goals. To maximize your depth of purpose and the ability to manifest it, write down what you want to have happen and how it can happen. Also, consider writing down what you believe about your goals. The more internal processing you do, the more you will achieve. Write your goals for all Four Worlds: Mental, Emotional, Spiritual, Physical, and Integrated. By recognizing that you live in multiple dimensions, you integrate all aspects of yourself and your values. This perspective is crucial in setting goals that manifest fully in your life. In addition, movement is essential for you. Tai Chi Gung may greatly benefit you because when doing it, you learn how to breathe and move energy to mobilize it to achieve your goals.

Your Keys to Empowerment
- Your connection to the depth of your soul drives your actions, consciously and unconsciously.
- You are a multidimensional being who recognizes that your choices impact your health and sense of fulfillment.
- Writing down your goals in all Four Worlds and the Integrated World allows you to align your values and manage your resources in all Worlds.
- Only commit to goals that honor you in all Four Worlds. It is essential for you to love what you commit to pursue.

Action Points for Manifesting Your Dreams
- Read what you wrote as your goals in all Four Worlds and the Integrated World daily.
- Always defer to a higher power who guides your path. Meditate daily to stay connected with your spiritual self.
- Use Meditative breathing to rebalance and realign when stressed.
- Daily movement and detoxing, such as Tai Chi Gung, walking, and Sauna treatments, are beneficial for you.

Mental World
Channel 32-54 *(Libra-Capricorn)*

Keywords: Transformation, Sustenance, Duration, Goals

You are more motivated to achieve your goals when they align with your spiritual values.

You have great wisdom and inner knowing. At your core, you want to achieve your goals and transform your life to honor your life mission. Your values are strong, and your physical well-being depends on you having the right balance of accomplishment. To maximize your depth of purpose and the ability to manifest it, write down what you want to have happen and how it can happen. Also, consider writing down what you believe about your goals. The more internal processing you do, the more you will receive inner guidance and achieve.

Write your goals for all the worlds: Mental, Emotional, Spiritual, Physical, and Integrated. By recognizing that you live in multiple dimensions, you integrate all aspects of yourself and your values. This perspective is crucial in setting goals that manifest fully in your life. In addition, movement is essential for you. Tai Chi Gung practice integrates movement and consciousness and can significantly benefit you. It teaches how to breathe and move energy so you can mobilize it to achieve your goals. Meditation, especially Transcendental Meditation, is an excellent way to discipline your mind so you connect to your higher, deep self. Honoring that aspect of yourself is crucial to feeling peaceful and fulfilled.

Your Keys to Empowerment
- Your connection to the depth of your soul drives your actions, consciously and unconsciously.
- Honoring and spending time in meditation promotes clarity.
- Write down your Goals in all Four Worlds and the Integrated World to align your values and manage your resources in all Worlds.
- When you feel challenged, assess where you are achieving your goals and revise your plans for your current situation.

Action Points for Manifesting Your Dreams
- Read what you wrote as your goals in all Four Worlds and the Integrated World daily.
- Modify your goals appropriately for your current situation.
- Always defer to a higher power who guides your path. Meditate daily to stay connected with your spiritual self.
- Use breathing to rebalance and realign when stressed.
- Daily movement and detoxing, such as Tai Chi Gung, walking, and Sauna treatments, are beneficial for you.
- Use breathing to rebalance and realign when stressed.
- Daily movement and detoxing, such as Tai Chi Gung, walking, and Sauna treatments, are beneficial for you.

Physical/Biological World
Channel 32-54 *(Libra-Capricorn)*

Keywords: Transformation, Sustenance, Duration, Goals

You are more motivated to achieve your goals when they align with your spiritual values.

What you set as your goals and how you physically manage to achieve them affects your health and physical stamina. Your underlying unconscious motivations impact you because you internalize your goals, whether you write them down or not. To use this energy effectively, be strategic in your goal setting so you do not take on more than is healthy for you. Pay attention to stress and have self-care practices that relieve stress.

You have great wisdom and inner knowing. At your core, you want to achieve your goals and transform your life to honor your life mission. Your values are strong, and your physical well-being depends on having the right energy balance in all Four Worlds to accomplish your goals. To maximize your depth of purpose and the ability to manifest it, write down what you want to have happen and how it can happen. Also, consider writing down what you believe about your goals. The more internal processing you do, the more you will achieve. Write your goals for all Four Worlds: Mental, Emotional, Spiritual, Physical, and Integrated. By recognizing that you live in multiple dimensions, you integrate all aspects of yourself and your values. This perspective is crucial in setting goals that manifest fully in your life. In addition, movement is essential for you. Tai Chi Gung may greatly benefit you because when doing it, you learn how to breathe and move energy to mobilize it to achieve your goals.

Your Keys to Empowerment
- Your connection to the depth of your soul drives your actions, consciously and unconsciously.
- You are a multidimensional being who recognizes that your choices impact your health and sense of fulfillment.
- Writing down your goals in all Four Worlds and the Integrated World allows you to align your values and manage your resources in all Worlds.
- Meditation, such as Transcendental Meditation, can powerfully quiet the mind and tune you into your body.

Action Points for Manifesting Your Dreams
- Read what you wrote as your goals in all Four Worlds and the Integrated World daily.
- Always defer to a higher power who guides your path. Pay attention to your physical sensations and make sure you stay well-hydrated and balanced physically and emotionally.
- Use breathing to rebalance and realign when stressed.
- Daily movement and detoxing, such as Tai Chi Gung, walking, and Sauna treatments, are beneficial for you.

Channel 34-57

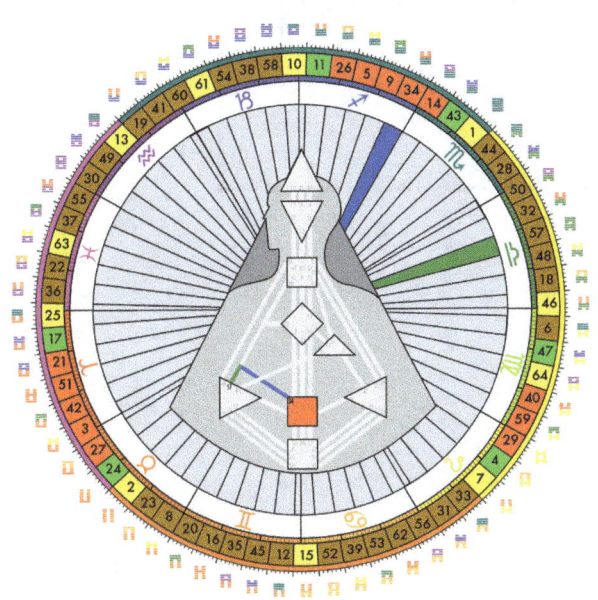

Mental World

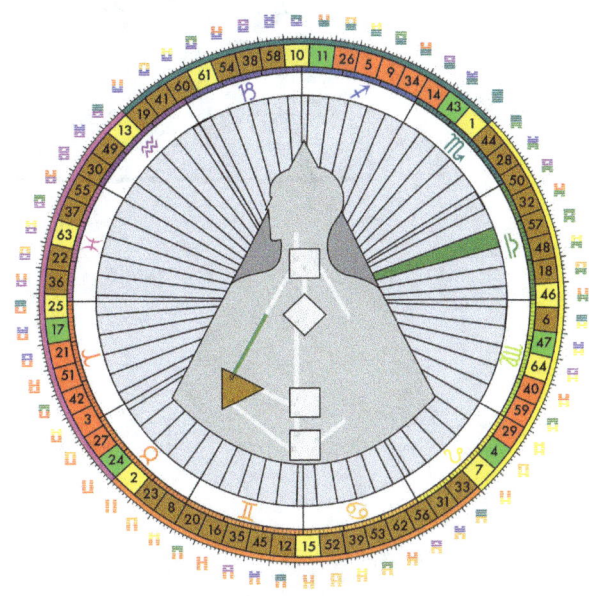

Spiritual World

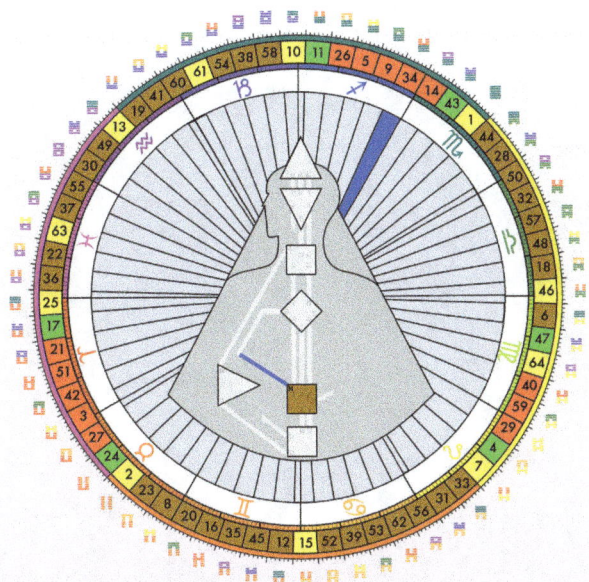

Emotional World

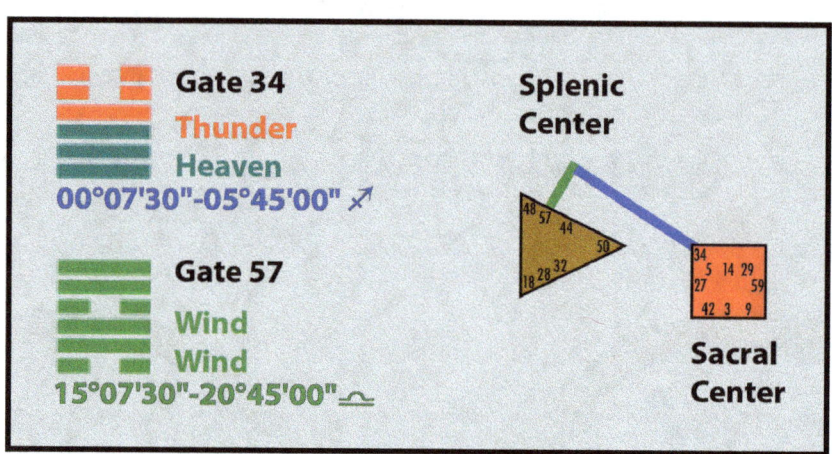

Channel 34-57

Integrated Mental, Spiritual/Archetypal Portal and Emotional/Angelic Portal
Channel 34-57 *(Sagittarius-Libra)*

Keywords: Potential, Power, Intuitive Knowing

Although your strong intuition drives you toward action, waiting until the timing is right to do so serves you well.

You are highly perceptive and intuitive. You tune in to the energy around you, and you know things that are not available to those not sensitive at that level of awareness. Your strong intuition and instinct drive you to manifest whatever you feel warrants your energy. However, because of your instinctive drive to manifest what comes into your awareness, you must intervene on behalf of your highest consciousness and make choices that optimize your energy.

Hence, you focus on what you truly value. Take time to process your internal direction of Self and make sure you align your inner Self with current considered actions. Go Slow. You have plenty of time. Knowing what aligns with your goals and life purpose requires you to wait until you know the appropriate timing for the best outcome. Patience and mindful attention benefit you by allowing your perceptions to go deep within and anchor your actions in what aligns with your highest purpose. Make sure you meditate daily in your own space, with your pets, if you have them, so you listen for the voice of wisdom that guides your truth.

Your perceptive intuition may motivate you toward acting. However, waiting to know what aligns with your goals and life purpose may require waiting until you know that any action is timed correctly for the best outcome. Patience and mindful attention benefit you by allowing your perceptions. Stay focused on what you truly value. Take time to process your internal direction of Self and make sure you align your inner Self with current considered actions. Go Slow. You have plenty of time.

Use the Four Worlds Clarity Worksheet to review factors you consider about any major decisions to ensure you are balanced and aligned in all worlds before acting. In addition, meditate daily in your own space, allowing your pets to be with you so you listen for the voice of wisdom that guides your truth.

Your Keys to Empowerment
- Your intuitive gut instincts drive you toward manifesting. Wait for the right time.
- Always consider how your intuitive knowing aligns with what you value. Use your power of knowing wisely.
- Stay focused on what you truly value.
- You know more than you think you know. Wait for clarity and be patient.

Action Points for Manifesting Your Dreams
- When you know what you know and no one can tell you otherwise, wait for an opportunity to speak or act. Be patient and strategic.
- Use the Four Worlds Clarity Worksheets to review factors you consider about any significant decisions.
- Your perceptiveness is multidimensional and beyond what other people perceive.
- Use your power of knowing to send healing energy to those around you.
- Meditate daily while listening for your inner voice of wisdom to guide you. Transcendental Meditation is an excellent choice for you.

Integrated Mental and Spiritual/Archetypal Worlds
Channel 34-57 *(Sagittarius-Libra)*

Keywords: Potential, Power, Intuitive Knowing

Although your strong intuition drives you toward action, waiting until the timing is right to do so serves you well.

You are highly perceptive and intuitive. You tune in to the energy around you, and you know things that are not available to those not sensitive at that level of awareness. Your strong intuition, along with your strong gut instincts, drives you to manifest whatever you feel warrants your energy. Because of your drive to manifest what comes into your awareness, you must intervene on behalf of your highest consciousness and make choices that optimize your power.

Your perceptive intuition may motivate you toward acting. However, waiting to know what aligns with your goals and life purpose may require waiting until you know that any action is timed correctly for the best outcome. Patience and mindful attention benefit you by allowing your perceptions. Stay focused on what you truly value. Take time to process your internal direction of Self and make sure you align your inner Self with current considered actions. Go Slow. You have plenty of time.

Use the Four Worlds Clarity Worksheet to review factors you consider about any major decisions to ensure you are balanced and aligned in all worlds before acting. In addition, meditate daily in your own space, allowing your pets to be with you so you listen for the voice of wisdom that guides your truth.

Your Keys to Empowerment

- Your intuitive gut instincts drive you toward manifesting. Wait for the right time.
- Always consider how your intuitive knowing aligns with what you value. Use your strength of powerful knowing wisely.
- Stay focused on what you truly value.
- Timing is crucial for you. Go slow and wait for the right time to speak or act.

Action Points for Manifesting Your Dreams

- When you know what you know and no one can tell you otherwise, wait for an opportunity to speak or act. Be patient and strategic.
- Use the Four Worlds Clarity Worksheets to review factors you consider about any significant decisions.
- Your power comes from what you know. Do not compromise your values.
- Meditate while listening for your inner voice of wisdom to guide you. Transcendental Meditation is an excellent choice for you.

Integrated Mental World and Portal to the Emotional/Angelic
Channel 34-57 (Sagittarius-Libra)

Keywords: Potential, Power, Intuitive Knowing

Although your strong intuition drives you toward action, waiting until the timing is right to do so serves you well.

You are highly perceptive and intuitive. You tune in to the energy around you, and you know things that are not available to those not sensitive at that level of awareness. Your strong intuition, along with your strong gut instincts, drives you to manifest whatever you feel warrants your energy. Because of your drive to manifest what comes into your awareness, you must intervene on behalf of your highest consciousness and make choices that optimize your power.

Hence, you focus on what you truly value. Take time to process your internal direction of Self and make sure you align your inner Self with current considered actions. Go Slow. You have plenty of time. Knowing what aligns with your goals and life purpose requires you to wait until you know the appropriate timing for the best outcome. Patience and mindful attention benefit you by allowing your perceptions to go deep within and anchor your actions in what aligns with your highest purpose. Make sure you meditate daily in your own space, with your pets, if you have them, so you listen for the voice of wisdom that guides your truth.

Use the Four Worlds Clarity Worksheet to review factors you consider about any major decisions to ensure you are balanced and aligned in all worlds before acting. In addition, meditate daily in your own space, allowing your pets to be with you so you listen for the voice of wisdom that guides your truth.

Your Keys to Empowerment
- Your intuitive gut instincts drive you toward manifesting. Wait for the right time.
- Always consider how your intuitive knowing aligns with what you value. Use your strength of powerful knowing wisely.
- Stay focused on what you truly value.
- Timing is crucial for you. Go slow and wait for the right time to speak or act.

Action Points for Manifesting Your Dreams
- When you know what you know and no one can tell you otherwise, wait for an opportunity to speak or act. Be patient and strategic.
- Use the Four Worlds Clarity Worksheets to review factors you consider about any significant decisions.
- Your power comes from what you know. Do not compromise your values.
- Meditate while listening for your inner voice of wisdom to guide you. Transcendental Meditation is an excellent choice for you.

Integrated Spiritual/Archetypal Portal and Emotional/Angelic Portal
Channel 34-57 *(Sagittarius-Libra)*

Keywords: Potential, Power, Intuitive Knowing

Although your strong intuition drives you toward action, waiting until the timing is right to do so serves you well.

You are highly perceptive and intuitive. You tune in to the energy around you, and you know things that are not available to those not sensitive at that level of awareness. Your strong intuition and instinct drive you to manifest whatever you feel warrants your energy. However, because of your instinctive drive to manifest what comes into your awareness, you must intervene on behalf of your highest consciousness and make choices that optimize your energy. Hence, you focus on what you truly value. Take time to process your internal direction of Self and make sure you align your inner Self with current considered actions. Go Slow. You have plenty of time. Knowing what aligns with your goals and life purpose requires you to wait until you know the appropriate timing for the best outcome. Patience and mindful attention benefit you by allowing your perceptions to go deep within and anchor your actions in what aligns with your highest purpose. Make sure you meditate daily in your own space, with your pets, if you have them, so you listen for the voice of wisdom that guides your truth.

Your Keys to Empowerment

- Your intuitive gut instincts drive you toward manifesting. Wait for the right time.
- Always consider how your intuitive knowing aligns with what you value. Use your power of knowing wisely.
- Stay focused on what you truly value.
- You know more than you think you know. Wait for clarity and be patient.

Action Points for Manifesting Your Dreams

- When you know what you know and no one can tell you otherwise, wait for an opportunity to speak or act. Be patient and strategic.
- Use the Four Worlds Clarity Worksheets to review factors you consider about any significant decisions.
- Your perceptiveness is multidimensional and beyond what other people perceive.
- Use your power of knowing to send healing energy to those around you.
- Meditate daily while listening for your inner voice of wisdom to guide you. Transcendental Meditation is an excellent choice for you.

Mental World
Channel 34-57 *(Sagittarius-Libra)*

Keywords: Potential, Power, Intuitive Knowing

Although your strong intuition drives you toward action, waiting until the timing is right to do so serves you well.

Because of your drive to manifest what comes into your awareness, you must intervene on behalf of your highest consciousness and make choices that optimize your energy. Although your perceptive intuition may motivate you toward acting, waiting to know what aligns with your goals and life purpose requires that you know your actions are timed correctly for the best outcome. Patience and mindful attention benefit you by allowing your perceptions to go deep within, so you anchor your actions to what aligns with your highest purpose. Make sure you meditate daily in your own space, with your pets, if you have any, so you listen for the voice of wisdom that guides your truth. Take time to process your internal direction of Self and make sure you align your inner Self with current considered actions. Stay focused on what you truly value. Go Slow. You have plenty of time.

Your Keys to Empowerment
- Your intuitive gut instincts drive you toward manifesting. Wait for the right time.
- Your intuition is powerful. Make sure any considered actions align with what you value.
- Your strength comes from the core of your being. Recognize your power.
- Timing is crucial for you. Go slow and wait for the right time to speak or act.

Action Points for Manifesting Your Dreams
- When you know what you know and no one can tell you otherwise, wait for an opportunity to speak or act. Be patient and strategic.
- Use the Four Worlds Clarity Worksheets to review factors you consider about any significant decisions.
- Recognize when you perceive other dimensions and wait for the right moment to make your knowing visible.
- Meditate daily while listening for your inner voice of wisdom to guide you. Transcendental Meditation is an excellent choice for you.

Channel 35-36

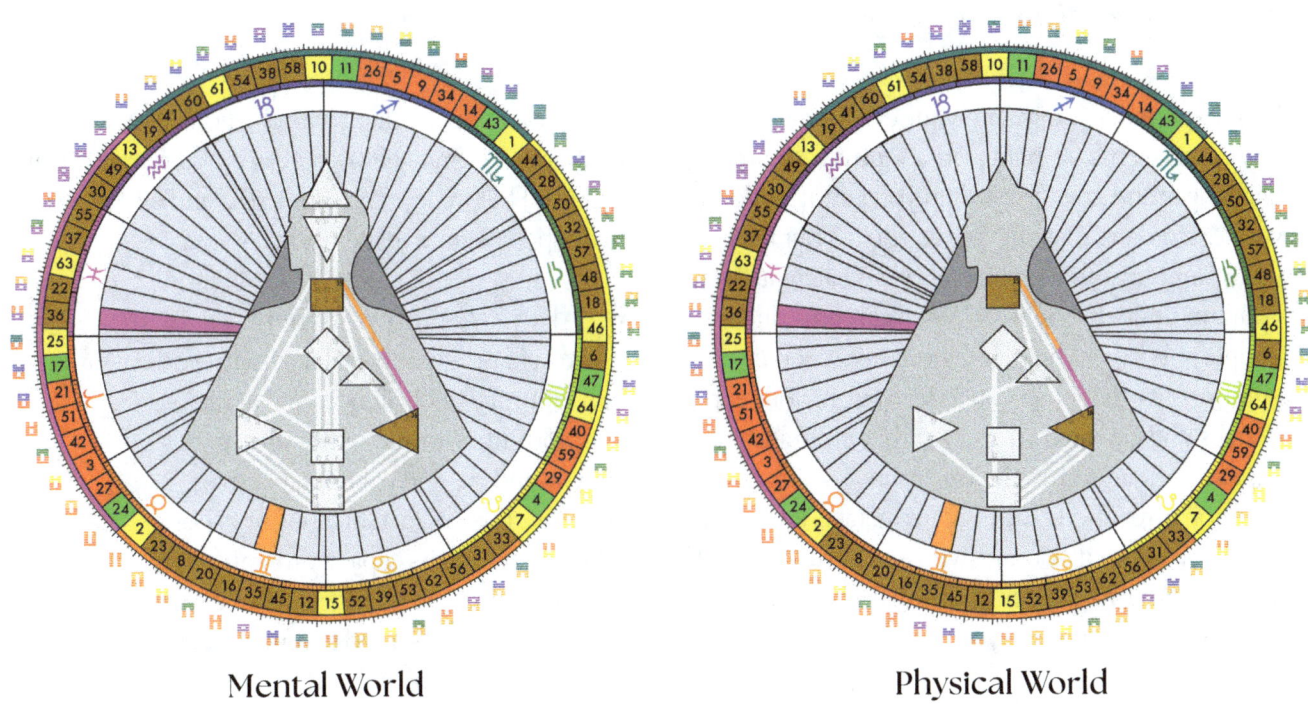

Mental World — Physical World

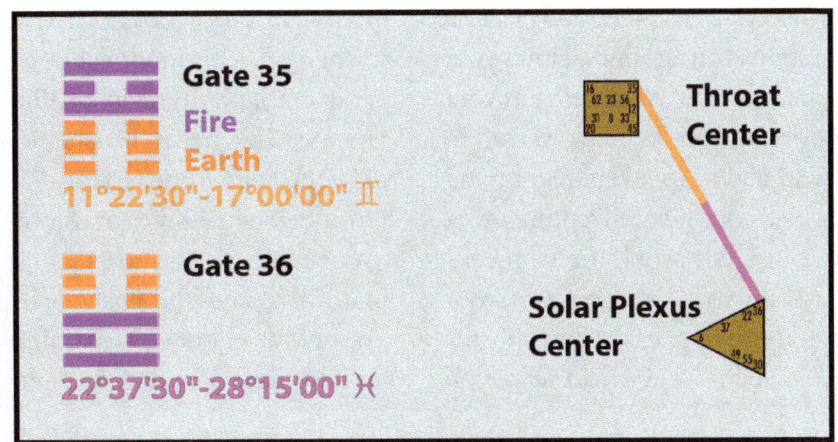

Channel 35-36

Integrated Mental and Physical/Biological Worlds
Channel 35-36 *(Gemini-Pisces)*

Keywords: Process, Transitoriness, Discernment

You love exploring new experiences and do well when you embrace change and transform emotional reactions spiritually.

Your experiences stimulate your emotions and give you a true sense of being on a journey with many challenges and great joy. When you pay attention to your desires and how they serve you in your process, you gain a lot of awareness about what matters to you and your uniqueness. When circumstances or people stress you, you may experience reactivity and emotionality that push you to learn from your experiences and be open to change that embraces new experiences and growth. The more you transform emotional reactions into higher octave awareness, the more aligned you are with your true-life path. You are here to master emotional challenges and transform them to serve you.

You are fun to explore with because you like to taste different varieties of life experiences. Make sure when you go exploring that you are grounded and clear on your intentions. Emotions can, at times, cloud your vision. So be cautious. Go Slow. Meditating in your own space, preferably with your pets, allows you to clear your energy field and keep a beginner's mind with which to consider your next adventure. Also, the practice of Tai Chi Gung would be beneficial because it would expand your experience of your energy body and teach you to release energy that is no longer serving you. Such a skill would serve you well. In addition, working with the Four Worlds Clarity Worksheet may help you clarify your emotional goals and help you transform stress and angst into a higher perspective that empowers you.

Your Keys to Empowerment
- As you master emotional reactivity, you embark on a journey of challenges and great joy.
- Explore areas and activities that spark joy in you and expand your perspectives.
- Consider doing Tai Chi Gung to experience the energy and its capacity to transform emotions into a higher perspective.
- Keep a beginner's mind to remain present in the now and to release the past.

Action Points for Manifesting Your Dreams
- Do what you love and love what you do.
- When you feel emotional, be alone and rebalance your emotions by asking: "What is so important for me to learn that this situation challenges me?"
- Use the Four Worlds Clarity Worksheet to understand how to transform your emotions into goals.
- Growth comes through your experiences. Be bold and courageous while holding firmly onto your values and integrity.

Mental World
Channel 35-36 *(Gemini-Pisces)*

Keywords: Process, Transitoriness, Discernment

You love exploring new experiences and do well when you embrace change and transform emotional reactions spiritually.

Your experiences stimulate your emotions and give you a true sense of being on a journey with many challenges and great joy. When you pay attention to your desires and how they serve you in your process, you gain a lot of awareness about what matters to you. You learn from your experiences and are open to change that embraces new experiences and growth. You are fun to explore with because you like to taste different varieties of life experiences. Make sure when you go exploring that you are also grounded and clear on your intentions. Emotions can, at times, cloud your vision. So be cautious. Go Slow. When you are emotionally reactive, take all the time you need to go within and transform your reactivity into a higher octave energy. Meditating in your own space, preferably with your pets, allows you to clear your energy field and keep a beginner's mind with which to consider your next adventure. Also, the practice of Tai Chi Gung would be beneficial because it would expand your experience of your energy body and teach you to release energy that is no longer serving you. Such a skill would serve you well. In addition, the Four Worlds Clarity Worksheet can help you recognize where you need to shift your perspective. Access Consciousness Bars may also be a helpful tool for you to learn.

Your Keys to Empowerment
- You are here to master emotional reactivity; thus, you are on a journey of challenges and great joy.
- Explore areas and activities that spark joy in you and expand your perspectives.
- Consider doing Tai Chi Gung to experience the energy and its capacity to transform emotions into a higher perspective.
- Consider releasing past traumas and experiences by learning Access Consciousness Bars.

Action Points for Manifesting Your Dreams
- Do what you love and love what you do.
- When you feel emotional, be alone and rebalance your emotions by asking: "What is so important for me to learn that this situation challenges me?
- Use the Four Worlds Clarity Worksheet to understand how to transform your emotions into goals.
- When you are emotionally reactive, take time to be alone and consider what you want to have happen from here.

Physical/Biological World
Channel 35-36 *(Gemini-Pisces)*

Keywords: Process, Transitoriness, Discernment

You love exploring new experiences and do well when you embrace change and transform emotional reactions spiritually.

Pay attention to how you care for your body and manage your emotions. When circumstances or people stress you, you may experience reactivity and emotionality. Remember that your experiences stimulate your feelings and give you a true sense of being on a journey with many challenges and great joy. Pay attention to your desires and how they serve you in your process. Thus, you gain a lot of awareness about what matters to you. Learn from your experiences and be open to change that embraces new experiences and growth.

You are fun to explore with because you like to taste different varieties of life experiences. Make sure when you go exploring that you are also grounded and clear on your intentions. Emotions can, at times, cloud your vision. So be cautious. Go Slow. Meditating in your own space, preferably with your pets, allows you to clear your energy field and keep a beginner's mind with which to consider your next adventure. Also, the practice of Tai Chi Gung would be beneficial because it would expand your experience of your energy body and teach you to release energy that is no longer serving you; this skill can serve you well. In addition, Self-Care routines are important for your well-being.

Your Keys to Empowerment
- You are here to master emotional reactivity; thus, you are on a journey of challenges and great joy.
- Explore areas and activities that spark joy in you and expand your perspectives.
- Consider doing Tai Chi Gung to experience the energy and its capacity to transform emotions into a higher perspective.
  Leave past traumas and memories in the past. Stay present in the now.

Action Points for Manifesting Your Dreams
- Do what you love and love what you do.
- When you feel emotional, be alone and rebalance your emotions by asking: "What is so important for me to learn that this situation challenges me?"
- Use the Four Worlds Clarity Worksheet to understand how to transform your emotions into goals.
- Emotional Reactions are for your growth. Ask what you can learn from what you are feeling.

Channel 37-40

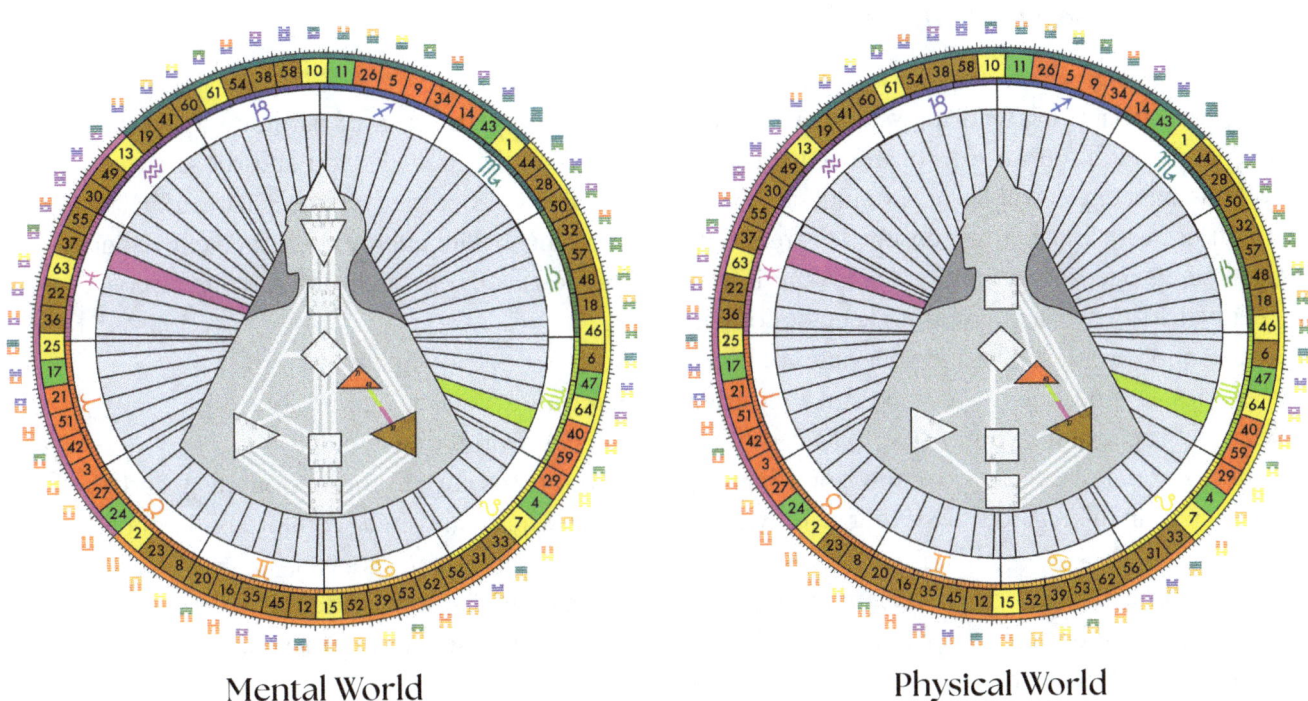

Mental World　　　　　　　　　　　Physical World

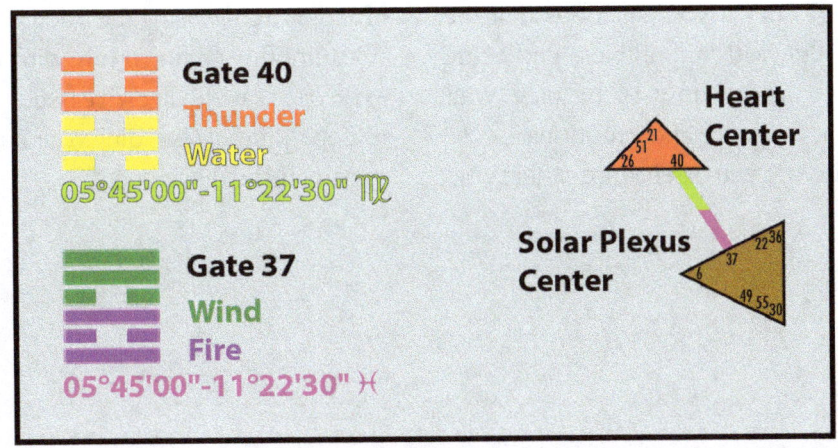

Channel 37-40

Integrated Mental and Physical/Biological Worlds
Channel 37-40 *(Pisces-Virgo)*

Keywords: Boundaries and Community

When you set clear boundaries and expectations, you can take care of your needs and participate in social situations.

You are a social being who enjoys time with family and time alone. If you are upset or around people you feel misaligned, you will likely have digestive issues if you eat with them. Your sensitivities are strong, and you have feelings about what you want in your energy field and what you want to keep out of your aura. Honor your instincts and your physical body's messages. It is healthy to set boundaries regarding what is beneficial for you or not. Expect those in your close circle to honor your boundaries. Stand up for yourself in this regard. Honor your sensitivities.

You live in a physical body. Pay attention to the health and well-being of your body. Take time to sleep, eat, dress. Self-care for you is essential because your love of life's pleasures and joys arises from your core sense of inner balance and chemistry. You may also have digestive issues if you eat foods that are not good for you. But, with mindfulness and acute perceptiveness, you assess how to balance your digestion. Use your instincts and emotional sense of balance to guide you; you can inspire others who recognize your sense of harmony with your body and how that benefits you and those around you. Use the Microcosmic Orbit regularly to balance yin and yang in your energy field. And keep a journal to stay conscious of your health and related goals.

Your Keys to Empowerment
- You are a social being who also needs to protect time alone.
- You are sensitive to your surroundings and do well when maintaining comfortable boundaries.
- Self-care is essential for you.
- Be alert to digestive issues and consider what is healthy for you.

Action Points for Manifesting Your Dreams
- Set clear boundaries regarding your time alone.
- Meditate daily using the Microcosmic Orbit.
- Be mindful of who you are with and what you eat to avoid digestive issues.
- Keep a journal regarding your health goals and be disciplined.

Mental World
Channel 37-40 *(Pisces-Virgo)*

Keywords: Boundaries and Community

When you set clear boundaries and expectations, you can take care of your needs and participate in social situations.

You are a social being who enjoys time with family and alone. If you are upset or around people you feel misaligned, you will likely have digestive issues if you eat with them. Your sensitivities are strong, and you have feelings about what you want in your energy field and what you want to keep out of your aura. Honor your instincts and your physical body's messages. You live in a physical body. Pay attention to the health and well-being of your body. Take time to sleep, eat, dress. Self-care for you is essential because from your core sense of inner balance and chemistry arises your radiance of life's pleasures and joys. If you use your instincts and your emotional sense of balance to guide you, you can inspire others who recognize your sense of harmony with your body and how that benefits you and those around you. Use the Microcosmic Orbit regularly to balance yin and yang in your energy field.

Your Keys to Empowerment
- You are a social being who also needs to protect time alone.
- You are sensitive to your surroundings and do well when maintaining comfortable boundaries.
- Self-care is essential for you.
- Meditate daily using the Microcosmic Orbit.

Action Points for Manifesting Your Dreams
- Set clear boundaries regarding your time alone.
- Disciplined Self-care is essential for your health and well-being.
- Be mindful of who you are with and what you eat to avoid digestive issues.
- Keep a journal regarding your health goals.

Physical/Biological World
Channel 37-40 *(Pisces-Virgo)*

Keywords: Boundaries and Community

When you set clear boundaries and expectations, you can take care of your needs and participate in social situations.

You are a social being who enjoys time with family and alone. If you are upset or around people you feel misaligned, you will likely have digestive issues if you eat with them. Your sensitivities are strong, and you have feelings about what you want in your energy field and what you want to keep out of your aura. Honor your instincts and your physical body's messages. Setting boundaries regarding what is healthy for you and expecting those in your close circle to honor your boundaries is healthy. Stand up for yourself in this regard. Honor your sensitivities.

You live in a physical body. Pay attention to the health and well-being of your body. Take time to sleep, eat, dress. Self-care for you is essential because from your core sense of inner balance and chemistry arises your radiance of life's pleasures and joys. When you feel emotionally agitated, disengage from the situation you are in. Your only path through emotional reactivity is to breathe and release or to move into a spiritual place within. When you master detachment, you have attained mastery in awareness. If you use your instincts and your emotional sense of balance to guide you, you can inspire others who recognize your sense of harmony with your body and how that benefits you and those around you. Use the Microcosmic Orbit regularly to balance yin and yang in your energy field.

Your Keys to Empowerment
- You are a social being who also needs to protect time alone.
- You are sensitive to your surroundings and do well when maintaining comfortable boundaries.
- Self-care is essential for you.
- Emotional reactivity derails you. When emotional, take time to breathe and release.

Action Points for Manifesting Your Dreams
- Set clear boundaries regarding your time alone.
- Disciplined Self-care is essential for your health and well-being.
- You have three options when in an uncomfortable situation: change yourself, change the other, or change your environment. Choose what benefits your health.
- Keep a journal regarding your health goals.

Channel 39-55

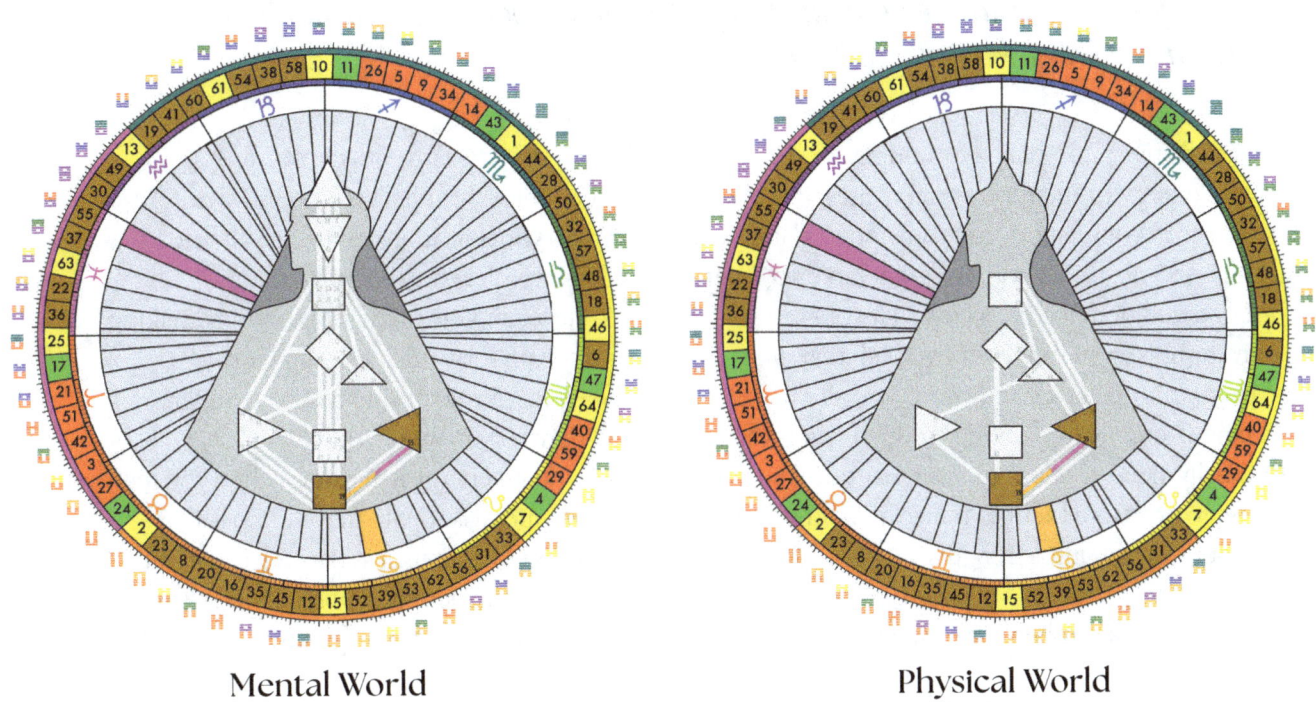

Mental World　　　　　　　　Physical World

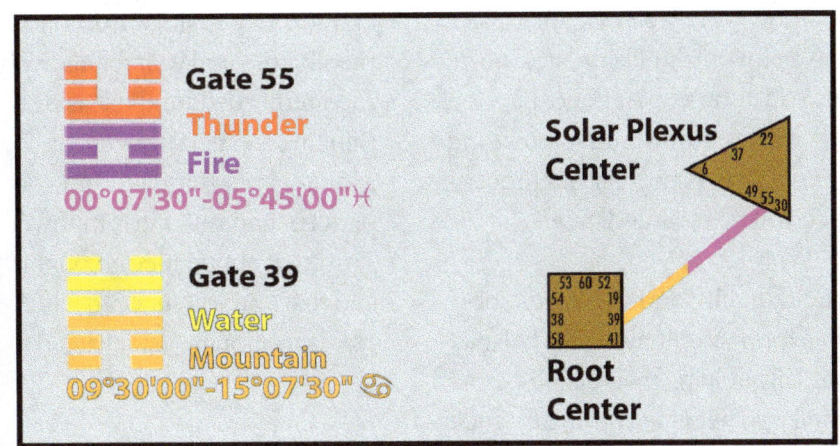

Channel 39-55

Integrated Mental and Physical/Biological Worlds
Channel 39-55 *(Cancer-Pisces)*

Keywords: Sensitivities, Obstruction, Self-Reflection, Emoting, Abundance, Acting Decisively

Because you are sensitive emotionally, pay attention to your self-talk and trust that overcoming challenges strengthens and transforms you.

Your sensitivity to your surroundings and the collective energy of the moment activates you toward mastery of your emotions. You notice daily challenges and obstacles and are vulnerable to feeling discouraged or defeated. Know that your emotional activation is a message from God that you can master your obstacles and overcome all challenges. Timing is crucial in working through whatever you internally need to clear in your attitude and emotions to rise above them to transcend and transform your sensitivities into strengths.

Once you work through the obstacles, you will likely feel abundance and relief from your challenges. Pay special attention to how your physical health impacts your energy and how you react to situations and people. Notice how your self-talk influences your perceptions. Negative self-talk creates more obstacles and keeps you away from inner expansion and self-reflection. Practice empowered self-talk and use Access Consciousness Bars to clear old thought patterns that will free you up to abundance.

Breathe through any difficulty and use meditation, especially the Sun/Moon Meditation, to balance yourself. In addition, daily tapping that releases stress neurologically is vital for helping you clear stuck emotional energy. Tai Chi Gung practices would be highly balancing for you.

Your Keys to Empowerment
- Recognize that challenges transform when you go within and find a still place from which action is appropriate.
- Your sensitivities activate emotions, making your path forward confusing. Consider ways to transform your feelings to align with what you want to have happen.
- Abundant energy is available when you rely on your inner wisdom to map your path forward.
- Access Consciousness Bars release stuck energy and open to all possibilities. Using Bars would benefit you greatly.

Action Points for Manifesting Your Dreams
- When you face challenges and feel confused about your path forward, consider all possibilities and wait for clarity before acting.
- Meditating daily and releasing negative thinking is crucial for you.
- Monitor your self-talk. Eliminate negative thought patterns and shift into empowered thinking.
- Trust that abundance is your birthright and that you will succeed when you clear emotional obstacles.

Mental World
Channel 39-55 *(Cancer-Pisces)*

Keywords: Sensitivities, Obstruction, Self-Reflection, Emoting, Abundance, Acting Decisively

Because you are sensitive emotionally, pay attention to your self-talk and trust that overcoming challenges strengthens and transforms you.

Your sensitivity to your surroundings and the collective energy of the moment activates you toward mastery of your emotions. You notice daily challenges and obstacles and are vulnerable to feeling discouraged or defeated. Know that your emotional activation is a message from God that you can master the mental world that carries emotions and challenges. You can rise above them to transcend and transform your sensitivities into strengths.

As you work through daily challenges, be mindful of your self-talk. If negative thought patterns are prevalent, shift them into empowered self-talk instead. What you think manifests over time. Be aware of your thoughts, especially when you are emotional and discouraged. God puts challenges before us to strengthen our character and test our faith. Know that abundance is yours when you act decisively and align with your highest potential.

Breathe through any difficulty and use meditation, especially the Sun/Moon Meditation, to balance yourself. In addition, daily tapping releases stress neurologically and is vital for helping you clear stuck emotional energy. Tai Chi Gung practices would be highly balancing for you.

Your Keys to Empowerment
- Explore possibilities for transforming challenges into opportunities. Trust your process.
- Your sensitivities activate emotions, making your path forward confusing. Align your feelings with what you want to have happen.
- Abundant energy is available when you rely on inner wisdom to map your path forward.
- Access Consciousness Bars release stuck energy and open to all possibilities. Using Bars would benefit you greatly.

Action Points for Manifesting Your Dreams
- When you face challenges and feel confused about your path forward, consider all possibilities and wait for clarity before acting.
- Meditate daily and release negative thinking to rebalance.
- Monitor your self-talk. Eliminate negative thought patterns and shift into empowered thinking.
- Trust yourself and your inner process and take time to gain clarity.

Physical/Biological World
Channel 39-55 *(Cancer-Pisces)*

Keywords: Sensitivities, Obstruction, Self-Reflection, Emoting, Abundance, Acting Decisively

Because you are sensitive emotionally, pay attention to your self-talk and trust that overcoming challenges strengthens and transforms you.

Your sensitivity to your surroundings and the collective energy of the moment activates you toward mastery of your emotions. You notice daily challenges and obstacles and are vulnerable to feeling discouraged or defeated. Know that your emotional activation is a message from God that you can master your emotions and challenges. You can rise above them to transcend and transform your sensitivities into strengths. Your physical well-being and emotional reactions indicate that you need to reassess and rebalance. Take all the time you need to self-reflect and to know what action is warranted. Be firm in your self-care, and do not compromise your integrity.

Breathe through any difficulty and use meditation, especially the Sun/Moon Meditation, to balance yourself. In addition, daily tapping that releases stress neurologically is essential for helping you clear stuck emotional energy. Tai Chi Gung practices would be highly balancing for you. In addition, Access Consciousness Bars may help you through difficult times.

Your Keys to Empowerment
- Explore possibilities for transforming challenges into opportunities. Trust your process.
- Your sensitivities activate emotions, making your path forward confusing. Align your feelings with what you want to have happen.
- Abundant energy is available when you rely on inner wisdom to map your path forward.
- Access Consciousness Bars release stuck energy and open to all possibilities. Using Bars would benefit you greatly.

Action Points for Manifesting Your Dreams
- When you face challenges and feel confused about your path forward, consider all possibilities and wait for clarity before acting.
- Meditate daily and release negative thinking to rebalance.
- Monitor your self-talk. Eliminate negative thought patterns and shift into empowered thinking.
- Trust yourself and your inner process, and take time to gain clarity.

Channel 42-53

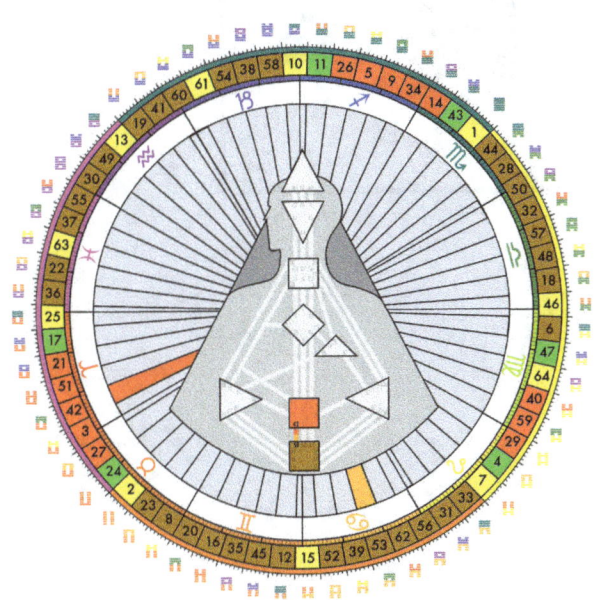

Mental World

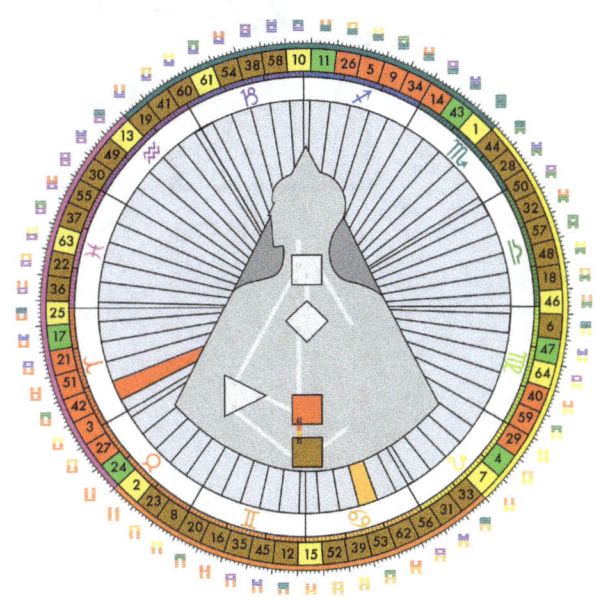

Spiritual World

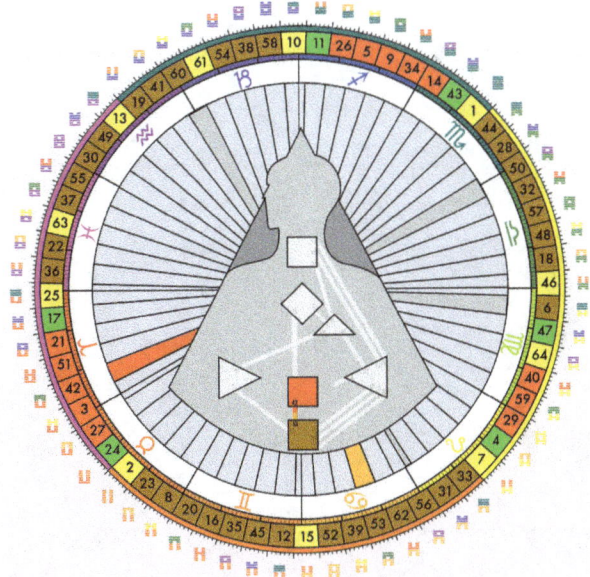

Physical World

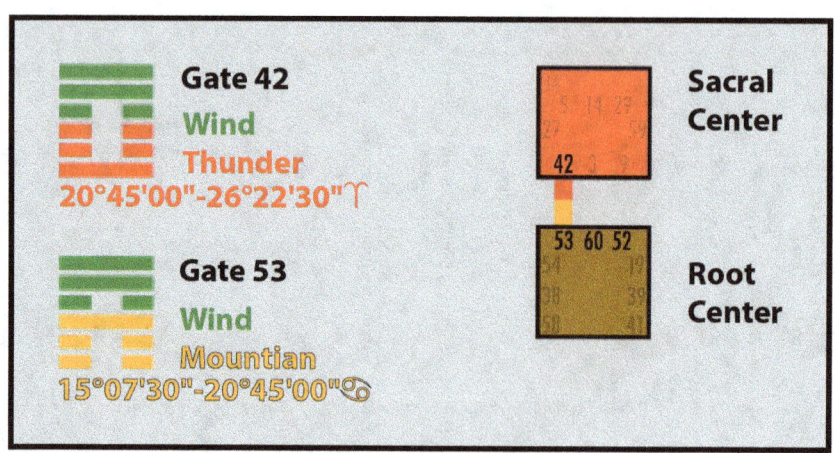

Channel 42-53

Integrated Mental, Spiritual/Archetypal, and Physical/Biological Worlds
Channel 42-53 *(Aries-Cancer)*

Keywords: Self-preservation, Maturation, Freedom, Connection, Enrichment, Faithfulness, Persistence

You value your freedom to choose what you spend time and energy doing. When you commit to something that resonates with you, you excel.

You have a strong innate sense of the cyclic nature of life and its processes. You recognize that balance and stability develop gradually and endure because they are more deeply rooted. When you start something, you prefer to see it come to completion and work to make it happen. On the other hand, you also like to have your freedom; you need time to find your place and get your grounding before committing to a process because you want what you do to have significance for those you care about. You will most likely flourish when you take command of your personality and remain loyal and committed to your inner truth. You are here serving your spiritual self, not your mental self. Because you connect to the spiritual world, a dog or cat as a pet can help anchor your energy and comfort you when you are struggling to persist.

Pay attention to your patterns and consider all alternatives in creatively innovative ways. When you push yourself to be creative within your comfort zone of focus, you will likely get inspired and involved in your projects beyond your expectations.

Your initial enthusiasm requires self-introspection to determine whether you feel aligned and committed to completing what you are considering. Take all the time you need to be confident of what you commit to when it involves time and energy. You are right to be protective of how your projects might impact your health and energy reserves. Recognize the importance of your freedom to choose your commitments and honor this quality in yourself.

When problems get solved, everything flourishes. Since you have a sense of living in multiple dimensions, you must commit to things you have energy for and are healthy for you. Then have the courage of your convictions, let your ideas and projects emerge in their own time, and trust that your Spiritual Self is guiding you.

Daily meditation and journaling are essential since you must integrate the Mental, Spiritual, and Physical Worlds when taking on any project. Stay true to yourself.

Your Keys to Empowerment
- Balance and stability are essential because you want what you do to be significant to those you care about.
- You like the freedom to do things your way and in your own time. Honor your timing.
- Consider your physical health and energy reserves when making commitments.
- Do what you love and love what you do.

Action Points for Manifesting Your Dreams
- Always defer to your Spiritual values when making choices and consider their impact on your life and health.
- Take time alone for inner work and honor your timing on decisions.
- Meditate Daily using either the Microcosmic Orbit or Transcendental Meditation.
- Keep a "To Do" list to track your projects, ideas, and creative inspirations. And have Faith.

Integrated Mental, Spiritual/Archetypal Worlds
Channel 42-53 *(Aries-Cancer)*

Keywords: Self-preservation, Maturation, Freedom, Connection, Enrichment, Faithfulness, Persistence

You value your freedom to choose what you spend time and energy doing. When you commit to something that resonates with you, you excel.

You have a strong innate sense of the cyclic nature of life and its processes. You recognize that balance and stability develop gradually and endure because they are more deeply rooted. When you start something, you prefer to see it come to completion and work to make it happen. On the other hand, you also like to have your freedom; you need time to find your place and get your grounding before committing to a process because you want what you do to have significance for those you care about. You will most likely flourish when you take command of your personality and remain loyal and committed to your inner truth.

You are here serving your spiritual self, as well as your mental self. Because you connect to the spiritual world, a dog or cat as a pet can help anchor your energy and comfort you when you are struggling to persist.

Pay attention to your patterns and consider all alternatives in creatively innovative ways. When you push yourself to be creative within your comfort zone of focus, you will likely get inspired and involved in your projects beyond your expectations. Your initial enthusiasm requires self-introspection to determine whether you feel aligned and committed to completing what you are considering. Take all the time you need to be confident of what you commit to when it involves time and energy. Do only what honors your deep self and say "no" to projects that do not activate a sense of joyfulness in you.

When problems get solved, everything flourishes. Since you have a sense of living in multiple dimensions, you must commit to things you have energy for and are healthy for you. Then have the courage of your convictions, let your ideas and projects emerge in their own time, and trust that your Spiritual Self is guiding you.

Daily meditation and journaling are essential since you must integrate the Mental, Spiritual, and Physical Worlds when taking on any project. Stay true to yourself.

Your Keys to Empowerment
- Balance and stability are essential because you want what you do to be significant to those you care about.
- You like the freedom to do things your way and in your own time. Honor your timing.
- When you feel spiritually connected to your projects, you thrive.
- Do what you love and love what you do.

Action Points for Manifesting Your Dreams
- Defer to your Spiritual values when making choices and consider their impact on your life and health.
- Use a journal to assess what your priorities are.
- Meditate Daily using either the Microcosmic Orbit or Transcendental Meditation.
- Keep a "To Do" list to track your projects, ideas, and creative inspirations. And have Faith.

Integrated Mental and Physical/Biological Worlds
Channel 42-53 *(Aries-Cancer)*

Keywords: Self-preservation, Maturation, Freedom, Connection, Enrichment, Faithfulness, Persistence

You value your freedom to choose what you spend time and energy doing. When you commit to something that resonates with you, you excel.

You innately sense the cyclic nature of life and its processes. Before you commit to any project, take the time to consider the impact that what you are thinking will have on your health. Pay attention to your patterns and consider all alternatives in creatively innovative ways. When you push yourself to be creative within your comfort zone of focus, you will likely get inspired and involved in your projects beyond your expectations. The depth of your attachment to your projects comes from your inner sense of higher purpose connected to it. Your initial enthusiasm requires self-introspection to determine whether you continue to feel aligned and committed to completing your tasks. Take all the time you need to be confident of what you are committing to when what you are committing to involves time and energy. You are right to be protective of your time and energy. You may tend to take on more than is healthy for you. Pay attention to your physical resources and make self-care a priority.

Recognize the importance of your freedom to choose your commitments and honor this quality in yourself. Because you connect to the Spiritual/Archetypal World, a dog or cat as a pet can help anchor your energy and comfort you when you are struggling to be clear.

Meditate daily using the Sun/Moon Meditation. It circulates your energy and allows you to connect to the yang and the yin energy, so it is essential for you to integrate into your body.

In addition, Access Consciousness Bars can help you release what is not productive for your process.

Your Keys to Empowerment
- Balance and stability are essential because you want what you do to be meaningful and enhance the lives of those you care about.
- You like the freedom to do things your way and in your own time. Honor your timing.
- Consider your physical health and energy reserves when making commitments.
- Meditate daily as part of your Self-Care routine and keep notes.

Action Points for Manifesting Your Dreams
- You flourish when you solve challenges and have a clear idea going forward.
- Take time alone for inner work and honor your timing on decisions.
- Meditate Daily using the Sun/Moon Meditation. Keep notes in a Journal.
- Make Self-Care a disciplined priority and have a routine you stick to.

Mental World
Channel 42-53 *(Aries-Cancer)*

Keywords: Self-preservation, Maturation, Freedom, Connection, Enrichment, Faithfulness, Persistence

You value your freedom to choose what you spend time and energy doing. When you commit to something that resonates with you, you excel.

You have a strong innate sense of the cyclic nature of life and its processes. You are most comfortable when projects develop over time, so they have deep roots that give them stability and endurance. When you start something, you prefer to see it come to completion and work to make it happen. On the other hand, you like to have your freedom; you need time to find your place and get your grounding before committing to a process. You have a Spiritual connection and deep Faith. Stay in tune with those aspects of yourself and give them authority over real-world opinions. You are your best self when you are serving your spiritual purpose.

Pay attention to your patterns and consider all alternatives in creatively innovative ways. When you push yourself to be creative within your comfort zone of focus, you will likely get inspired and involved in your projects beyond your expectations. Your initial enthusiasm requires self-introspection to determine whether you feel aligned and committed to completing your consideration. Take all the time you need to be confident that what you envision and commit to involves the time and energy you have to commit. You are right to be protective of your time and energy. Recognize the importance of your freedom to choose your commitments and honor this quality in yourself. When problems get solved, everything flourishes.

Your Keys to Empowerment
- Balance and stability are essential because you want what you do to be significant to those you care about.
- You like the freedom to do things your way and in your own time. Honor your timing.
- Consider your physical health and energy reserves when making commitments.
- Always consider your spiritual values before committing to a project.

Action Points for Manifesting Your Dreams
- You flourish when you solve challenges and have a clear idea going forward.
- Take time alone for inner work and honor your timing on decisions.
- Meditate Daily using either the Microcosmic Orbit or Transcendental Meditation.
- Keep a "To Do" list to track your projects, ideas, and creative inspirations. And have Faith.

Spiritual/Archetypal World
Channel 42-53 *(Aries-Cancer)*

Keywords: Self-preservation, Maturation, Freedom, Connection, Enrichment, Faithfulness, Persistence

You value your freedom to choose what you spend time and energy doing. When you commit to something that resonates with you, you excel.

You innately sense the cyclic nature of life and its processes. Thus, when you start something, you prefer to see it complete and work to make it happen. On the other hand, you also like to have your freedom; you need time to find your place and get your grounding before committing to a process you will likely want to see to its end. You always straddle the Spiritual and Mental Worlds because it is through the Spiritual/Archetypal World that you manifest your Spiritual values and process.

Pay attention to your patterns and consider all alternatives in creatively innovative ways. When you push yourself to be creative within your comfort zone of focus, you will likely get inspired and involved in your projects beyond your expectations. The depth of your attachment to your projects comes from your inner sense of higher purpose connected to it. Your initial enthusiasm requires self-introspection to determine whether you continue to feel aligned and committed to completing what you are considering. Take all the time you need to be confident of what you are committing to when what you are committing to involves time and energy. You are right to be protective of your time and energy.

Recognize the importance of your freedom to choose your commitments and honor this quality in yourself. Because you connect to the Spiritual/Archetypal World, a dog or cat as a pet can help anchor your energy and comfort you when you are struggling to be clear.

Meditate daily using the Sun/Moon Meditation. It circulates your spiritual energy and allows you to connect to the yang and the yin energy, so it is essential for you to integrate into your body.

Your Keys to Empowerment
- Balance and stability are essential because you want what you do to be significant to those you care about.
- You like the freedom to do things your way and in your own time. Honor your timing.
- Consider your physical health and energy reserves when making commitments.
- Before making any commitments, self-reflect and release Mental World concerns.

Action Points for Manifesting Your Dreams
- You flourish when you solve challenges and have a clear idea going forward.
- Take time alone for inner work and honor your timing on decisions.
- Meditate Daily using the Sun/Moon Meditation. Keep notes in a Journal.
- Keep a "To Do" list to track your projects, ideas, and creative inspirations. And have Faith.

Physical/Biological World
Channel 42-53 *(Aries-Cancer)*

Keywords: Self-preservation, Maturation, Freedom, Connection, Enrichment, Faithfulness, Persistence

You value your freedom to choose what you spend time and energy doing. When you commit to something that resonates with you, you excel.

You innately sense the cyclic nature of life and its processes. Before you commit to any project, take the time to consider the impact that what you are thinking will have on your health. Pay attention to your patterns and consider all alternatives in creatively innovative ways. When you push yourself to be creative within your comfort zone of focus, you will likely get inspired and involved in your projects beyond your expectations. The depth of your attachment to your projects comes from your inner sense of higher purpose connected to it. Your initial enthusiasm requires self-introspection to determine whether you continue to feel aligned and committed to completing your tasks. Take all the time you need to be confident of what you are committing to when what you are committing to involves time and energy. You are right to be protective of your time and energy. You may tend to take on more than is healthy for you. Pay attention to your physical resources and make self-care a priority.

Recognize the importance of your freedom to choose your commitments and honor this quality in yourself. Because you connect to the Spiritual/Archetypal World, a dog or cat as a pet can help anchor your energy and comfort you when you are struggling to be clear.

Meditate daily using the Sun/Moon Meditation. It circulates your energy and allows you to connect to the yang and the yin energy, so it is essential for you to integrate into your body. In addition, Access Consciousness Bars can help you release what is not productive for your process.

Your Keys to Empowerment
- Balance and stability are essential because you want what you do to be significant to those you care about.
- You like the freedom to do things your way and in your own time. Honor your timing.
- Consider your physical health and energy reserves when making commitments.
- Meditate daily as part of your Self-Care routine and keep notes.

Action Points for Manifesting Your Dreams
- You flourish when you solve challenges and have a clear idea going forward.
- Take time alone for inner work and honor your timing on decisions.
- Meditate Daily using the Sun/Moon Meditation. Keep notes in a Journal.
- Make Self-Care a disciplined priority.

Channel 47-64

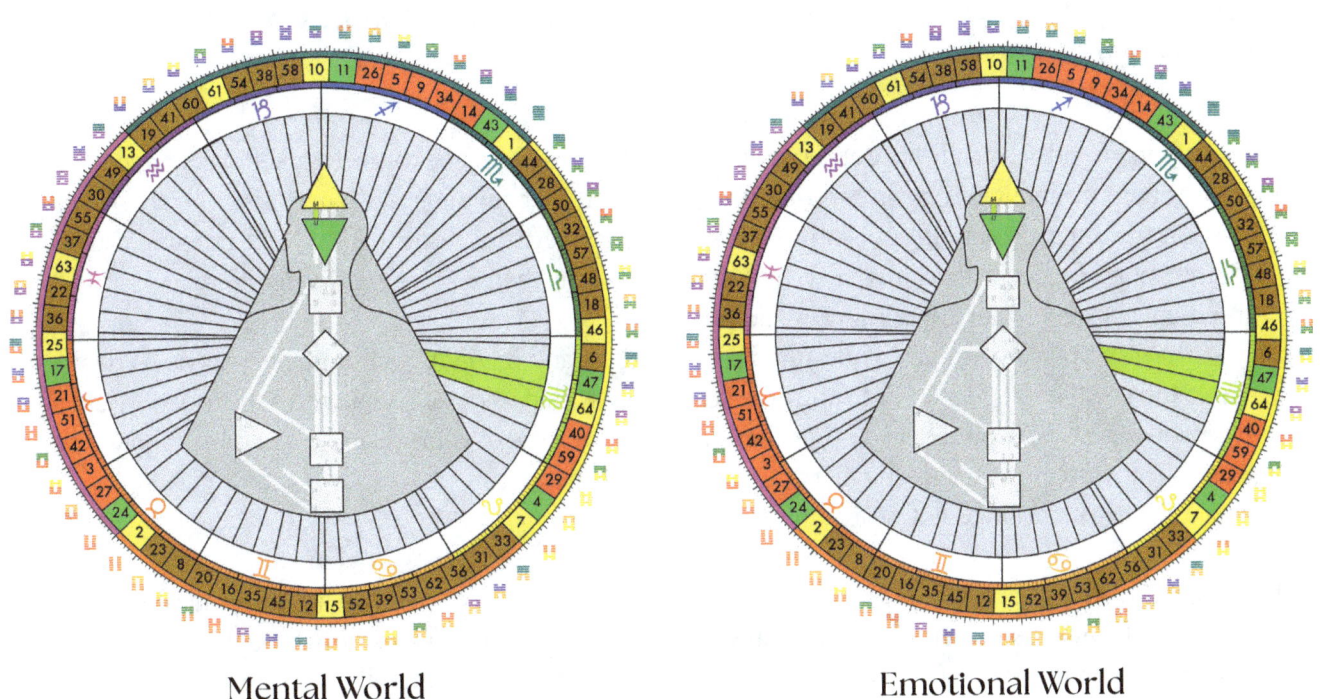

Mental World   Emotional World

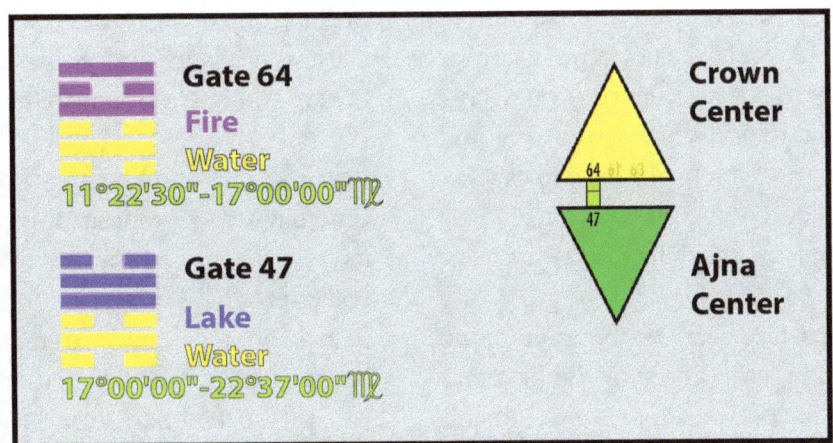

Channel 47-64

Integrated Mental and Emotional/Angelic Worlds
Channel 47-64 *(Virgo-Virgo)*

Keywords: Thoughtfulness, Abstraction, Expansion, Bringing Order Out of Confusion, Not Yet Fulfilled

Your probing mind pushes you to expand your consciousness as you seek knowledge and understanding.

Because you are brilliant and think about all topics that raise questions about the universe and how things are, you may often find yourself alone in your pursuit of truth. You probe deeply for answers to questions you sense will expand your consciousness and push you forward in your growth and understanding of yourself and your life experiences. You must use your inner resources to overcome outside pressures and manage negative, oppressive self-talk that arises from feelings of exhaustion and test of your faith.

Understand yourself and your process. You are driven by a deep sense of purpose when you want answers; sometimes, you are impatient because you feel exhausted and alone in your quest for knowledge. Trust the universal orchestration and relax. Ask for clarity and trust that you will receive answers. However, answers do not always appear as you expect them to appear. Suppose you deeply trust a higher orchestration of understanding and knowledge. In that case, you might be able to relax your sense of urgency to know and let yourself perceive beyond the veil for other dimensional answers.

Your task is to recognize that you bring harmony to disharmony and order to chaos by thinking and reacting to what is before you. Your confusion and stress are a natural part of the process, and by clarifying your goals and the outcome you want, you can find the right strategy for gaining resolution. Be cautious, alert, and flexible. Change your thinking and goals as you move toward resolution if you recognize that your thinking and approach to your situation need revision. Be flexible and take the time you need to rest when you are overloaded.

Rest and meditation are crucial for you. When you go within spiritually, you access the root of your faith in the core of yourself and your connection with the Divine.

Your Keys to Empowerment
- Accept every situation with faith and ease.
- Learn from your situation through self-reflection and self-correction.
- Take time to rest and reorient when you are frustrated or stressed. Exercise like Tai Chi Gung or going out into nature can restore energy.
- Trust your process and resilience and believe you will overcome difficulties.

Action Points for Manifesting Your Dreams
- Carefully analyze your situation and its components and envision what you want to have happen.
- Remain optimistic and use empowering language in your self-talk. Trust that you will succeed. Stay strong.
- Use the Sun/Moon Meditation daily and take time in nature.
- Relax and let go of your concerns when tired and burnt out. You have plenty of time

Mental World
Channel 47-64 *(Virgo-Virgo)*

Keywords: Thoughtfulness, Abstraction, Expansion, Bringing Order Out of Confusion, Not Yet Fulfilled

Your probing mind pushes you to expand your consciousness as you seek knowledge and understanding.

You are brilliant, and you think about all topics that raise questions about the universe and how things are in the world. You can probe deeply for answers to questions you sense will expand your consciousness and push you forward in your growth and understanding of yourself and your life experiences. Be understanding of yourself and your process. You are driven by a deep sense of purpose when you want answers, and sometimes, you are impatient with your process. Trust the universal orchestration and relax your timing. Ask and trust that you will receive answers. However, answers do not always appear how you expect them to appear.

Situations you are in may overwhelm you, and you may feel lost and tired of trying to make sense of things in your life. It is natural at times for you to feel exhausted and discouraged. Know that you are tested in your depth of commitment to your life mission and purpose and that you will succeed if you set goals and are patient. You know more than you think you do, and you can overcome obstacles and soar to great heights.

Your Keys to Empowerment
- Accept every situation with faith and ease.
- Learn from your situation through self-reflection and self-correction.
- Take time to rest and reorient when you are frustrated or stressed. Exercise like Tai Chi Gung or going out into nature can restore energy.
- Trust your process and resilience, and believe you will overcome difficulties.

Action Points for Manifesting Your Dreams
- Carefully analyze your situation and its components and envision what you want to have happen.
- Remain optimistic and use empowering language in your self-talk. Trust that you will succeed. Stay strong.
- Use the Sun/Moon Meditation daily and take time in nature.
- Relax and let go of your concerns when tired and burnt out. You have plenty of time.

Emotional/Angelic World
Channel 47-64 *(Virgo-Virgo)*

Keywords: Thoughtfulness, Abstraction, Expansion, Bringing Order Out of Confusion, Not Yet Fulfilled

Your probing mind pushes you to expand your consciousness as you seek knowledge and understanding.

You are brilliant and think about various topics that raise questions about the universe and how things are in the world. You may often find yourself alone in your pursuit of truth. Probe deeply for answers to questions you sense will expand your consciousness and push you forward in your growth and understanding of yourself and your life experiences. Be patient and understanding of yourself and your process. You are driven by a deep sense of purpose when you want answers, yet sometimes, you are impatient with your process. You may feel and be alone in your quest for knowledge. Trust the universal orchestration and relax your timing.

Ask and trust that you will receive answers. However, answers do not always appear as you expect them to. Suppose you deeply trust a higher orchestration of understanding and knowledge. In that case, you might be able to relax your sense of urgency to know and let yourself perceive beyond the veil for other-dimensional answers.

Your Keys to Empowerment
- Accept every situation with faith and ease.
- Learn from your situation through self-reflection and self-correction.
- Take time to rest and reorient when you are frustrated or stressed. Exercise like Tai Chi Gung or going out into nature can restore energy.
- The more you relax and trust a higher power, the more success you will have.

Action Points for Manifesting Your Dreams
- Meditate on your situation envisioning what you want to have happen.
- Remain optimistic and use empowering language in your self-talk. Trust that you will succeed. Stay strong.
- Use the Sun/Moon Meditation daily and take time in nature.
- Conserve your energy by resting and meditating when you are stressed. Allow your unconscious spiritual connection to do the work for you.

Acknowledgments

When I began working with the Human Design material and with Ra Uru Hu in 1996, I had no idea of the complexity and dimensionality I would be studying. Although my background in research as a social scientist, psychologist, astrologer, and psychic gave me a wealth of knowledge to draw from, writing in detail about it for others presented me with a daunting task.

When I began releasing Noble Energy Maps® to the public as a downloadable report, it became clear that I had to document every Integrated Channel and all possible combinations and permutations of how the Channels in the Four Worlds and the Integrated World would combine and impact consciousness. This task required a great deal of self-reflection and documentation of the reliability and validity of the information I shared. I have done thousands of Noble Energy Maps® readings for people. This manual presents the Channel Materials as I describe them in all the Worlds and with relevant practices.

My husband, Marvin M. Portner, M.D., my soul mate and partner for the past 46 years, has been a fantastic support, encourager, and editor. Marvin is always with me as I document my work and stands with me as I struggle to clarify, expand, and research it. He recognizes the divine creative energy when I channel it and provides a nurturing and protective space when I need it. Together, we are better than if either one of us were alone. Our love story, orchestrated by God, has fulfilled our dreams. We wish for others a love as strong and as deep as our love for each other.

Writing all the Channels had its challenges. My son, Charles Haspel, has been instrumental in helping me with this project. Charles set up a database for me to work with and coded all the information I wrote about each Channel into the database. The data could then be programmed into a report for a computer program and this book. Charles helped me figure out how to code the data and present it.

Cindy O'Connor Smith and I have worked together since 2007. As a fellow traveler, Cindy and I share the values of honesty, integrity, kindness, and user-friendly materials. We spend time discussing how to present the material best, and we consider everything from its design to the color-coding of its elements that make it resonate and communicate on all Four World levels of consciousness. Cindy is a very dear friend of mine, a fellow traveler, and an inspiration. We both have a God-given mission to bring truth and awareness to our audience while honoring the science and integrity of Noble Sciences material.

Michelle M. White implemented the design of my books, *Astrology Essentials, Cosmic Secrets, First-Degree Reiki Manual, Second-Degree Reiki Manual and Workbook, Cosmic Guidance for Mastering Your Life*, and now *Beyond Human Design: Turbocharge Your Practice with Integrated Channels in All Four Worlds*. Michelle's sharp eye and acute sense of design make my work easier and my products the best I can imagine. I am very grateful to have Michelle on my team.

Melanie Herschorn helps guide my thinking and way of presenting material. She encourages me, supports my visions, and helps crystallize the practical applications of my work. When my complex thinking needs clarification, Melanie is my go-to person. She understands the mind and soul of a writer.

Erin Keller posts on social media and creates exceptional copy using my words and thoughts. Erin's ability to capture the essence of my work is creative, brilliant, and spot-on. With Erin's help, I am reaching more people than I could otherwise, and her help is a true blessing.

When Susie Schaefer joined my team, she brought professionalism and support to the project. I can count on her to watch for missed details and inform me of nuances in the publishing industry that I would otherwise be uneducated about. With Susie on my side, I know my books get the exposure they require and the energy that makes them appealing. She is always ready to help with valuable and very much welcomed suggestions. I am very blessed to have Susie working with me and my team.

Nick Lush has worked with me for more than twenty years. Nick's attention to detail, willingness to pitch in and do what needs to get done, and ability to work with my database and manipulate its parameters in ways I want to analyze have been constructive. Nick is a supportive friend, loyal employee, and adopted family member. With Nick on my team, I know I have someone with impeccable ethics and loyalty.

To all my clients, webinar participants, and Human Design colleagues, I am deeply honored and grateful to have your trust. Since I started my career, I have been blessed to love what I do and to do what I love. As I prepare to teach about The Four Worlds and Noble Energy Maps®, I recognize that I am entering an unmapped area of psychological personality theory and research. If, along with all my students, I can help heal hurt souls, I will have accomplished my mission. It is an honor to have your trust.

In Loving Light,
Dr. Eleanor®
Mount Pleasant, South Carolina
June 2024

About the Author

It is my great honor and privilege to share my knowledge with you and to use it to help you live a life of fulfillment and recognition of your divinity.

My interest in astrology began in 1971 when I was told that astrology is the most scientific of the esoteric disciplines. At the time, I had just completed my doctorate at the University of Chicago, was well versed in psychology, sociology, anthropology, and biology, and had done extensive research on world religions; however, hearing that astrology was scientific intrigued me.

I found an astrology bookstore near my home and proceeded to learn how to calculate an astrology chart. It proved to be the hardest thing I had ever attempted to learn. The language was symbolic and the mathematical calculations were complex. But I persisted and began to understand basic astrological work.

Two years later, I was deeply honored and blessed to book an astrological reading with Katherine de Jersey. The reading with her showed me the power and depth of astrology in the hands of a Master. I studied astrology privately with several astrologers and was also in training as a Jungian Analyst. I also focused on Kundalini energy and meditation because I was having Kundalini energy experiences, and I wanted to understand them and my psychic abilities.

In 1996, I encountered the Human Design Mandala, a complex, yet intriguing system that intertwines psychology, astrology, and developmental science. My fascination with the Human Design System deepened with each passing year.

Through my research, I had a staggering revelation: 95% of humanity possesses the inherent potential to manifest their true selves. Tragically, the majority of people remain oblivious to the existence of the Four Worlds — the Mental, Spiritual, Emotional, and Physical dimensions that govern our daily reality.

While their lack of awareness is not inherently "bad," it is a missed opportunity for growth and fulfillment. When individuals are unaware of the Four Worlds, they navigate life without understanding the diverse dimensions of their consciousness. They may feel disconnected, struggling to align actions with their true selves and miss out on the profound impact that recognizing and harmonizing with these dimensions can have on their overall wellbeing.

It was then that my mission crystallized in my mind: to illuminate these dimensions to guide individuals towards a conscious existence that embraces the essence of their soul.

Noble Energy Wellness®

Noble Energy Wellness® focuses on Energy Medicine and Holistic options for healing and health. Dr. Marvin and Dr. Eleanor® teach energy wellness in their weekly Manifest Your Dreams Webinar. Through the webinar, you can learn how to live authentically while manifesting your actual potential by understanding and integrating the Four Worlds into your daily life. Register to learn how you can manifest your dreams by attending these weekly webinars.

https://www.nobleenergywellness.com

Noble Energy Maps®

Noble Energy Maps® focus on Dr. Eleanor's proprietary and innovative system for mapping how cosmic energy impacted you during your childhood development and how you can use this knowledge to optimally time your decisions, identify your life purpose, and live a self-realized life. Dr. Eleanor® statistically validated her system through over 45,000 cases and uses Noble Energy Maps® to guide clients toward wholeness and empowerment.

https://www.nobleenergywellness.com/energy-map/

The Noble Logo has a special place in Dr. Eleanor's heart. Her first cat, Noble, lived to age 22 and was an inspiration and guide during important times in Dr. Eleanor's growth and studies. He worked with her and Dr. Marvin when they hosted weekend groups for over ten years. Noble always helped guide them toward whom to work with next, as well as to the area that clients needed to work on. Dr. Eleanor® uses calculations based on research done on her two home-grown twin kittens. The critical human developmental times used in Dr. Eleanor's proprietary Noble Energy Maps® have proven accurate clinically and statistically. They map the Four Worlds in a person's energy field and how they can best function.

The Mandala of Synthesis® describes the elements coded into Dr. Eleanor's proprietary Noble Energy Maps®. The Mandala of Synthesisr® includes the Kabalistic Tree of Life, Chakras, Astrology, the Hexagrams of the I-Ching, and critical times in early Human Development. Dr. Eleanor® calculates her maps and integrates the information coded into a graphic illustrating the way you use your energy, where the flow of energy becomes clear. Dr. Eleanor's extensive education as a social scientist, researcher, and clinician has empowered her to formulate a complete system that recognizes the complexity of your consciousness and shows how you can best use it for growth and expansion of consciousness.

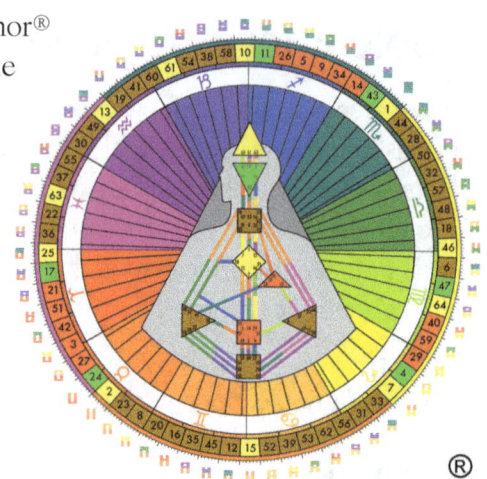

https://www.nobleenergywellness.com/mandala-of-synthesis

Weekly Wisdom

Join our free "Weekly Wisdom" course and embark on a journey of personal growth and empowerment. Each week, receive insightful and actionable wisdom designed to enhance your well-being, balance your energy, and elevate your life. Led by Dr. Eleanor, a renowned expert in Human Design and The Four Worlds, this course provides you with the tools and inspiration to thrive in all aspects of your life.

Scan The QR code to Subscribe now and start transforming your mind, body, and spirit with our exclusive weekly insights!

www.ingramcontent.com/pod-product-compliance
Lightning Source LLC
Chambersburg PA
CBHW081442070526
44586CB00019B/2201